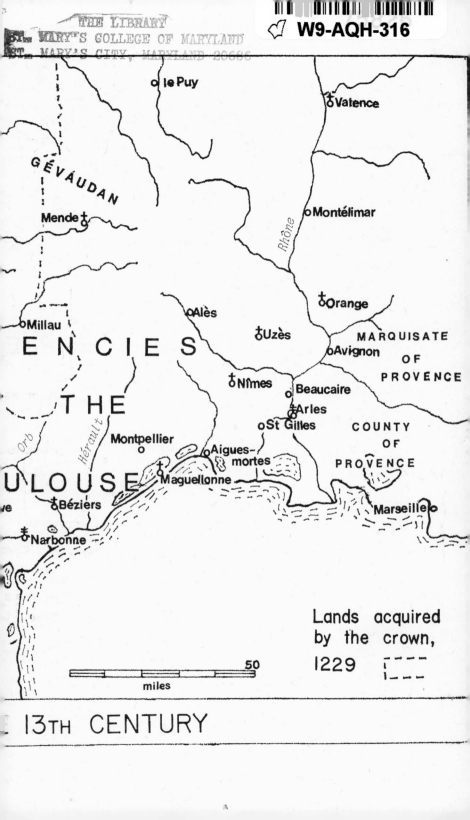

le Puy

Valence

GÉVAUDAN

Mende

Rhône

Montélimar

Alès

Millau

Orange

Uzès

MARQUISATE

E N C I E S

Avignon

OF

PROVENCE

Nîmes

Beaucaire

T H E

Arles

St Gilles

COUNTY

Montpellier

Aigues-
mortes

OF

PROVENCE

U L O U S E

Maguellonne

Béziers

Marseille

Narbonne

Orb

Hérault

Lands acquired
by the crown,
1229

50

miles

13TH CENTURY

# Heresy, Crusade and
# Inquisition in Southern France

# Heresy, Crusade and Inquisition in Southern France 1100-1250

WALTER L. WAKEFIELD

UNIVERSITY OF CALIFORNIA PRESS

Berkeley and Los Angeles 1974

First published in 1974

UNIVERSITY OF CALIFORNIA PRESS
Berkeley and Los Angeles, California

ISBN 0-520-023803
Library of Congress Catalog Card Number: 72-93524

Printed in Great Britain

# Preface

This book had its beginning when, having translated the short and lively account by William Pelhisson of the early years of the Inquisition in Toulouse and of events in which he had a part, I undertook an introduction to the document. To establish the historical setting called for a description of the heresies which the inquisitors pursued, as well as comment on the failure of either peaceful persuasion or force in the form of a crusade to subdue them. In addition, more information than William Pelhisson provides on how the tribunal operated in its formative years seemed desirable. The introductory comment grew into this book on the rise of heresy in Languedoc, the Albigensian crusade, and the work of the Inquisition in the first decade and a half of its existence; to it, Pelhisson's chronicle and a few other contemporary documents are appendixes.

To justify that expansion of the original project one may point out that there is interest today in examining the history of dissent and its repression, for, despite the ecumenical movement in religion, we have our own experience with controversy among secular creeds and with attempts to curb or punish those who disagree with established authority. Yet, while studies of medieval religious movements, notably the heresies, by Herbert Grundmann, Antoine Dondaine, Mlle Christine Thouzellier, Raoul Manselli, and Kurt Selge; histories of Languedoc and Toulouse prepared by Philippe Wolff; narratives of the Albigensian Crusade by Pierre Belperron and Michel Roquebert; and analysis of the thirteenth-century Toulousan Inquisition by Yves Dossat (to name only a few of the scholars who have written on these subjects) have been produced in Europe in recent years, the results of their work have not been conveniently available in English.

The extent to which this book rests on the researches of the scholars just named and others deprives it of a claim to originality. I have, however, consistently gone to the original sources for corroboration and detail. In the interest of readers who are, perhaps, approaching the subject for the first time there are explanations of matters perfectly familiar to the specialist. Also, in a compromise between a desire to let the reader know the bases on which this narrative rests and an unwillingness to crowd the pages with citations, brief statements are provided in the notes of the works to which I am most indebted, while full publication data on them and others which may usefully be consulted are reserved for the bibliography.

The texts translated in the appendixes illustrate certain aspects of the narrative other than descriptions of the heresies, for which one may be referred to existing translations. Because only the first of these pieces has already appeared in English translation they are accompanied by more elaborate documentation than is found in the preceding pages.

Errors found here are entirely my own. I owe thanks to Miss Chantal Esposito and Miss Gail Smith for help in preparing parts of the typescript. I acknowledge my gratitude to readers unknown to me whose comments saved me from mistakes, more particularly to Mlle Christine Thouzellier, Malcolm Lambert, and Jeffrey B. Russell for my profit from discussions with them of subjects related to this book. If we did not always agree, our differences were most amicable.

*State University College*
*Potsdam, New York*

# Contents

# Maps

# Abbreviations

# I The Rise of Heresies

Heresy, crusade, and inquisition are words often used today in contexts quite different from those in which they were coined. Hence – and this is particularly true of heresy – we need to be aware of the meaning the words had in the Middle Ages.

## What Is Heresy?

Medieval Christians, searching for God and anxious to do His will, knew that He had given them through Jesus Christ the message of salvation. Eternal life, they were assured, could be attained through belief in Christ, membership in the church which He had instituted on earth, and acceptance of its teaching and discipline as God's will. Yet there could be situations in which that teaching was not entirely clear, for even in the eleventh century the doctrine of the church was not fully developed. Although it did comprise a body of generally accepted tenets based on Scripture, affirmed by fathers of the church, and stated in ancient creeds, diversity was still to be found in modes of worship and interpretation of certain dogmas. There were important questions which had not yet been definitively answered, areas of uncertainty in which were encountered religious ideas of which it was not possible to say: 'To be a Christian, you must hold this belief'; or 'If you believe that, you are not a Christian.'

Part of the religious history of the Middle Ages, notably in the twelfth and thirteenth centuries, was the reduction of these areas of uncertainty, yet it was a long process to achieve clear and authoritative statements on disputed matters. The church, enmeshed in a changing society, was itself changing in its structure, wealth, influence, and power, as well as in its methods of making decisions. Meanwhile, not only were old questions being raised anew, but new trends in thought posed novel problems.

No matter how familiar literate churchmen might be with the struggles of the early church to establish unity of structure and doctrine, they were not well prepared to meet the kind of new challenges which now appeared. The dissent from received doctrine in the high Middle Ages was much more a product of affirmation about the highest principles of Christian life than a reiteration of ancient heresies. The dissenters proposed answers to the big questions of good and evil, the nature of man and of the church, the proper conduct of life, and the end of man which, however much open to criticism, had their roots in the Gospels. Yet their affirmations often so emphasized certain beliefs or certain ways of behaviour that other long-accepted ones were downgraded or denied. As they found hearers, groups or sects formed, and when the ideas they shared seemed to differ too widely from prevailing norms, the cry of heresy was raised.

'Heresy' (in Latin *haeresis*) derives from a Greek word meaning 'a choosing'. Long before the twelfth century Christians were using the word to designate a wrong choice, a personal and wilful contradiction of common and necessary beliefs. But in debatable cases where was to be found the standard of right belief, that is, orthodoxy? In practice, when non-conformity or dissent seemed to exist, the first decision about what was permissible and what was pernicious had to be made on the spot by local authority, bishop or synod, who would condemn errors they discerned, demand that they be corrected, and excommunicate the individuals who persisted in them. Obedience thus became a crucial issue. The heretic was one who was declared to be such because he did not choose to accept correction from ecclesiastical authority in a certain time and place. When the church became more centralized and popes held the reins of authority more firmly, isolated decisions gave way to pronouncements from the Holy See or from councils convened by it and the standard of authority was generally accepted to be doctrine sanctioned by Rome. Once that was stated, a choice to reject it was heresy.

Heresy could not be a casual matter when religion was so vital an element in life. It had to be regarded as the most grievous sin and crime into which man could fall, for by denying the magistracy of the church which Christ had established, over which His vicar in Rome presided, the heretic became a traitor to God himself. Moreover, he imperilled others by his words and example; medieval writers were fond of likening heresy to a loathsome and contagious disease.

Christian duty was, first of all, to reclaim the sinner and usually when heresy was identified sincere efforts were made to persuade its proponents to abandon it. There was no room for the dissident to plead personal sincerity or the right to believe as he chose. Most medieval men were quite incapable of admitting that one could in good conscience continue in heresy once truth was pointed out. The choice must have been made deliberately to sin. Therefore, anyone who stubbornly refused to accept the proferred correction abandoned hope of eternal life, fell prey to the powers of darkness, and deserved only to be cut off from the Christian community. So noxious was the crime that unless it were resolutely dealt with many other souls might be gravely endangered. Secular officials put heretics to death in the conviction that one faith in one church was the indispensable cement of Christian society. Mobs who burned accused heretics were moved equally by horror at their wickedness and fear of God's wrath if it went unpunished on earth.

What of the accused? Heresy was an easy word to bandy about and sometimes a convenient stick with which to beat one's enemies. But the religious ideas which caused the greatest stir were deeply held convictions which gained adherents among the laity as well as clergy, the more dangerous the more they were attractive to ordinary men and women. The peril of such dissent to the church was shown by the fact that only a few who were accused submitted, being convinced by argument or instruction or converting out of fear. Far more commonly the charge of heresy was denied and the accused retorted that theirs was the truly Christian way and that they were unjustly persecuted. Some, indeed, went further to insist that not they but the accusers were the heretics, that the Roman church had turned aside from Christ's purpose. Well into the twelfth century heated discussions occurred when alleged heretics justified their position by appeal to the Scriptures and their captors and judges replied in the same fashion. Rarely did these debates end other than in punishment by ecclesiastical or secular officers after a formal condemnation or more rudely at the hands of a mob which interrupted the proceedings and put the suspects to death.

## The Earliest Heresies

In some areas of western Europe as early as the eighth century, churchmen had been disturbed by iconoclastic ideas, divergent ideas about the eucharist, outbursts from self-declared prophets, and rather vague aspirations for reform of the church. Southern France was relatively unaffected. The ensuing years were quiet until between AD 1000 and 1052 in Italy, France, the Low Countries, and Germany groups were detected who challenged

B

practices such as veneration of the cross or of saints or burial in consecrated ground, regarded eating certain foods, especially meat, as sinful, criticized priests and hierarchy unmercifully, and sometimes were accused of worshipping demons. As we shall see in the next chapter there has been scholarly debate over the explanation of these episodes. Information for southern France in that time is sparse. One chronicler reported that about 1018 people in Aquitaine were being led astray by 'Manichaeans' who denied the validity of baptism and refused to venerate the cross. In diet and piety they resembled monks but secretly, it was said, they were debauched. A council in 1026 discussed action that might be taken, with results unknown, but some persons were burned in Toulouse.

In the last half of that century there was a lull everywhere and no mention of heretical outbreaks appears in the sources, apart from the quarrels generated by the Gregorian reform programme.[1] The quiet ended as the twelfth century began. For nearly two hundred years thereafter the contest of orthodoxy and heresy, nowhere more bitter than in southern France, was a major element in religious life and political affairs as well. The story of that conflict should be approached by way of a discussion of its causes.

### The Problem of Causes

Among the numerous explanations advanced in general terms for the rise and spread of the medieval heresies the one most frequently encountered is that they were a product of resentment against a 'corrupt' clergy in a church that had become wealthy, worldly, and forgetful of its mission. Another theory is that the heresies were protests, expressed in religious terms, against socio-economic dislocations and inequities. Alienation from the church for these reasons is presumed to have opened the way for such seductive doctrines as religious dualism, which explained good and evil by dividing creation between principles or gods of spiritual and material realms; after being rejected by the early church such ideas had been preserved in various sects in the Balkans and Asia Minor and found their way westward some time after AD 1000. It has also been suggested that the great intellectual advances of the Middle Ages had a part in stimulating opinions which diverged into heresy.

In specific instances of radical dissent one or another of these causes may be found to be dominant, but none of them alone is sufficient to explain the whole range of heretical movements of the high Middle Ages. Challenge to the existing religious order would not have reached such serious proportions unless minds and hearts had already been prepared for a general renovation. The rise of the heresies is explicable only in the light of that revival of piety which occurred everywhere in western Europe at every level of society. It took the form of new religious orders, of enhancement of episcopal and papal power, of mystic exaltation for some, of application of intellect to theological problems for others. Not confined to clerical circles, the desire for spiritual experiences also animated many laymen. While warriors marched on crusade to the Holy Land and pilgrims thronged the routes to famous shrines, other men and women also scrutinized religious ideas closely and critically in their desire to find the most authentic forms of Christian life.[2]

A desire for personal spiritual perfection and an emphasis on purity of life within a group can be discerned in certain episodes of dissent as early as the eighth century and more clearly in those of the eleventh century, and with them a diminution of the sense of need for clergy and sacraments. In the twelfth century a movement away from the church as then constituted was accentuated by two related but subtly different sentiments. One developed from criticism of the church for its failures as a spiritual institution, the other out of enthusiasm for a more satisfying form of religious practice. The first, keenly felt among those whose primary aim was reform of Christian life without giving up traditional fundamental doctrines, will be the theme of the remainder of this chapter. From the second came the acceptance of a different theology, that of dualism, which will be discussed in the following chapter.

### Reform, Apostolic Life, and Heresy in the Twelfth Century

Repeatedly in Christian experience over centuries sensitive individuals who observed a contrast between the church of their own day and that described in the New Testament have sought to restore religious institutions to the earlier model. In the medieval church targets for criticism were plentiful: a papacy which sometimes seemed more intent on political programmes than spiritual leadership; bishops who loved pomp, prerogative, and power; priests who were careless, ignorant, incelibate. Strong forces were aroused within the church in attempts to remedy its defects by withdrawing ecclesiastical property and offices from secular patronage, by asserting the superiority of religious over civil authority, by renovating monastic orders or forming new ones, by promoting morality in the priesthood through the canonical movement and closer ecclesiastical supervision. They succeeded in part but without entirely removing the causes of criticism. At the same time, the idea of reform also awakened among laymen the impulse to achieve the fullest kind of Christian life on earth.

When the response of the hierarchy and clergy was an attempt to silence their critics or when proposals for renovation of the church encountered apathy or resistance, resolute advocates of a new spirit in religious life might go from reform to rejection. Refusing to admit limitations on what could be accomplished or to be constrained by obedience, they took their case to the people, inspiring sects which were declared to be heretical. Even though the critics might share with reformers within the church the vision of revived evangelical Christianity they parted company with them on the way to achieve the ideal. A few rebellious critics concluded that there was no need of church or clergy to mediate between God and man. Most, however, took the theme that the Roman church had somewhere taken a wrong path and lost its divine authority, so that it must be superseded by 'a true church of Christ', which they were disposed to find only among themselves and their followers. Theirs was the authentic faith and they alone were true Christians.

One aspect of this upswelling of piety accompanied by criticism deserves special attention in discussing the relationship of reformist movements and heresy in southern France. It was the concept of the *vita apostolica*, life based on Gospel precepts, lived in imitation of the apostles, which at the end of the eleventh century was beginning to take an important place among popular religious ideas.

It is an historical irony that the very success of the Gregorian programme to free the church from civil control and to promote celibacy and good order in the priesthood inspired men who would be troublesome to the church and clergy. They were advocates of the apostolic ideal who felt the ambition to go further and to promote among the laity a new sense of religious commitment. To do this they had, perforce, to move out among the people, to abandon cloister and cathedral for the roadside and the marketplace. As they preached the message that the perfect Christian life, the apostolic way to salvation through repentance, chastity, poverty, and evangelism, was open to all men, they awakened aspirations that could not be readily satisfied within the church as it was then constituted and that sometimes led into heresy.

No element in the concept of the apostolic life was a novelty. Chastity and humility had always been regularly praised if not always practised; asceticism was extolled in the lives of the saints. The power of the apostolic ideal as it was now put forward was in the proposal that all men could pursue a Christian life that had hitherto been confined to hermitage or monastery, and in the emphasis placed on two further elements: the need to preach the evangelic way and the profession of voluntary poverty.

The urge to preach was a natural product of the zeal of the reformers and of the fact that, in a largely illiterate society, preaching was the necessary method of instruction. Traditionally, this was the bishop's function and could be undertaken by others only with his consent, but the exhortations that had accompanied the call to the First Crusade had whetted appetites for the word of God and put a strain on the old limitations. Enthusiasts refused to be forbidden. When challenged with Paul's question, 'How can men preach unless they are sent?', they quoted the command of Christ to teach all nations. With or without permission, they preached, and disciples gathered about them to do the same.

Poverty, in the sense of inability to maintain oneself above a bare level of existence, was a harsh fact in a rural economy often hurt by natural disasters and war. Commercial revival had not reduced the proportion of the poor in society, while the increase in population forced many men out of the rural community into vagabondage or into the precarious life of the labourer in towns, where to be poor was to be anonymous, part of a faceless crowd, a state more painful by contrast with the affluence which urban life could afford to others. Awareness of the fact of poverty did not lead to the suggestion that it could be abolished. It was part of the social order, permitted by God to exist as a consequence of sin, as a test for the righteous, or as an opportunity for the fortunate to give charity. As a social condition it did give rise to some discussion of the mutual rights and duties of the well-to-do and the poor and about the justice of a claim by the latter on the bounty of an earth given by God to all men.

Voluntary poverty in imitation of Christ and the apostles was another matter, not a social condition but a religious state. It had been institutionalized in the monastery, which normally, however, protected members from real destitution. Hermits in the eleventh and twelfth century, as they had earlier, took absolute poverty as part of their renunciation of the world. In dwelling on the ideal of voluntary poverty the preachers of apostolic life were less innovators than reinforcers of a tradition, but they gave tradition a wider application by enthusiastically echoing Jerome's words that one served God best who 'naked followed a naked Christ'. They emphasized the sentiment, which would be even more strikingly put into action by the end of the twelfth century, that holiness and poverty were inseparable, that the great act of religious commitment was to rid oneself of material possessions.

What the preachers of apostolic life did by offering their ideal to all men was to give their hearers a sense of participation in religion, thus resetting in part the balance in worship between clergy and laity which had tipped in favour of a greater role for the former. They were listened to with respect among the nobles who were often at odds with clerical proprietors over land and income. Peasants could venerate them and comfort themselves with the thought that their humble lot, even if involuntary, had God's blessing. A merchant too occupied with business for more than lip service might allow his womenfolk more enthusiasm and eventually consecrate his wealth to charity. Groups of labourers might be persuaded to find their religious vocation in chaste lives of labour, prayer, and communal sharing. Thus, there was the likelihood that the regular services of the church might fall into disrepute.

More dangerous still was the dissemination of the idea that holy authority rested less on ordination than on the personal purity that was demonstrated by voluntary poverty, asceticism, and evangelism. The contrast between the wandering preachers and many of the clergy could all too often lead to repudiation of the latter as demonstrably unworthy and incapable of spiritual leadership.

The influence of the apostolic ideal in stimulating heretical movements should not be over-stated, for most wandering preachers of the early twelfth century did stimulate a popular piety that could be expressed within orthodox limits. Among such who came to southern France was Robert of Arbrissel who preached repentance before the coming of the kingdom of God. He demonstrated his sincerity in his personal asceticism and founded a religious house to carry on his work, inspiring also a native Toulousan, St Raymond Gayrard to preach and devote himself to care of the poor. Another of Robert's disciples, Gerald of Sales, probably also worked in parts of Languedoc. These men, despite a certain amount of suspicion on the part of the clergy, found it possible to win support from the episcopacy and the papacy and remained within the church.[3]

Dissemination of the ideal of apostolic life could, however, contribute to the appearance of dissent so radical as to become heresy if its proponents chose to offer themselves as better leaders than the church provided toward goals which they believed had been forgotten by the church. Two such men appeared in southern France in the first half of the twelfth century.

## Peter of Bruys and Henry

In the region near the mouth of the Rhône, some time between 1112 and 1220, Peter of Bruys, a priest, began to preach an individualistic faith based on the Gospel but differing in important points from orthodox teaching. He is known only through the writings of his opponents who sought to refute his errors; if there was a more positive element in what he said it is lost to us. Peter denied the need of church buildings for worship, repudiated infant baptism as worthless, the Eucharist as unnecessary, and prayers for the dead as futile. So radical, indeed, was his attitude that it has been suggested that he approached the Protestant doctrine of salvation by faith alone. This is a less valid appraisal than that he was somehow influenced by the extreme opposition to the established church then current in Balkan heresies which will be mentioned presently. After two decades of preaching, first in the region along the Rhône, then further west toward Toulouse, Peter of Bruys went too far in his scorn of conformity and was murdered by a crowd, horrified when he made a bonfire of crosses to show his repugnance for what he called an instrument of torture rather than a sacred symbol. By that time, however, he had already established a relationship with another itinerant preacher who would have even greater influence.

Peter of Bruys' successor was Henry, who, in an earlier appearance in the northern city of Le Mans in 1116, had set the people fiercely at odds with their clergy. Already the young preacher had won a great reputation for piety, which was borne out by his appearance. Bearded, long-haired, barefoot, Henry seemed to be the very personification of a prophet. The unsuspecting Bishop Hildebert of Le Mans gave him permission to preach Lenten sermons in the city, then departed to attend a council; in his absence, Henry set Le Mans in uproar. What he taught is not recounted in detail by the one reporter of events, a cleric of the city, who depicts Henry vividly although at times made almost incoherent by his dislike. We are told that the preacher tried to redeem women from prostitution and find them husbands. His other activities can only be judged by the result: hearers aroused to such antipathy for the clergy that the count had to interfere to protect some unfortunate clerics from mobs. When Bishop Hildebert at last returned he was jeered at by his own people, but set about restoring order. With considerable difficulty, and probably not without assistance from the count, Hildebert finally succeeded in driving Henry out. The preacher thereupon moved southward, creating turmoil like that in Le Mans as he went. Yet, although he was a great disturber of religious peace, from what is known of him to this point, he cannot fairly be called an heretic.

At some time within a decade after he left Le Mans, Henry made contact with Peter of Bruys and probably adopted more radical ideas from him. His self-appointed mission of preaching was interrupted, however, by arrest at the hands of the archbishop of Arles and condemnation by pope and council at Pisa in 1135. He was sent to a monastery, probably Clairvaux, but soon fled and resumed his unauthorized, now anathematized, preaching in the region around Toulouse.

Henry has been called a disciple of Peter of Bruys, but he did not merely echo the latter's teaching. While he did repeat the Petrobrusian verdicts that church buildings were not needed for worship and that prayers for the dead were valueless he respected the symbol of the cross, as Peter of Bruys did not, but went beyond Peter in denying the concept of original sin. A Catholic writer reported a debate he claimed to have engaged in with Henry about 1135. When challenged to show his authority to preach Henry declared that God desired him to deliver a message of love. 'I obey God rather than man,' he said. 'He who sent me said, "Thou shalt love thy neighbour as thyself".' The true church was a spiritual one, he insisted, a congregation of the pure, and thus sinful priests of the Roman organization had no power to consecrate the Eucharist or to impose penance. The hierarchy should give up its wealth and honors. Men need only confess their sins to one another. Only faith made the sacrament of baptism valid. Adam's sin was not visited upon his descendants, and surely a merciful God would not condemn children for it. Marriage was a human relationship.

By 1145, the influence of Henry and other dissidents, who profited by the unrest he was creating, had produced a situation most distressing to the churchmen in Toulouse and the surrounding area. Churches were without congregations, congregations without priests, priests without respect, men perished in their sins and children were denied salvation – so wrote the saintly Bernard of Clairvaux, who joined a preaching mission to visit the region and seek to recall the populace from error. Henry did not challenge the abbot in person and thereafter disappears from view, but the Catholic party had a mixed reception.[4] They found that, in addition to Henry's teaching, a heresy in which they discerned a revival of the Arian denial of the Trinity had spread among the common people, especially weavers, and that feudal nobles were fostering opposition to the church, no doubt out of jealousy aroused by the extensive lands and revenues in the hands of bishops and abbeys. One participant in the mission perceptively remarked that much preaching would be needed to win back allegiance to the church. The truth of the observation was soon proved, for dissent in the reforming tradition continued and by the end of the century was widely spread by the sect of Waldenses or Poor of Lyon. A more serious danger to the church was the rapid spread of the new heresy of the Cathars which, also claiming apostolic validity, proposed to substitute for traditional Christianity a theology based on a dualistic concept of God and the world. Between them the two movements threatened to carry the whole area from the Alps to the Pyrenees out of communion with Rome.[5]

# References

1. J. B. Russell, *Dissent and Reform in the Early Middle Ages*, discusses religious controversies from the eighth to the twelfth century. For incidents of the eleventh century see especially Ilarino da Milano, 'Le eresie popolari del secolo XI', *Studi Gregoriani*, II, 43–89.
2. J. B. Russell, 'Interpretations of the Origins of Medieval Heresy', *Mediaeval Studies*, XXV (1963), 25–53, surveys various theories of causation of heresy. See also C. Thouzellier, 'Tradition et résurgence dans l'hérésie médiévale' in her *Hérésie et hérétiques*, 1–15. The volume in which that article first appeared (*Hérésies et sociétés*, J. Le Goff [ed.)] has other studies pertinent to the questions discussed here.
3. A summary of the apostolic impulse and its effects is E. W. McDonnell, 'The *Vita apostolica*: Diversity or Dissent?', *Church History*, XXIV (1955), 15–31. More detailed is H. Grundmann, 'Eresie e nuovi ordini religiosi' in *Relazione del X Congresso internazionale di scienze storiche*, III, 357–402 (also in the revised edition of his *Religiöse Bewegungen*). Poverty is discussed in articles by Gilles Couvreur, 'Pauvreté et droits des pauvres à la fin du XIIe siècle', and Jacques Paul, 'Mouvements de pauvreté et réflexion théologique au XIIIe siècle', both in *La Pauvreté: Des sociétés de pénure à la société d'abondance*, 13–37 and 38–46, respectively. See also M. Mollat, 'La Notion de la pauvreté au moyen âge', *RHEgF*, LII (1966), 6–23; and T. Manteuffel, *Naissance d'une hérésie*. Best on the wandering preachers is J. von Walter, *Die ersten Wanderprediger Frankreichs*.
4. The doctrines of Peter of Bruys and Henry, as interpreted by their opponents,

are found in documents translated in Wakefield and Evans, *Heresies of the High Middle Ages*, 118–21, and 107–17, respectively. Two excellent studies of the heretics are those by R. Manselli: *Studi sulle eresie del secolo XII*, 1–67; and 'Il monaco Enrico e la sua eresia', *Bulletino dell'Istituto storico Italiano . . . e Archivio Muratoriano*, LXV (1953), 1–63. J. Fearns, 'Peter von Bruis', *Archiv für Kulturgeschichte*, XLVIII (1966), 311–35, suggests that Peter was influenced by Bogomilist ideas but was not a dualist. E. Magnou, 'Note critique sur les sources de l'histoire de Henri l'hérétique', *BPH* (1962), 539–47, argues for dating Henry's appearance at Le Mans about 1100. The mision of Bernard of Clairvaux is described in E. Vacandard, 'Les Origines de l'hérésie albigeoise', *RQH*, LV (1894), 50–83.

5. Attention is called here, as it will be in later places to the existence of heresy as a European phenomenon, not confined to southern France. Evangelism, apostolic life, and repudiation of the Roman church and its sacraments were the themes of a reformer-prophet named Tanchelm, who had gathered a following in Flanders about a decade before Peter of Bruys began to preach. Near Soissons about 1115 and in Trier, not long afterward, were small sects with antisacramental views; the doctrines of another one in Liège in 1135 are obscure. A crazed prophet named Eudes, in Brittany after 1145, challenged the church by setting up his own hierarchy. About 1143–1144, side by side with the Cathars who will be described in following pages, there were in Köln heretics who denigrated the papacy and accepted no religious practice not clearly attributable to Christ and the apostles. Arnold of Brescia caused a stir between 1149 and 1155, especially in Rome, where his passionate attacks on the wealth and secular involvements of the hierarchy and his advocacy of apostolic poverty gave him extraordinary influence for a time.

# II Cathars and Waldenses

Dualism is a term for religious thought which elevates the contrast between the spiritual and the material, the eternal and the temporal, into a theory of two creators and two creations. Man is a creature whose soul belongs to the realm of good but is caught in flesh which was created by the evil one. Doctrines of this sort antedate Christianity. In the early centuries of the Christian era they had been taught in Manichaeism and a variety of Gnostic sects; recurrently in later years they were to be encountered in religious groups in the Near East and the Balkans. In the second half of the twelfth century dualism was also the central theme of a heresy very widespread in western Europe. How much that heresy of the Cathars, a generic name for medieval western dualists, owed to the ancient tradition, how it came to be implanted in the West, are questions which cannot be answered with certainty.

## The Bogomils

It is, however, generally agreed that the Cathars were much influenced by a sect, known as the Bogomils after their founder, which grew up in Bulgaria in the tenth century. Bogomil, a priest, had taught that a life of repentance, prayer, and simple worship was the way of escape from a wicked world that was under the rule of a prince of darkness. He had been a rebellious son of God who, expelled from heaven, had formed the earth and imprisoned in human bodies the angels who fell with him. This concept of creation is known as 'mitigated' dualism since it accepts God as the unique creator but assigns to a lesser and evil maker the actual shaping of the material world. God's younger son, Christ, had come then from heaven as a spirit, never assuming human flesh, to bring a message of forgiveness and salvation confirmed by a baptism of the spirit, a ceremony performed not in water but by the imposition of hands. For those who received it rigorous chastity became a rule of life, meat and other foods produced by coition must be avoided, material possessions were forbidden. For the Bogomils the Old Testament was the work of the evil one, the New Testament revealed the word of the true God, which only they properly interpreted. Christ had not instituted the established church, whose teaching about images, saints, infant baptism, about the virgin birth, crucifixion, and resurrection was all false.

As the Bogomil creed spread it acquired a body of myth to explain its beliefs and there was introduced the doctrine of 'absolute' dualism, which entirely separates the origin of good and evil. There are two creations by two coeternal principles or gods, one wholly spiritual and good, the other forever evil. This may have been borrowed from other cults, or it may have been an internal development in Bogomilism, as more sophisticated minds grappled with problems of how evil could appear from good, how a spiritual Christ could participate in the life of a wicked world. Various 'churches' soon existed, differing in their acceptance of mitigated or absolute dualism, but practising substantially the same rites.

The Bogomils no doubt owed many of their beliefs to a tradition of dualism expressed in the ancient Manichaean and Gnostic sects, although the way it was passed along over the centuries is not clearly demonstrated. If they were, indeed, inheritors, they were by no means servile imitators. The Cathars likewise derived some of their theology from the Bogomils. The problem of when and how that Bogomil-Cathar link was established has been much discussed.

One interpretation, advanced most explicitly by Father Antoine Dondaine, is that Bogomil infiltration of western Europe gave rise to the various heresies which appeared in the half century after the year 1000. Dondaine argues that the similarity of doctrines, such as rejection of baptism in water, refusal to eat meat, detestation of the cross, and denunciation of marriage, together with the rather sudden appearance of the sects and the fact that they drew from all classes of society must convince us that the eleventh-century heresies were Bogomil-inspired. A very different statement has come from Raffaelo Morghen who insists that the early western heresies were native products, not inspired by eastern intervention but thrown up by a groundswell of piety and shaped by desires for church reform and a purer faith. Since no contemporary document mentions the doctrine of two creators the traits that seem to be dualistic, Morghen believes, should be explained as the result of the tension between spirit and flesh which has always existed in Christian thought. The debate is non-sectarian and international. Ernst Werner, for example, supports Dondaine's thesis; Jeffrey B. Russell has placed himself at Morghen's side. Other scholars, such as Malcolm D. Lambert and R. I. Moore, have taken an intermediate position, from which they see native western aspirations for moral reform, asceticism, and deeper spirituality as basic to the western heresies, but do not exclude attempts by the Bogomils to win converts in the West.[1]

The question is of some importance to the interpretation of Catharism. If Bogomil influence brought an ancient tradition to western Europe in the eleventh century, a proto-Catharism existed then as an alien intrusion before popular enthusiasm for religious renovation and reform was widespread. But if there were little or no effective Bogomil penetration of the West in those years, the criticism and rejection of the Roman church, perhaps with overtones of dualism, should be regarded as spontaneous dissent, and thus the subsequent Catharism of the twelfth century may be regarded as a theology adopted by men who already in their pursuit of moral and ethical rigour, had rejected the Roman church. Their minds had been prepared by their own religious searchings; doctrines absorbed from the Bogomils shaped their dissent into a counter-church, but were not its cause.

It is incontrovertible that Bogomils and Cathars had close relationships after the middle of the twelfth century. Eminent scholars like H. C. Puech, Christine Thouzellier, and Raoul Manselli have concluded that only then was the impact of eastern heresies significant.[2] This is certainly true of southern France. If the 'Manichaeans' who were noticed there between 1018 and 1026 were, indeed, Bogomils their activity ceased to be noticed for many decades thereafter. In the early twelfth century, while Peter of Bruys was probably affected by certain Bogomil ideas, he did not adopt the basic theme of dualism. No dualistic teaching at all can be found in the activity of his successor, Henry. When Catharism did become clearly evident, about a decade and a half after Henry disappeared from the scene, it was an importation from the Rhineland through northern France and from Italy.

Circumstances of the time facilitated the importation. Bogomils had spread in Bulgaria, Serbia, and Bosnia. Crusaders, pilgrims and merchants travelled back and forth. Moreover, religious enthusiasts in the West were receptive to the new ideas. Tales of the devil were commonplace and it was not entirely strange to hear that he exercised an independent creative power. Would a beneficent God visit famine, plague and epidemic on His own people; for such malevolence in Nature must there not be a malevolent cause? The dualistic explanation of the existence of evil appealed to men who were meditating on the contrast between spirit and matter. The disposition to impose puritanical restraints on the flesh was always present among advocates of rigorous moral reform. Furthermore, the wandering preachers of apostolic life, by their criticism of the clergy and the discredit they cast on the authority of the church, had prepared the ground where the new heresies flourished. Men like Peter of Bruys and Henry and their counterparts in dissent all over western Europe were forerunners of the Cathars, not in anticipating their dogma, but because they attacked corruption and wealth in the church violently, weakened dependence on the clergy, and popularized the idea that the warrants for spiritual leadership were outward signs of chastity, poverty, asceticism, and humility. For wherever the Cathars appeared they too presented themselves as Christians in a truly apostolic mode, giving by every external sign of holiness proof of the truth of their teaching.

## The Albigensian Heresy

Between about 1140 and 1160 the 'new' dualist heresy spread from northern Europe where it appeared in cities such as Köln and Liège southward. We cannot be sure of the moment – it was probably about 1150 – that it penetrated Languedoc. The name 'Cathars' was first applied to the heretics in the north about 1160. As they spread they acquired others: Publicans was often used in the north; in Italy they were called Patarines. The connection with Balkan sects gave rise to the name Bulgars (*bougres* in French). Opponents also revived ancient sect-names – Arians, Manichaeans, Marcionites – to apply to them. All Europe soon knew those who congregated in southern France as the Albigenses.

Although the town of Albi was not the sole, nor even the most important centre of heresy, circumstances combined to give its name to the southern dualists. The earliest such incident occurred in 1165, when a group of alleged heretics under the leadership of one named Oliver were induced to come before an assembly of ecclesiastics and prominent laymen at the village of Lombers, not far from Albi. In response to questions they admitted to rejecting the Old Testament, denied that baptism by a priest was necessary, and gave noncommital but suspect answers to questions about marriage and confession. In the heat of subsequent debate with the Catholic party they were vitriolic in denunciation of the prelates, who, however, had the last word when they condemned the Lombers group as heretics, although no punitive action followed.

The Catharist theology first taught in the West was, like that of the early Bogomils, a mitigated dualism in which the devil was a fallen angel or perhaps even a rebellious son of God, whose role had been to shape the inchoate elements already created by God into a world of matter. There, the evil one had imprisoned in bodies of his devising the angelic souls which had fallen with him from heaven. This creed was soon challenged by missionaries from Constantinople who came to Italy to teach the absolute dualism of two implacably opposed, coeternal deities. The chief missionary, Papa (that is, priest) Nicheta is said to have crossed the Alps sometime between 1167 and 1172 to meet Catharist leaders from northern and southern France at the village of St Fèlix de Caraman, where he persuaded them to be rebaptized in the absolute dualist tradition. To supplement the group already existing near Albi, three new churches or bishoprics were set up for heretics of Toulouse, Carcassonne, and Agen (or perhaps of the Val d'Aran in the county of Comminges, although that seems quite unlikely). The document describing this important event has been vigorously challenged as fraudulent and as vigorously defended as substantially accurate. Whatever its status, the Languedocian Cathars subsequently were organized in those divisions and the doctrines of absolute dualism held general sway among them in the last decades of the century.

The Cathars rapidly made converts and by the end of the twelfth century they constituted an organized rival of the Roman church. Some reasons for their success in southern France will be suggested later; here we will be concerned with a description of the heresy.

*Organization of the Catharist Church*
Members of the Catharist church were men and women who had been baptized in the true faith of Christ by the consolamentum, a baptism and gift of the spirit by imposition of the hands of persons already in the sect. Catholics referred to them as 'perfected' or 'consoled' heretics, names never used by the Cathars themselves; 'robed heretics' was another name derived from their habitual black garb. The Cathars chose to be called 'Christians' or 'Good Christians' and their followers commonly referred to them as 'the Good Men'. Such fully professed heretics were, as

we shall see, always relatively few. The strength of the Albigensian heresy lay in the much larger number of persons, called 'believers', who were its adherents but who had not yet been baptized. They were persons who accepted the teaching of the Good Men, venerated and supported them by their service and gifts, and attended their ceremonies. Believers took as implicitly true that their eternal salvation lay in dying 'in the hands of the Good Men', that is, receiving the consolamentum, but normally they postponed that ceremony until their death beds.

Bishops of the churches of the Cathars, whose geographical limits in part paralleled the lines of Catholic dioceses, were elected by the community of perfected heretics and were established in office by a special repetition of the consolamentum. No one was superior to another, although their opponents in the thirteenth century spread the report that there was a pope of the sect with his see in the Balkans. Each bishop had two elected assistants, called 'elder son' and 'younger son', respectively; the titles had nothing to do with family connection or age but only indicated the order of succession to the episcopate. Several deacons were subordinate to each bishop. Bishops and sons travelled about, preaching and baptizing; the deacons were usually supervisors of hospices which sheltered other perfected men and women. All who had received the consolamentum could perform that spiritual baptism for others, all had the duty of preaching and counselling believers. When they gathered in the absence of one of the hierarchy the Good Man who had been longest in the faith presided with the title of 'elder'. Administrative decisions, such as the marking out of dioceses at Saint Félix or the creation of a new diocese of Razès in 1225, took place in assemblies of the perfected.

The public teaching which won so many followers was buttressed by constant reference to the New Testament. The true Christian, the Good Men told their hearers, obeyed literally the precepts of Christ which forbade taking oaths, lying, stealing, or killing and required men to live in chastity and charity. The Christian put his trust in the true church which they represented; he knew that in this world his lot was to suffer and his duty was to forgive his persecutors. Sometimes passages were read from the Scriptures in the vernacular – the passion of Christ was a favourite subject – and the Good Man commented on the verses. Or the preacher might draw the contrast between the spirituality of the church of Christ, preserved in the apostolic succession of the Good Men, and the actuality of the Roman organization, described as an institution of this world and its evil maker, whose works were vain, whose priests were without sacramental power because of their greed and worldly lives. Bread of the Eucharist differed in no way from ordinary bread. It was a favoured quip to say that if the body of Christ was really in the bread in quantity as great as a mountain, priests would long ago have eaten it all up. The Mass and baptism in water, like other sacraments and burial in consecrated ground, were silly foibles fostered by the clergy for their own profit. Prayer for the dead and invocation of saints were useless. It was no better to pray in a church than in a stable.

As the Albigensian preachers gained the confidence of their hearers, other themes would be introduced, for, however much they profited by the hostility to the established church and the enthusiasm for apostolic life which their predecessors had generated, they were missionaries of a creed which challenged orthodox Christianity in its fundamentals. The evil of this world, they declared, arose because its maker was the prince of darkness. God wished to redeem His lost souls from the power of Satan and Jesus Christ had come in His spiritual nature to show men the way to salvation. He had never really assumed human flesh but deluded mortal eyes by seeming to do so. Redemption of the soul was possible only when one learned to pray in the name of Christ and entered the apostolic fellowship of His church by receiving the consolamentum. Without that the soul remained a prisoner in flesh, passing from body to body. There would be no resurrection of bodies which could never enter the spiritual heavens; there is no purgatory. Works of the world served only the evil one. Sexual acts which produced new bodies to inhabit the temporal realm had no divine sanction; thus legal matrimony was no better than prostitution.[3]

The exposition of these themes to lay audiences was buttressed by carefully chosen passages of Scripture, unencumbered by philosophical or theological subtleties which the auditors were little prepared to understand. In Italy at that time quarrels among groups of Cathars were sharpening statements of doctrine and refining theological arguments. Internal disputes were not unknown in Languedoc but they were muted after 1170. There the impact of Catharism was more emotional than intellectual.

Although the public preaching of the Albigensian heretics was a relatively simplified statement of their theology, within the hierarchy were certain leaders quite willing to defend themselves in more elaborate fashion in numerous casual encounters with

C

defenders of orthodoxy and in the organized debates with Catholics which were to occur in the first decade of the thirteenth century. For these they were prepared by knowledge of a fairly substantial literature.

### Catharist Literature

The major literary resource of the Cathars was the Bible in the Vulgate tradition which they often used in vernacular translation. Portions of the New Testament were carried about and often left with literate believers. The Gospels and the Epistles of the New Testament furnished spiritual instruction, the Apocalypse provided proof of their interpretation of creation and of the struggle between good and evil. The Pentateuch and historical books of the Old Testament clearly showed the wicked power at work in the tales of wrath, rapine, and murder. Expository writings were also circulated: glosses on the Lord's Prayer, explanations of the nature of the true church, books written to sustain the controversy between factions and between the Cathars and orthodox Christians, and old apocryphal scriptures which buttressed their doctrines on the creation and destiny of this world.

Absolute dualists, the dominant faction in Languedoc after about 1170, taught that Lucifer, son of the eternal principle of evil, had made his way into heaven. A myth current among some Albigenses about 1210 was that this invasion was in retaliation for the theft by the good God of two beings the devil had already created. Lucifer, by his handsome appearance and wiles, won the affection of some of God's heavenly creatures; some Cathars said that he deluded even God, who made him a steward over the angels. In any event Lucifer eventually seduced and drew out of heaven a third part of the angels.[4] Before the fall the angelic beings had a triple constitution: body, soul, and spirit. The souls were seduced by Lucifer and fell from grace, leaving the bodies and spirits abandoned in heaven. In the world of matter which evil had created, captive souls were incarcerated in human bodies made by the devil. Some said that this earth, in fact, was one of many realms of the wicked god and the lowest hell. In pity God sent Christ, an angel of superior merits, to redeem His lost people, but Christ never exchanged His angelic nature for a material body nor did He suffer the infirmities of human flesh, except as an illusion to human eyes. His mother Mary was an angel sent before him into the world. Another doctrine common to both some of the Albigenses and some Italian absolute dualists was that Christ's real birth, death, and resurrection had actually taken place in 'another world', a higher realm than this earth, from which the people of God had fallen and to which redeemed souls would return to await the general resurrection or absolute separation of the domains of good and evil.

The mitigated dualists of Languedoc, who were fewer in numbers after 1170, also spoke of a sole God, creator of the spiritual realm as He was also creator of undifferentiated and formless matter. Lucifer, a creature of the good God – some Cathars said that his heavenly name had been Lucibel and some accepted the Bogomilist teaching that he was God's son – rebelled in heaven and was cast out with his followers. Explanations of the rebellion differed: one version was that his revolt sprang from pride and envy; another was that Lucibel had ventured into the chaos outside of heaven and encountered a four-faced evil spirit by whose prompting he was led to sin. After his expulsion from heaven Lucifer made the world, that is, he gave form to the undifferentiated elements created by God, and in it placed the bodies of Adam and Eve, giving them life with the aid of a good angel sent by God for the purpose and then repaying his helper by thrusting him into the body of Adam. Some mitigated dualists believed that the souls of all men were the angels who had sinned, others that human souls were born of the souls of Adam and Eve, just as bodies were born of their bodies. There were disagreements as to whether all souls would eventually be saved. There were also various teachings about Christ. Most Cathars insisted that Christ, Mary, and John the Evangelist were all angelic beings; a few admitted that Christ and Mary had assumed human flesh, but taught that they had abandoned it on ascension to heaven.

To illustrate and explain their theological teaching both factions among the Albigenses used a number of myths, some of which derived from old apocryphal writings. One especially in favour among the absolute dualists of Languedoc was *The Vision of Isaiah*, a version of a very ancient work, which was imported from the Bogomils by way of Italy after 1190. In it, Isaiah was described as having traversed the seven heavens to the highest court of God, beholding wonderful things and witnessing the descent of Christ to earth, His fate, resurrection, and reascension. To Isaiah was also revealed the reward of the blessed in the last days, when they would be reunited with God in the seventh heaven. A source of edifying instruction for the mitigated dualists was *The Secret Supper of John the Evangelist*, also called *The Questions of John*, a Bogomil work, in which the evangelist, in spiritual communion with Christ, is told of the origin of the world, the devil's work therein, and the final judgement to come.

Albigensian theologians were also capable of discourses of some subtlety, although their enemies declared them jejune and deceptive. In confrontations with heretical spokesmen at Lombers in 1165 and in Toulouse in 1178 Catholics were puzzled and infuriated by their opponents' affirmations of faith in one God, their approval of the sacraments, and their other affirmations of orthodoxy, despite a reputation for teaching the contrary. A clue to the true intent of such statements is disclosed in an anonymous treatise by an Albigensian heretic, written soon after 1220, of which only fragments have survived. The heretic begins by declaring his belief in one true and highest God, maker of 'heaven and earth, the sea, and all things that are in them', but subsequent passages reveal that he is referring only to 'all things' of the spiritual universe and that he believes that there are in truth two kingdoms, two distinct and separate realms, of which one is utterly wicked. The exposition of this interpretation is made by profuse citation of biblical verses.[5]

There is not space here to discuss the full variety of Catharist beliefs. From sources originating outside Langeudoc we know that there were bitter disputes between factions over various theological points. In the early thirteenth century a few dogmas seem to have been evolving toward an approximation of Catholic beliefs. Also, from the reception of heresy at all social levels, we might guess, but without documentary proof, that Catharist teaching was adaptable by variations of emphasis to the desires and needs of all classes, appealing in one light to workers, in another to merchants, and, with changes in nuance, to feudal aristocrats. Yet Catharism was classless in the sense that any man or woman was welcome among the believers and the humblest person could rise to an important place in its hierarchy.

## The Consolamentum

The great majority of believers postponed the consolamentum to the last moments of life. The relatively few who aspired to an earlier baptism and full membership in their church, with the intention of living out their lives in the faith, undertook a rigorous and demanding existence. Often they prepared themselves by an initiatory year of fasting and instruction in one of the hospices endowed and protected by a noble family in a town or castle where a deacon presided. Such houses were also places of rest for the Good Men on their travels or, under the direction of holy women, were shelters for the daughters of the nobility. When judged ready, the believer was presented to assembled Perfect and believers for a two-part ceremony, the ritual for which is known in two versions: one is written in Provençal, the other was originally composed in that language but now survives in a Latin text. The essentials of the ceremony are similar in both, although there are differences in the suggestions for the sermon to be delivered by the ministrant.

For the first part of the rite, in which he received the authority to say the Lord's Prayer (until this had been granted no one in the devil's realm of this world could properly call on God as Father), the believer was led forward by a sponsor in a room where the company had gathered around a table covered with a white cloth, on which lay the Gospels. The ministrant, a bishop or deacon or one among the Good Men who had been longest in the faith, welcomed them with an exchange of greetings, genuflections, and prayers for mercy in formal phrases, and then gave a short sermon. That suggested by the ritual in Provençal reminds the believer that the church he was about to join comprised the heavenly people of God, who by deception had been separated from their Holy Father, but were to be restored by Jesus Christ. In the church he would receive the Holy Spirit, just as Christ and Paul had promised. The first requirement was to say the Lord's Prayer with true discernment. According to the Latin ritual the full meaning of the prayer might then be explained. Its phrases referred to the Father of those who were to be saved, to Him whose law was hallowed. The kingdom to come meant both Christ and the people of God, those who prayed to do His will. The 'supersubstantial bread' – words which among the Cathars replaced the 'daily bread' of the prayer in the Gospel of Matthew – was the law of Christ, the spiritual commandment which Christ 'broke', that is, gave to his disciples. In the Lord's Prayer the Cathars also included a doxology not used in the Roman church, in which 'the kingdom, and the power, and the glory' were respectively explained as referring to God's people, acknowledging His power to save, and giving Him due honour, 'forever,' that is, in His divine creation.

Under certain circumstances the actual baptism might be deferred for a time; usually the Cathars proceeded at once to that ceremony. Again there were genuflections and repetitions of the Lord's Prayer and ritual requests for forgiveness of sin. When the believer made a formal request for baptism he heard a sermon, largely comprised of the teaching of Christ and the evangelists about baptism, the texts chosen to demonstrate that it had been preserved unchanged among the Good Men from the time of the apostles. The Gospel commandments which the believer now accepted were emphasized: Do not commit adultery, kill, tell a lie, swear an oath, or steal. Do unto others what you wish done to you. Pray for persecutors and turn to them the other cheek. If any one steals your coat, give him also your cloak. Furthermore, hold the world and all its works in hatred. So goes the sermon preserved in the Provençal text; that in the Latin is not greatly dissimilar, emphasizing the effect of baptism in forgiveness of sins and in regenerating souls which had been fouled by contact with evil. One must henceforth love God in truth, kindliness, humility, chastity, and in all good virtues; be faithful in worldly things; obey the commandments of Christ; never eat cheese, milk, or the flesh of birds or animals. Hunger, thirst, and persecution will be the lot the true Christian endures for the love of God.

The believer's promise to follow unfalteringly all these precepts brought him to the most solemn moment. After an exchange of prayers by the participants the minister held the Gospels over the believer's head and all the Cathars placed their hands on his body. The minister read the first seventeen verses of the Gospel of John and recited a litany of requests for mercy, alternated with repetitions of the Lord's Prayer. Thus the believer became a Good Christian and his soul was forgiven its sin in heaven. The ceremony ended with a kiss of peace, given from man to man and woman to woman – women touched men only on shoulder or elbow – or by kissing the Gospels, followed by a general confession of sins.

The 'Good Christian' thereafter wore the black robe which showed his status. When persecution eventually made this distinctive garb dangerous, it was sometimes replaced by a black thread worn next to the body. Women, after receiving the consolamentum, were apt to retire to quiet life in a hospice or as honoured guests of the believers. A Good Man entered on a life of preaching and teaching, travelling always with a companion, praying constantly, owning nothing, visiting believers, blessing bread and distributing it to those with whom he dined and, when called upon, performing the consolamentum for those who asked for it on their death bed.

In that abbreviated ceremony the invalid was questioned on his attitude toward the church he wished to enter, whether he owed it any unpaid pledge, and if his resolve was firm. Satisfied on these points the ministrant might give brief instruction on the usages of the Cathar church and the commandments which must be observed or, at need, would proceed at once to administer the prayer and consolamentum.[6] Although the Cathars disparaged the necessity of burial in consecrated ground and there is some mention of cemeteries of the heretics in the sources, they also utilized Catholic cemeteries for their dead.

The consolamentum was a sacrament of surpassing importance for the Cathars, yet it could be repeated, as it was when used to consecrate a bishop. In certain other circumstances a new baptism was also deemed essential. If one were persuaded to change allegiance between the mitigated and absolute traditions of dualism, as perhaps occurred at Saint Félix de Caraman, he was rebaptized. Furthermore, the redeeming value of the sacrament depended on the personal purity of the ministrant; thus, if he who performed it was discovered to have been guilty of sin, those whom he had consoled had to receive a new consolamentum to be assured of salvation. A Good Man who confessed to so much as entertaining sinful thoughts must have the baptism anew after doing suitable penance of fasting.

Public religious ceremonies other than the consolamentum were simple but often repeated. At meals food was consecrated by blessing, requests for forgiveness of sin, and repetition of the Lord's Prayer; the consecrated bread was distributed to all who were present. Believers were also welcomed when the Good Men gathered, usually once a month, for the Service, a confession of minor faults such as careless thoughts or failure to say the Lord's Prayer as required. (Catholic writers referred to this ceremony as *apparellamentum*).[7]

### Religious Life of the Cathars

The personal life of the perfected Cathar was marked by constant prayer and rigid asceticism. The Lord's Prayer, normally repeated sixteen times in one sequence, was said at stipulated times during the day, as well as at any incident out of the ordinary, such as on entering a town. Meat, eggs, cheese, and milk were absolutely forbidden; even shellfish were usually avoided, except in illness. Three days of every week were devoted to fasting on bread and water and there were three forty-day periods of restricted diet, during one week of which only bread and water were taken. Contact of the sexes was kept to the minimum. Men and women associated in religious services and, in later days of persecution, they travelled together to disarm suspicion, but physical touch was avoided as much as possible.

The Cathars admitted that even one who had received the consolamentum might be tempted by weaknesses of the flesh, although the great sin had been that committed by their angelic souls at the time of the fall from heaven. There were persistent reports, however, from the malicious or ill-informed among their opponents that behind the appearance of piety were concealed lives of immorality. It was not infrequently alleged that because the Good Men shunned physical relationship between the sexes they were addicted to homosexuality. Such charges are contradicted and more than offset by the abundance of testimony from persons who had best reason to know the rigid ascetic standards the Cathars observed.

Disdain for the temporal world did not deter the Cathars from accumulating property as the common possession of their church, while professing to own nothing as individuals. Their Catholic and Waldensian opponents reproached them for accumulating lands, livestock, and other wealth through gifts or bequests and for lending at usurious interest to their believers. Enemies also asserted that perfected heretics sometimes travelled in the role of merchants while searching for converts and pursued gainful occupations as they proselytized.

A great deal has also been written, some of it little short of nonsense, about the supposed hatred of Cathars for human life. There is no doubt at all that their attitude toward existence in this world was deeply pessimistic. They thought of the world and the flesh as the work of an evil god from which divinely created souls could escape only through membership in their church. They spoke harshly of procreation as perpetuating the devil's realm in human bodies, which encased the souls fallen from heaven; they expected only persecution, as Christ had been persecuted; and they astonished observers by their calm acceptance of death. However, to attribute to them a hatred for all life and the wish to see it extinguished is grossly to exaggerate the Cathars' conviction, shared by orthodox Christians, that this world is only a temporary abode of the soul.

In particular, a supposed practice of *endura*, that is, suicide by fasting or the murder of a newly-baptized person to prevent contamination of his purified soul, has been over-emphasized. Rumours about holy suicide or murder were in circulation about 1250 and were stoutly denied by one well-informed orthodox writer in Italy. There are reports of death by endura in Languedoc in the late thirteenth and early fourteenth centuries, but by that time a furtive existence was fostering vagaries and extravagances in belief and practice. One ought not to deny that there may have been individuals fanatical enough to commit suicide as a way of attesting their faith or of calling attention to persecution, for dramatic gestures of that sort are not unknown among all kinds of groups devoted to all kinds of ideals, even today. The mistaken idea that death by endura was a normal Catharist practice, however, seems to have arisen from over-emphasis on incidents in which Good Men who were too ill to repeat the Lord's Prayer refused unsanctified food or when a prisoner of the Inquisition preferred death to the dungeon. Suicide was not a characteristic practice when the religion was flourishing and reports about it, like those of nasty sexual aberrations – and, we may add, of secret lore preserved from ancient esoteric cults – must be regarded with scepticism, as tales purveyed by rumour and encouraged by credulity and hostility, medieval and modern.[8]

*Believers of Heretics*

Believers of the Cathars were much more numerous than the leaders and teachers. The term 'believer' has sometimes been interpreted as designating only such followers as had received the right to say the Lord's Prayer. If it once had so limited an application, that had been lost in the early thirteenth century; witnesses and inquisitors used 'believer' to refer to any person who believed that the heretics taught a good faith and who proposed to receive the consolamentum before death. Requirements placed on them were not heavy. As has been said, they were welcomed at the religious ceremonies of the Good Men, and such instruction as they heard there was reinforced when they gathered to hear the preaching of the itinerant preachers. The believers learned to greet and part from the perfected heretics with three deep bows or prostrations to the ground, accompanied by a three-fold repetition of the phrase, 'Bless us, have mercy upon us,' usually adding, 'Pray God that He will make me a good Christian and bring me to a good end.' The good end meant reception of the consolamentum. To this the Good Man responded, 'May God bless you,' adding the requested prayer for death in the sect. This was the *melioramentum*, which Catholic observers, supposing that the Cathar himself was worshipped or the Holy Spirit residing in him, called 'adoration'. It was an act also of commitment, a pledge of allegiance, and an acknowledgement of faith. By the middle of the thirteenth century it could be reinforced by the *covenensa*, the believer's promise eventually to receive the consolamentum, with the reciprocal assurance from the Good Men that it would be bestowed even if power of speech had been lost.

Believers entertained the Good Men as they travelled about preaching, sent them food, guided them from place to place, concealed and defended them in time of danger. Not infrequently they made bequests to the church; opponents were fond of repeating stories about the difficulties sometimes encountered in collecting these. We should not be surprised to find that the warmth of devotion varied, that under persecution some believers were easily persuaded to abandon their allegiance, while others chose to die rather than do so.

There were also variations among believers in their knowledge of the theology of the Cathars. Our information about how much of the niceties of doctrine was taught them is not abundant; it was theology as known to the perfected heretics that Catholic polemicists described (and no such treatise is known to have been written in Languedoc before the last years of the twelfth century), while inquisitors, in the years before 1250, seem to have been more interested in recording guilty acts than doctrine and normally asked persons accused as believers only a few general questions about teaching they had heard. However, Peter Garcias, who in 1247 was induced to reveal his beliefs in what he thought was a private conversation,[9] probably exposed the major points the Cathars made in their public teaching: belief in a dual creation, the fall of angels, and a docetic interpretation of Christ, as well as detestation of the Roman church.

Enemies in that day and some historians since then have alleged that the impact of Catharist teaching on the believers was unwholesome. These critics have insisted that condemnation of the material world and teaching that to procreate human bodies was to do the devil's work encouraged licentiousness, loosened family relationships, and threatened to dissolve the moral bases of society. It is easier to make such charges than to produce evidence to substantiate them. There are references in inquisitorial records to concubinage among believers of the heretics, but also to those who lived chastely. Neither was unknown in orthodox circles. Ardent believers married and begot children no less frequently than their Catholic neighbours. Another charge is that the Cathars' teaching on the sinfulness of taking an oath endangered the medieval social order. Yet good faith and mutual support among believers is too amply attested to let us suppose that social bonds were being dissolved.

It may be argued, moreover, that the moral and ethical standards which the Good Men demonstrated in their own lives, their sobriety, and their abhorrence of violence and lies would encourage the same among their believers. Surely, in gaining their initial favourable reception and winning the reputation of good men teaching a good faith, the Cathars profited less from theology than from the way in which their appearance and actions conformed to the currently popular ideal of apostolic behaviour. Therein they had the advantage over the Catholic clergy of southern France in the twelfth century. Indeed, the only consistent opposition to them in evangelization in the streets, in shops and homes and noble courts, came not from the orthodox clergy but from another religious group which the church had also declared to be heretical. They were the Poor of Lyon, or Waldenses, who also emphasized in the strongest terms the necessity of the apostolic life.[10]

*Waldes of Lyon and the Waldenses*
In the city of Lyon some time between 1173 and 1176 a prosperous merchant named Waldes[11] underwent a religious experience. One account is that he was deeply affected on hearing from a street singer the popular legend of St Alexis. Waldes went to a teacher of theology to ask how he could be saved, who quoted to him the words of Christ: 'If thou wilt be perfect, go sell what thou hast and give to the poor, and come and follow me.' If this event, indeed, is what precipitated Waldes's decision, it seems evident that he had already been moved by the spirit of the *vita apostolica* which was then being widely discussed and by its emphasis on poverty as essential to salvation. As Francis of Assisi would do a few years later, Waldes took the words of Christ literally. Making a property settlement on his wife and providing for his daughters in a nunnery, he distributed his remaining wealth to the poor and began to preach a message of repentance in the streets. Some people, of course, thought him mad; others, as was also almost inevitable in that day, joined him to follow his example; for their instruction, Waldes procured translations of the Scriptures and of some excerpts from the writings of the church fathers. When reproached by the archbishop of Lyon for his unauthorized evangelism, he is said to have made the same answer that the heretic Henry had uttered forty years before: 'It is better to obey God than man.' No doubt it was the antagonism of the clergy of Lyon that induced Waldes and his companions to seek papal approval of their lives of poverty and preaching. At the Third

Lateran Council of 1179 a few of the clergy laughed at the simplicity of these would-be followers of the apostolic life because of their ignorance of theology, but the pope applauded their devotion to poverty. The right to preach he denied them unless they first obtained permission from their bishop.

Even if Waldes observed the papal restriction for a time after his return to Lyon, suspicion of him persisted among the clergy. In 1180, or perhaps 1181, Henry, former abbot of Clairvaux, now cardinal, visited the city as papal legate, the memory of an encounter with Cathars in Toulouse fresh in his mind.[12] Waldes was called before the cardinal at a diocesan synod, where, to attest his orthodoxy, he swore to a profession of faith. It was based on ancient Christian forms brought up to date by additions which specifically rejected the major points of Catharist teaching. To this credo Waldes appended a statement of his intention to live in holy poverty. The conviction, derived from the Gospels, that this was the way to follow Christ has never been more explicitly stated: 'Whatever we had', said Waldes on behalf of himself and his fellows, 'we have given to the poor as the Lord advised, and we have resolved to be poor in such fashion that we shall take no thought for the morrow, nor shall we accept gold or silver or anything of that sort from anyone, beyond food and clothing sufficient for the day. Our resolve is to follow the precepts of the Gospel as commands.'

Undeniably, at that moment Waldes was entirely orthodox in belief; the fault which soon incurred the censure of the church was disobedience, for he and his companions could no more resist the compulsion to preach than the clergy, under a new archbishop, could tolerate that trespass on their function or endure criticism of their way of life arising from its contrast with that of these evangelists. Waldes and his followers were excommunicated and expelled from Lyon about 1182. The paths they took cannot be exactly traced. For most of them it lay southward. Now calling themselves the Poor in Spirit and known to others also as the Poor of Lyon, they were excommunicated with other sects in the general condemnation of heresy issued by Pope Lucius III in 1184.

A new sect thus appeared in Languedoc. By 1190 the Poor of Lyon or Waldenses, as they were also then known, were attracting unfavourable comment from the clergy in Narbonne and Montpellier; two decades later the area of their activity was described as extending 'from Catalonia to the sea at Narbonne and thence to the sea at Bordeaux'. The wandering preachers had adopted sandals cut in a special pattern to signify their apostolic profession in which they remained true to Waldes's original intent, owning nothing, not even an extra cloak, begging their daily food, taking shelter where they could find it. Perhaps it was inevitable that by analogy with the Cathars these evangelists before long were called 'the perfect', in distinction from their devotees who were 'believers'.

The enthusiasts formed a loose society in the early days. As long as Waldes's leadership prevailed, the preachers were forbidden to labour at any task other than teaching the Gospel or to set up an organization that might constrain their itinerant evangelism. Waldes died, probably not long after 1205. By 1218 the problem of leadership had been resolved in Languedoc by the annual election of two provosts or rectors who spoke for the group in important matters, such as an attempt to heal a schism between French and Italian factions in 1218.[13] Contemporary sources also mention persons who were charged with supervision of recent converts, indicating that hospices or retreats were coming into existence.

The errors which had earned papal condemnation in 1184 were of practice, not doctrine; the danger to the church arose from disobedience and from the contrast of the Waldensian way of life with that of the orthodox clergy. 'They go about two by two, barefoot, clad in woollen garments, owning nothing, holding all things in common like the apostles, naked following a naked Christ,' wrote Walter Map, who saw them in Rome in 1179, and his conclusion was that 'if we admit them, we shall be driven out'. After their excommunication, not unsurprisingly, the Poor of Lyon developed further disagreements with the Roman church; there is reason to believe that some of these were stimulated by the absorption of the legacy of discontent left by Peter of Bruys and Henry in Languedoc, yet the Waldensian preachers insisted that they were in the direct tradition from early Christianity. In a book written a few years after 1190 by a companion of Waldes, an enemy was made to ask derisively: 'Where was the church between the advent of the Savior and your coming?' The Waldensian reply was: 'The church of God is ever there where a congregation of the faithful exists, holding right faith and fulfilling it by works.' Waldensian preachers who appeared at Narbonne in 1190 were challenged to a debate by Catholic clergy before an elected judge, and at its conclusion were declared to be heretics. The errors censored then were rejection of the authority of pope, prelates, and priests and the insistence on preaching, in which women joined. A few years later the learned Alan of Lille heatedly denounced the Poor of Lyon, not only for unauthorized preaching but also for teaching that confession to God alone sufficed, that indulgences were worthless, and that preachers must not labour in any other way. He found them in error, also, for absolutely banning oaths and condemning the penalty of death for crime.

What the share of Waldes was in widening the breach with the church is unknown. One influential member of his following never moved very far from orthodoxy. He was Durand of Huesca (*Osca*), who was ardent in controversy against the Cathars. In the work mentioned in the preceding paragraph, entitled *A Book Against Heresy* [*Liberantiheresis*], he warmly defended fundamental Christian tenets: belief in the unity of God, acceptance of both Testaments, faith in Christ, validity of the sacraments, and belief in resurrection. From the orthodox point of view, his words were chiefly suspect in the declaration against manual labour by preachers, certain remarks about predestination, and the assertion that the faith of Waldes was derived by grace of God directly and solely from the Gospels. In 1207 Durand and a few friends yielded to the arguments of Catholic missionaries in a debate at Pamiers, and in the following year were received again into the church by Pope Innocent III, who authorized them to form a society known as the Poor Catholics, with the aim of combating Catharism.[14]

The unreconciled Waldenses, however, continued to move among the people of Languedoc, preaching, hearing confessions. Some gained a reputation for medical knowledge and were consulted even by believers of the Cathars and orthodox persons. The Waldenses baptized children, also sometimes rebaptizing adults. Some of them who insisted that only adult baptism was efficacious formed a splinter group. In their teaching, the sandal-wearing preachers spoke constantly of the sinfulness of oaths, lies, and murder. They derided the garb and tonsure of priests because, they said, the mark of a priest, the right to preach, and the assurance of salvation came only with the profession of absolute poverty and the maintenance of personal purity. They were ready to admit that good priests might be found within the Roman church and willingly accepted the sacraments from such as won their approval, but they also soon developed their own fashion of consecrating the Eucharist. On the evening of Holy Thursday the leader of a group or household would convene others around a table spread with a white cloth on which were a goblet of wine and a loaf of unleavened bread. At first it was held that the ministrant must be in holy orders but this gave way to allowing any worthy man or woman to preside. After an invocation all knelt to repeat the Lord's Prayer seven times. The minister, making the sign of the cross over the bread and wine, gave each participant a morsel and a sip. Any leftover bread was kept for use at Easter and the bread and wine thus consecrated were also the food offered to those who fell ill. Some Waldenses also consecrated bread, fish, and wine in a service on Good Friday.[15]

The Waldenses were never as numerous as the Cathars in Languedoc and were usually regarded by orthodox Christians as less dangerous. They were, in fact, vigorous opponents of the dualists, despite agreement with them in rejecting the Roman church, in refusal to take oaths or tell lies, in reprobation of the death penalty, in emphasis on the Lord's Prayer, evangelism, and poverty. Debates between spokesmen for the two sects before interested lay audiences were not unusual. Neither traits in common nor the fact that occasionally certain people would treat both with courtesy or members of the same family would be found among devotees of each sect diminished their rivalry. The Cathars constituted a church which challenged and sought to destroy Rome; they entirely rejected Catholic theology and practised an ethical code based on the presumption of the fundamental wickedness of the world. The Waldenses, whose organization was simpler, expressed the evangelical impulse in a way so enthusiastic that they incurred the hostility and condemnation of the church. But they accepted Christian dogma and complained of the injustice of persecution for what seemed to them to be advocacy of the purest Christian ideals.

The question, 'Why did the Cathars and Waldenses flourish in Languedoc?' calls into account factors other than doctrine. Thus an attempt to explain the prevalence of heresy will be postponed[16] until certain features of Languedocian society, including the status of the church, have been passed in review and an attempt has been made to estimate how numerous, in fact, the heretics were.

# References

1. Dondaine's argument was stated in 'L'Origine de l'hérésie médiévale', *Rivista di storia della chiesa in Italia*, VI (1952), 47–78, in criticism of the views of Morghen, expressed in *Medioevo cristiano*, which have been restated several times and summed up in his 'Problèmes sur l'origine de l'hérésie au moyen âge', *RH*, CCXXXVI (1966), 1–16. Russell supports Morghen's

thesis in *Dissent and Reform*, 192–215. Werner supports Dondaine in παταρηνοι-patarini' in *Vom Mittelalter zur Neuzeit*, 404–19. Lambert's remarks appear in the commentary on maps he prepared for Herder's *Atlas zur Kitchengeschichte*, 41*, 57. Moore is rather more sceptical of Bogomilist influence in 'The Origins of Medieval Heresy', *History*, LV (1970), 21–36.

2. Puech, 'Catharisme médiéval et Bogomilisme' in *Convegno 'Volta'* ... *1956*, published in Accademia nazionale dei Lincei, *Atti*, 8th ser., XII (1957), 56–84; Thouzellier, 'Hérésie et croisade au XIIe siècle', *RHE* XLIX (1954), 855–72; Manselli, *L'eresia del male*.

3. The literature on the Albigensian Cathars is abundant and they enjoy a vogue among writers for popular audiences today. Among scholarly studies, indispensable are Borst, *Die Katharer*, and C. Thouzellier, *Catharisme et valdéisme en Languedoc* (2nd ed.). Two recent studies of the early years of the heresy are by E. Griffe: *Les Débuts de l'aventure cathare en Languedoc*, and *Le Languedoc cathare de 1190 à 1210*. Sect names are discussed in chapters on 'Patarins' and 'Albigenses' in Thouzellier, *Hérésie et hérétiques*. Whether the northern heretics called Publicans were, in fact, Cathars is a question deserving closer analysis than it has received. An account of the conference at Lombers is translated in Wakefield and Evans, *Heresies*, 189–94. Pros and cons of the debate over the authenticity of the sole document which reports the heretical council at St-Félix-de-Caraman are summarized by P. Wolff in *Documents sur l'histoire du Languedoc*, 99–105. Its reliability has most recently been defended by F. Šanjek, 'Le Rassemblement hérétique de St-Félix-de-Caraman (1167) et les églises cathares au XIIe siècle', *RHE*, LXVII (1972), 767–800.

4. The scriptural basis was Apocalypse 12:4, 9: 'His tail drew the third part of the stars of heaven and cast them to earth ... And that great dragon was cast out, that old serpent who is called the devil and Satan, who seduceth the whole world; and he was cast unto the earth and his angels were thrown down with him.'

5. New light has been cast on the beliefs of the Albigenses of the early thirteenth century by recently discovered documents mentioned in the text: an anonymous attack on them, published by Dondaine, 'Durand de Huesca et la polémique anti-cathare', *AFP*, XXIX (1959), 268–71; fragments of a tract by an Albigensian spokesman, edited by Thouzellier in *Un Traité cathare inédit*; and a Catharist exposition of the nature of the true church, edited by T. Venckeleer, 'Un Recueil cathare', *Revue belge de philologie et d'histoire*, XXXVIII (1960), 820–31. All are translated in Wakefield and Evans, *Heresies*, Nos. 37, 58, and 60, as are the two Bogomil myths mentioned in the text (*ibid.*, No. 56). The latter have been studied in E. Trudeneau. 'Apocryphes bogomiles et apocryphes pseudo-bogomiles', *Revue de l'histoire des religions*, CXXXVIII (1950), 22–52, 176–218.

6. If the invalid recovered and wished to persevere in the holy state he had entered in expectation of death, it was understood that he must present himself anew to the church for another baptism.

7. For descriptions of the religious ceremonies it is best to go to the sources, translated in Wakefield and Evans, *Heresies*, esp. Nos. 51 and 57. J. Guiraud 'Le Consolamentum cathare', *RQH*, LXXV (1904), 74–112, discusses the similarities between the consolamentum and baptismal ceremonies in the early Christian church.

8. Two recent sympathetic accounts of life among the Cathars are by J. Duvernoy, 'La Liturgie et l'église cathares', *CEtC*, XVIII, Nos. 33, 35 (1967),

3–16, 16–30; and R. Nelli, *La Vie quotidienne des Cathares du Languedoc.* They may be compared to older descriptions by C. Molinier, 'L'Eglise et la société cathare', *RH*, XCIV (1906), 225–48; XCV (1907), 1–22, 263–91; and J. Guiraud, *Histoire de l'Inquisition*, I, Chs 3–7. Controversy over the endura may be followed in these and in the articles of Molinier, 'L'Endura', *Annales de la Faculté des lettres de Bordeaux*, III (1881), 282–99; Y. Dossat, 'L'Evolution des rituels cathares', *Revue de synthèse*, XXIII (1948), 27–30; and J. L. Riol, *Dernières connaissances sur des questions cathares.*

9. See Appendix V.

10. To glance at other areas: In northern Europe the Cathars were under harsh attack by the beginning of the thirteenth century. The short-lived sect of Amalricians in Paris about 1210 showed the influence of Joachim of Flora and anticipated doctrines that would be widely spread in later years. In Italy Cathars were well established. Contemporary with them were two sects of quite different character: the Speronists, founded by Hugo Speroni of Piacenza, who taught a doctrine of predestination that made priesthood and sacraments unnecessary, and the Passagians in Lombardy, who differed from other heresies by accepting Old Testament law as binding in every respect.

11. *Valdesius* in Latin, to which followers in the late fourteenth century prefixed 'Petrus', as though to link him with the first apostle. There is little historical or phonetic justification for the 'Peter Waldo' much used by modern authors.

12. See pp. 83–5, below.

13. The Waldenses had soon spread to northern Italy where they absorbed some of the Humiliati, comprising pious labourers who, wishing to live communally and preach the Gospel, had been condemned in 1184. Some remnants of the followers of Arnold of Brescia were also picked up. At the beginning of the thirteenth century Innocent III persuaded some Humiliati to return to the church. Disputes also arose between the Italian and French factions of Waldenses over organizational matters. The former broke away to form the Poor Lombards. Doctrinal issues soon were joined to administrative differences, which frustrated the attempt to heal the schism in 1218. The Poor Lombards did not survive the thirteenth century.

14. In 1210 another group, probably recruited from among Poor Lombards, was reconciled under the leadership of Bernard Prim.

15. On the origin of the Poor of Lyon, see P. Pouzet, 'Les Origines lyonnaises de la secte des Vaudois', *RHEgF*, XXII (1936), 5–37; A. Dondaine, 'Aux Origines du Valdéisme', *AFP*, XVI (1946), 191–235; and C. Thouzellier, *Catharisme et valdéisme*, 16–38. Other comments appear in G. Koch, 'Neue Quellen und Forschungen über die Anfänge der Waldenser', *Forschungen und Fortschritten*, XXXII (1958), 141–9; R. Manselli, 'Il valdismo originario', *Studi sulle eresie*, Ch. 4, and K. Selge, *Die ersten Waldenser*, Vol. I (arguing that for Waldes poverty was a motive secondary to zeal for preaching). Among the works of a leading Waldensian historian, Giovanni Gonnet, may be cited his *Il Valdismo medioevale* and his publication of texts in *Enchiridion fontium Valdensium*, Vol. I. C. Thouzellier studied the *Liber antiheresis* of Durand of Huesca in Chs. 3–5 of *Hérésie et hérétiques* and in *Catharisme et valdéisme*. It has been published as Vol. II of the work of Selge just cited. On the Waldensian Eucharist see Thouzellier, *Catharisme et valdéisme*, 175–6. The use of bread and fish appears in testimony to inquisitors in 1241, in Bibliothèque nationale, Collection Doat, XXI, fols. 185–312, *passim*.

16. See pp. 77–80, below.

D

# III Languedoc

'Languedoc' derives from the Provençal language of the Middle Ages, which was spoken with dialectical variations in most of the region south of the mountains of central France from the valley of the Rhône River westward to somewhat beyond the Garonne. One of the Romance languages, Provençal was closer to those of northern Spain than to French. One distinctive difference from the latter was that in the south, one said 'oc' [yes] instead of 'oïl', as in the north. For the area where it was spoken there was no general geographical or political term during most of the Middle Ages; at the time of the Albigensian Crusade, northerners might refer to 'the Provençal land' or 'the Albigensian region', southerners to 'the land of our language'. Not until the end of the thirteenth century did the name 'Languedoc' come into use; it was then adopted by French royal officials to specify an administrative division smaller than the whole area of the distinctive speech. Nonetheless, it is a convenient term, which has long been used as it will be here, to refer to southern France as a whole.[1]

There were cultural traits other than language which, taken all together, set Languedoc off clearly from France of the north. Its governmental and social pattern was feudal, with less binding ties of homage and military obligations. Manorial institutions were rare. Urban growth proceeded more rapidly in the twelfth century than in the north. Many towns gained substantial autonomy and spread their influence over the adjacent countryside. Nobles and merchants alike were acquainted with other parts of the world. Southern knights fought the Moslems in Spain and Palestine; two counts of Toulouse died in the Holy Land; merchants had followed the crusaders and established commercial agents in the eastern Mediterranean. Ideas as well as goods moved along the trade routes from Spain and Italy and knowledge of other lands and other ways helped to produce a tolerance of diversity greater than normally encountered in Europe north of the Alps.

## The County of Toulouse

The most prestigious lords in Languedoc were the counts of Toulouse, who also used the old family name of St Gilles. They claimed jurisdiction over an area as large as that ruled by their nominal sovereigns, the kings of France, and also did homage for certain holdings to the kings of England and the German emperor, without admitting any real dependence in practice. There had been no solid political tie between the Capetians and the counts since the mid-tenth century, although King Louis VII, after failing in an attempt to seize Toulouse in 1141 in the name of his wife, Eleanor of Aquitaine, a descendant of a former count, intervened to save it from English invasion in 1159. Pressure from the English in Aquitaine continued until Raymond VI of Toulouse (1194–1222) married Joan, sister of Richard I of England, in 1196. At that time King Richard abandoned his pretensions to the county but required Raymond to do homage for the region of the Agenais.

A more dangerous power had moved against Toulouse in the later twelfth century. The counts of Barcelona, who had become kings of Aragon in 1137, fought Raymond V of Toulouse (1148–1194) over Provence and after 1181 mounted other attacks from the southwest. Open conflict had ceased after the accession of Pedro II (1196–1213) to the Aragonese throne, but, as the event would prove, he had not given up expansionist ambitions. He had important possessions in the Rouergue and Gévaudan; Narbonne, Carcassonne, and Béziers lay within his sphere of influence; and in 1204, in connection with his marriage to the heiress of Mont-pellier, Pedro arranged a tacit alliance with Raymond VI of Toulouse. Had the Albigensian crusade not intervened, Aragon might have put together a feudal state reaching from the Ebro across the Pyrenees to the Alps.

The role of the kings of Aragon made more complicated an already tangled feudal situation in Languedoc. While Raymond V and Raymond VI of Toulouse managed to avoid close oversight by royal lords, they were by no means masters of all the areas in which they claimed suzerainty. In theory, there was a feudal hierarchy; in fact there were two levels of aristocracy: the great houses bearing the titles of count or viscount and a far more numerous petty nobility scattered over the land with small holdings and few resources. Homage was so light a burden and loyalty so readily shifted for advantages of the moment that the 'feudal system' in Languedoc was not much more than an association of princes and knights pursuing family interests. The big families were able to manoeuvre profitably during the wars of the counts of Toulouse with Aragon. Notable in this respect were the Trencavels, viscounts of Albi, Béziers, Carcassonne, and Razès, who had succeeded by the end of the twelfth century in creating a feudal enclave that cut the county of Toulouse in two. The counties of Nîmes and Melgueil were connected with the count of Toulouse by only the lightest of political ties.

Even within regions in which they exercised substantial authority, the counts of Toulouse had to share rule of many localities with bishops and abbots or with urban governments. None of them would hesitate at a chance to increase their possessions or influence. On the other hand the unreliability of feudal bonds was offset to some degree by the fact that a large proportion of the arable land, perhaps as much as half, was held in free or allodial tenure, that is, was not subject to feudal relationships. Raymond VI of Toulouse probably depended much more on the resources of his own allods than on feudal services.

The absence of close ties of common interest among the powerful families was a weakness in the overall political structure of Languedoc, even though these important lords, the Trencavels as well as the counts of Toulouse, were moving toward a fairly well-ordered administration in their own courts. In the lower levels of the landholding aristocracy the habits and antipathies of violent years were not easily abandoned. Moreover, while the important houses worked to enlarge their power by marriage alliances and kept their possessions relatively intact by the succession of a male heir, the same was not always possible for others. There had developed in much of Languedoc a practice of free bequest rather than primogeniture, so that an estate might be divided among several heirs, including women. Thus, members of a family often shared a seignury consisting of a castle or two, with a few villages. Five or six coseigneurs were not uncommon; there were fifty lords of Lombers at one time, thirty-six of Montréal, thirty-five of Mirepoix. These petty nobles often ruled through a common court and shared revenues by intricate division – one-seventh of a third, a fifth of a half, and so on. Marriages might bring claims to other small fiefs or portions of a fief. Quarrels arising from these tangled relationships were inevitable even when one individual was recognized as head of a family, and local anarchy frequently resulted, despite elaborate rules to protect coseigneurs against each other and despite the use of money payments in lieu of other penalties for breach of feudal contracts. Few of the rural nobility were blessed with substantial income from their share of revenues from tenants, justice, and tolls; many, in fact, were almost impoverished. From the point of view of an overlord, a serious result was that the value of feudal aids was sharply reduced. Military service was hedged about with so many reservations as to be almost useless. Many a knight rode to war only for pay, and other feudal duties were much less burdensome in Languedocian custom than elsewhere. Liege homage was impossible, and vassals holding from several lords changed allegiance from one to another almost at will.

The weakness of the lesser feudality reduced the social distinctions between them and wealthy commoners, especially as rural nobles moved into the towns, intermarrying with prominent urban families with whom they co-operated in government and defence. The count of Toulouse readily accepted men from both classes as counsellors and officials. The class lines in urban communities were further blurred by military obligations of the townsmen, who, as their wealth increased, aspired to the military trappings of knights. Commoners also invested in villas and vineyards in the countryside, until the words 'fief' and 'vassal' could not be restricted to the noble class, but were applied to various kinds of estates and personal relationships.

The church, by virtue of property ownership, must be brought into a discussion of political relationships in Languedoc. The question of moral and spiritual influence of the clergy will be taken up later; here it is to be noted that many bishops and the greater abbots were seigneurial powers of importance. Neither self-interest nor political pressures swayed these ecclesiastical princes to habitual co-operation with secular authority. The close alliance of church and state, so important in Capetian history, did not exist in Languedoc, for the count of Toulouse placed little reliance on ecclesiastical counsellors, nor did churchmen see him a power sympathetic to their interests. Prelates were often virtually independent lords and on terms of active animosity with lay proprietors in their vicinity. The archbishop of Narbonne, for example, ruled part of that town directly and had the viscount as his nominal vassal for the rest, as well as holding substantial properties in the region roundabout. He had already established the basis for disputes over real property which would embroil his successors for many years. The bishop of Agde bore the title of viscount; in Albi and Béziers, the bishops were lords of part or all of the towns; the bishop of Mende, by grant of the French king, exercised all royal rights within his diocese. The town of Toulouse was an exception, however, in that its bishop played no important role in urban administration and the episcopal court was relatively unimportant. Great abbeys were less conspicuous as semi-autonomous powers, but some were rich: St Sernin, Lézat, La Grasse, Fontfroide, St Gilles, whose abbot governed that town, to name only a few.

Thus, the counts of Toulouse by 1200 had not been able to imitate the Capetians or the lords of Normany or Flanders in centralizing their authority. Despite Raymond VI's prestige and popularity and the marriage diplomacy which got him peace with England and Aragon, the count did not command the resources and loyalty on which to build a unified feudal state. The idea of representation of common interests of classes or estates had not yet appeared in his government. Feudal assemblies for the whole of the county were unknown; the count summoned to court for counsel the local nobility where he happened to be. The lack of a common bond among the aristocracy, their tendency to insubordination and private war, the poverty of the petty nobility, the dogged pursuit of self-government by the towns, and the hostility between lay and ecclesiastical lords were obstacles to efficient government which even a wiser prince than Raymond VI could scarcely have corrected. That division of political authority and the often rancorous relationships between officials of church and state played a part in permitting religious diversity to flourish.[2]

### Agriculture, Commerce, and Industry

The assertion has often been made that the Albigensian crusade (1209–1229) disrupted a cosmopolitan civilization in which a flourishing economy had supported a gay, sophisticated, and tolerant culture. Nostalgia and regional loyalties may have heightened the colours in that view of Languedoc before the war and blackened its post-war picture; Americans have seen something of the sort in treatment of the history of their own southern states.

Languedoc had developed a healthy economy in the twelfth century from its own resources and the profits of commerce. In addition to the basic cereal crops, hemp was grown, vineyards and orchards were everywhere, and oil from olives was an important product in the eastern regions. The rural economy varied from bare subsistence in out-of-the-way uplands to the productiveness of the river valleys which made the land seem rich to northern crusaders. The peasantry was on its long move out of serfdom, although this was no steady rise. A shift from ecclesiastical to lay lordship over villages was perceptible in the latter twelfth century, which reduced to a degree the personal freedoms of villagers. Yet some were able to bargain over rights with their seigneurs and a form of long-term lease which defined and stabilized the rights of the cultivators was becoming common.

Especially noteworthy is the rapid growth of population in the twelfth century and the pattern of rural settlement. Monasteries and lay lords founded planned villages (*salvetats*), attracting inhabitants by special privileges; one such was created by the count of Toulouse, lying partly within and partly outside the southern walls of the town. Also, frequent war and the danger from mercenary soldiers who became bandits in intervals of peace forced the rural population to draw together behind walls, often in the shelter of castles. Local markets and those in the bigger towns brought peasants into contact with urban life; the allodial plots cultivated by urban dwellers, both inside and outside their walls, the investment by burghers in agricultural property, the development of some industrial production, as of leather and textiles, in the villages served to blur differences of social condition and outlook between peasants and townsmen.

Urban communities also grew and prospered in the twelfth century. Along or near the seaboard, Arles, Avignon, Montpellier, Narbonne, and St Gilles had long profited from transport of pilgrims and supplies in the Palestinian crusades. Their rivalry for Mediterranean commerce occasionally gave rise to trade wars. St Gilles was a busy market town, with a September fair for international trade, privileges for its merchants at Tyre and Acre, and commercial treaties with Genoa and Pisa. Montpellier did a flourishing business dyeing northern textiles for re-export. In the western part of the county Toulouse thrived also as a centre for regional trade, while its leather, furs, and cloth were sold in the fairs of Champagne and its merchants carried wine through Bordeaux to England. The inland traffic was carried largely by mule train, sometimes by barges, through the town markets. Wine and oil were of great importance, along with grain, fish, and salt. Manufactures from the Levant, Italy, and Flanders were part of the trade, but in less bulk than the cloths, leather, and metalware of local production.[3]

Toulouse may serve also as an example of rapid urban growth. Immigration in the later years of the twelfth century provided labour for construction and industries, of which milling, using the water power of the Garonne, was among the earliest to develop.

Butchers and tanners formed the first trade confraternities which negotiated with the count for privileges and protection. Boatmen, bakers, butchers, construction workers, artisans in various aspects of production of metal goods, leather, and cloth are mentioned in twelfth century documents; an incomplete list of guilds at the end of the thirteenth century names cutlers; makers of kegs, dice, bridles, rope, tile, candles, and pastry; dealers in lumber, oil, wax, and secondhand clothes. Capitalistic practices developed in connection with the grain mills and in land speculation by the merchants of the town. Money-lenders were among the wealthy citizens. The prosperity of Toulouse is evidenced by the fact that the town government readily raised the funds to purchase from the count freedoms for its citizens or to finance military campaigns against adjacent nobility to gain exemption from tolls. Raymond VI and Raymond VII were able to borrow large sums from wealthy families during the Albigensian crusade.

The health of the southern economy lay in the balance of agriculture and trade, in production and distribution that was chiefly regional. Languedoc did not rival Lombardy in long-distance commerce, in which there were difficulties not easily overcome. For all their efforts the towns did not gain complete freedom from tolls. Bandits in some areas in troubled times were as dangerous to merchant caravans as to undefended monasteries. Italian, rather than Languedocian, shippers carried the bulk of seaborne commerce, and the outlet for trade to the Atlantic was dominated by Aquitaine and Bordeaux. Yet it has been suggested that control of trade routes was a factor in the strategy of conquest planned by leaders of the Albigensian crusade. Such plans are not well-attested but the land was prosperous enough to add the lure of material gain to the spiritual incentives of the northern invaders of 1209, economically sound enough, also, to emerge from twenty years of war damaged but not in collapse.[4]

## Social and Intellectual Life
We know little more of the recreations and pastimes of the people of Languedoc than what was common to most of medieval Europe. The courts of the greater lords perhaps displayed more ease of life and gaiety than their northern counterparts, and among aristocrats a certain prestige attached to prodigal expenditures. The southern aristocracy has also been accused of sexual licence unusual in that age, but it would be difficult to show that they produced any more bastard offspring than did members of their class elsewhere.

Nor, despite the wealth of its princely courts and the lighter bonds of feudal obligations, do the sources support the contention that in the Midi flourished a culture notably superior to that of other areas. True, the medical school at Montpellier was beginning to win a reputation. Initiatives toward the study of Roman law were made there also. In many places superb examples of the Romanesque style in architecture and sculpture still survive. Much of the legend of southern 'courtesy', however, derives from the special, if artificial, prestige given to women by the predilection in aristocratic circles for the verses of the troubadours.

That new form of vernacular poetry, which probably originated in Aquitaine about the beginning of the twelfth century and whose antecedents are matters of scholarly debate, became the passion of noble audiences. Of some four hundred poets whose names are known half were nobly born; even if a poet rose from humbler circumstances his audience was in the castles and courts. Satirical verses, lyrical elegies, celebrations of noble adventure were the themes of some, but the dominant subject was love, the passion of the poet for the lady. Love, as sung of by the troubadours, became a code – feudalization of love, it has been called – in which the lady was sovereign, so that, in a society where feudalism was ineffective as a political device, chivalric ideals were transposed to the relationship of the sexes. Veneration of the lady, it has also been said, paralleled the increasingly popular cult of the Virgin; the troubadours' attitude has, indeed, the aspects of a cult, but a secular worship with a secular morality.

Of the counts of Toulouse, only Raymond VI seems to have aspired to compose his own lyrics and other courts may have rewarded the poets more lavishly, but that of the count was rich and to it, sooner or later, came most of the famous poets of the time. The town of Toulouse also had its connection with them. Peire Vidal, one of the most famous troubadours, was son of a furrier there; Peire Ramon was another Toulousan. Fulk of Marseilles, composer of elegant aphorisms and satirical verses, gave up his career as a poet to enter religion in a Cistercian monastery about 1201, then was bishop of Toulouse during its most troubled days. The partisan southern account of the Albigensian crusade and the defence of Toulouse was composed by an anonymous poet, perhaps a citizen of the town, who completed the *Chanson de la croisade albigeoise* begun by William of Tudela.

Much ink and ingenuity has been used in the attempt to prove that the troubadour poets were advocates of the Albigensian

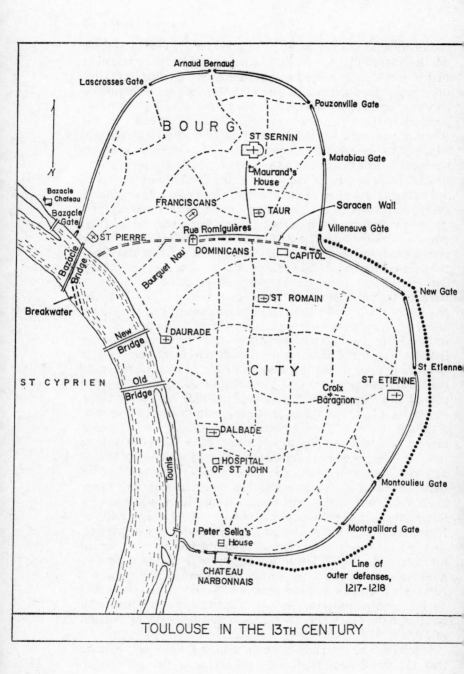

TOULOUSE IN THE 13TH CENTURY

heresy and subtly expressed it in their verses. However elegantly phrased, such arguments, on the whole, offer no more solid evidence of a connection between the poets and the heresy than that they existed at the same time in Languedoc. Some vitriolic denunciations of the clergy and the papacy were composed by the poets during the war, yet neither theologians nor inquisitors, who surely were not indifferent to nor uninformed about the expression of wicked doctrines, condemned the literature or any poet. The language and themes of the verses show rather that the authors were nominally Christian; a few, indeed, became active clergy in positions of some importance. Most of the poets, however, were little interested in advocating either conventional piety or radical dissent. They borrowed Christian phraseology and transmuted Christian ideals for a literary cult of love. Toward heresy most of them showed the tolerance which was, as we shall see, the general rule in the courts where they found their richest patrons.[5]

## The Town of Toulouse

Because the town of Toulouse by 1200 had become the chief residence of the counts and in a sense their capital, because of its ancient past and its innovations in government, because it became notorious for heresy, played a crucial role in the Albigensian Crusade, and was a centre of resistance to the Inquisition afterward, Toulouse deserves special mention here.

Toulouse stands on the right bank of the Garonne at a point where the river slows in its precipitate flow north-east from the Pyrenees and turns westward toward the Atlantic. The valley there is relatively broad, rolling up to low hills on each side. A natural route of travel up through the Pyrenees and along the Ariège River valley converges there with one coming westward from the Mediterranean and Narbonne and another from the Rhône. The value of the spot had not escaped the Romans, who, about 118 BC, built the first Toulouse on their main road from Italy to Spain, nor the Visigoths and Carolingians after them: the latter made Toulouse the capital of the March of Gothia defending against the Moslems in Spain. The town lay on a main line of pilgrim travel to St James of Compostella and had a claim to holiness in its own right by the number and age of its churches, notably St Sernin and Notre Dame de la Daurade, and the sacred value of their relics. Toulouse grew rapidly in the twelfth century by immigration from regions on the north and east and by AD 1200 was the largest town in Languedoc, yet it still bore the marks of existence on the 'frontiers' (of Gascony to the west,

Languedoc to the east) in an element of turbulence and toughness in its population and in the strength of its defences.

The impression that Toulouse stood guard over the valley of the Garonne was heightened by the looming bulk of the Château Narbonnais at its southern corner, residence of the counts, built on Roman foundations and tied into the walls of the town. From the castle, the buildings on the river bank followed the curve of the Garonne; on the east, walls circled out to come back toward the river about two-thirds of a mile downstream, where they met those of later construction, protecting the bourg of St Sernin. Inside the more than two hundred acres of the older city and in the suburb of St Sernin, which was about three-quarters as large, lived perhaps twenty thousand people in 1200. Mellow stone and brick gave the whole town a roseate glow. Everywhere there were towers: stubby defensive points along the walls, a Romanesque spire over the marvellous basilica of St Sernin, a square one above the cathedral of St Etienne; towers over the Cluniac Notre Dame of La Daurade with its golden mosaics, and over the white walls of the Dalbade church; towers over smaller churches, hardly taller than those of the houses which well-to-do citizens built for ostentation and defence – more than three hundred private towers were counted in 1226, even after destruction caused by siege and occupation.

Outside the walls of Toulouse were dwellings, shops, farms, hospices, and hospitals in unenclosed suburbs. The most populous of these was St Cyprien on the west side of the river, reached from the central part of the city by the Old Bridge and the New, also called the Daurade bridge. Another span had more recently been constructed further downriver, at the Bazacle gate. It was built of wood, unlike the older ones which were of brick and stone and fortified with towers.

In preceding paragraphs have appeared the words city, bourg, and town. The first two refer to divisions of the last and ought not be used interchangeably in speaking of Toulouse or any other southern community which combined the seat of episcopal administration with an important suburb. The city was the original settlement within the old walls, encompassing the cathedral of St Etienne, the episcopal palace, a multitude of shops, markets, and dwellings, but with some space also for gardens and vines. The bourg was the walled area to the north which had grown up around the monastery of St Sernin. It had mills along the river, a stage for river barges, some crafts, notably leathermaking, and hospices for pilgrims, yet was a less crowded and more residential area, where wealthy businessmen had houses. Toulouse did not fit the pattern of many other medieval towns in which a mercantile community grew up outside an older episcopal centre, for there had been space for merchants and artisans to settle within the original limits. Mercantile and industrial occupations were somewhat less numerous in the bourg than in the city, but there was not a sharp division of economic function between the two sections.

In other Languedocian towns lay or ecclesiastical seigneurs had often been able to play on the rivalry of subdivisions to keep control. The count had not done this in Toulouse. Although for some purposes city and bourg were administered separately and the Albigensian crusade produced issues that set the two districts at odds for a time, Toulouse was a political entity; in the government of the whole or in the defence of its interests, the distinction between citizen (of the city) and burgher (of the bourg) was unimportant; the consuls were selected in equal numbers from each part; the town hall was built along the old Saracen (actually Roman) wall, which was a common boundary for city and bourg. Citizen can thus be used as the term for all Toulousans, native or naturalized who performed public duties and acted in the numerous associations formed by men of common interests. The townsmen of AD 1200 were free – free from arbitrary exactions, free to handle property as they chose, free to move, and free to manage their individual and corporate affairs. No inhabitant could be claimed as a serf by a non-resident. Yet freedom did not dispense the citizens from duties to their count, whom they recognized as a legitimate ruler as long as he did not interfere with their self-governing ways and was content to draw limited and negotiated revenues from his rights.

Jews of Toulouse were not regarded as citizens but there, as throughout Languedoc, they were better situated than elsewhere in Europe. They were not the victims of that religious intolerance which appeared so virulently in the north with the First Crusade. Jews did business and owned property under the count's protection, and he used their skills in his administration. They had a hospice in the city which served as school and synagogue, but there was not a ghetto, since Jewish families could be found in various quarters. Within other Jewish communities, notably at Narbonne, developed the mystical strain of thought that produced the Kabbala, as well as tendencies toward asceticism which paralleled the practices of the Cathars. There may, indeed, have been interchanges of influence between Jews and the heretics.

It may be added that the poor and aged and ill were as well

cared for in Toulouse as in any medieval town. There were at least eleven hospitals and half a dozen leper houses within the walls and in the suburbs by 1200. Much of their maintenance came from the initiative of private individuals who turned their homes into places of shelter or contributed to the hospitals their pious bequests.

## The Rise of Self-Government

The story of Toulouse in the twelfth century, like that of most other towns of Languedoc, includes the development of civic rights and governmental autonomy. Toulouse moved faster and went farther in these respects than many others. The history of its rise to self-government has been told in John H. Mundy's *Liberty and Political Power in Toulouse, 1050–1230*.

At the beginning of the twelfth century, the count ruled Toulouse, taxing his subjects at will, dispensing justice, demanding services, and issuing licences to merchants and craftsmen, while other seigneurs in the vicinity possessed rights to tolls along the roads and river. In the first half of the century a body of townsmen bought freedom from certain dues for citizens, developed municipal courts, and began to share the duty of defence, and in 1152 a Common Council of city and bourg produced legislation limiting the count's rights. His prerogatives were further eroded in the second half of the century by negotiation, purchase, and a forceful struggle in the decade after 1180 which ended with the townsmen acquiring jurisdiction over their own essential affairs.

Leadership of the town was provided by a patrician oligarchy of rich merchants and knightly families who had moved into Toulouse, holding towers of the Saracen wall in fief, building fortified houses, investing in real estate, and intermarrying with prominent commoners. These patricians supplied the membership of the first consulate, a governmental body whose twenty-four members after 1189 were evenly apportioned between city and bourg. All citizens might be summoned for service in the militia or convened to ratify the selection of the consuls, and for ordinary administrative purposes city and bourg were each divided into six quarters. The great churches, with their clientele of worshippers, oblates, and servants, no doubt had a degree of influence in internal affairs as well.

Political division appeared in 1202, causing a peaceful electoral revolution in that year. The line between the parties was indistinct: the patricians' wealth rested heavily on land rents and real estate speculation; the newer group which now acquired political power included merchants, money-changers, and even a few tradesmen, and there may have been some rivalry between city and bourg also in play. The shift in the consulate was followed by vigorous expansion of urban influence over the surrounding countryside, forcing rural lords to abolish or curtail their tolls. But the 'popular party' of 1202 soon had to share or alternate in power with the patricians and did so during the years of the crusade. Issues of heresy and usury pressed by the bishop of Toulouse, then stirred up latent antagonisms between city and bourg and set borrowers against the moneymen, but the rough hand of Simon of Montfort as ruler in 1216 subordinated these quarrels to a common resentment which culminated in revolt. When Montfort was besieging the town in 1217–1218 all citizens united against him. For another decade the town was the backbone of southern resistance to the crusaders, but their common cause with Counts Raymond VI and Raymond VII did not deter the consuls from wringing more concessions in the matter of tolls and government from the counts, so that, when comital control over the choice of consuls was entirely withdrawn in 1222, Toulouse came very close to independence.

There were moves toward something like democratic government during the war years, especially in moments of extreme danger and in 1226–1227 the consulate was taken over by an ultra-patriotic group, including some small merchants and tradesmen, which has been said to resemble government by the people in arms. The older parties of patricians and populars, however, regained control in peace. In later years, the ability of the town to dominate the countryside waned, Raymond VII strove to rebuild his authority and between 1241 and 1248 even regained power to appoint the consuls, while ecclesiastical courts worked themselves free from civil influence. Toulouse passed into the hands of Alphonse of Poitiers, brother of the French king, in 1249, and in 1271 came directly under the crown. The autonomy of the town was respected in many ways by the new rulers, but the days of independence were over.[6]

# References

1. 'Provence', from the Roman *provincia Narbonnensis*, has a more restricted meaning today. 'Occitania', also based on linguistic usage, is coming into some favour: cf. J. Strayer, *The Albigensian Crusades*, 10.
2. Indispensable here, as for many other topics discussed in this book, is the *Histoire générale de Languedoc* of C. Devic and J. Vaissete, in the edition of

A. Molinier and others, Vols VI–VIII. There is a one-volume *Histoire du Languedoc*, prepared by Philippe Wolff, with an accompanying *Documents de l'histoire du Languedoc*. The much shorter E. Le Roy Ladurie, *Histoire de Languedoc* is informative. For the political situation I am indebted to the essay by A. Molinier, 'Étude sur l'administration féodale dans le Languedoc' in *HGL*, VII, 132–212; even more to P. Dognon, *Les Institutions politiques et administratives du pays de Languedoc*. Useful summaries are Y. Dossat, 'Le Comté de Toulouse et la féodalité languedocienne', *Revue historique . . . du Tarn*, IX (1943), 75–90; and G. Sicard, 'Monocratie et féodalité', *Recueils de la Société Jean Bodin*, XXI, Part 2, 405–28. Rivalry of the houses of Saint Gilles and Barcelona is treated in C. Higounet, 'Un Grand Chapitre de l'histoire du XIIe siècle' in *Mélanges . . . dediés à la memoire de Louis Halphen*, 313–22.

3. The variety of goods passing through a town market is shown by a thirteenth century schedule of brokerage fees at Narbonne, which lists, among other items, about two dozen kinds of textiles, eight kinds of leather, fur, dyes, thread, saddlery, iron and steel products, silver, oil, wine, grain, livestock, armour, ploughshares, hoes, wooden spoons, bottles, and slaves: R. Lopez and I. W. Raymond, *Medieval Trade in the Mediterranean World*, 131–5.

4. On the population and economy, see the general histories already cited (n. 2); also P. Ourliac, 'Les Villages de la région toulousaine au XIIe siècle', *Annales: économies, sociétés, civilisations*, IV (1949), 268–77; and the overviews by Y. Dossat, 'La société méridionale à la veille de la croisade albigeoise', *Revue historique et littéraire de Languedoc*, I (1944), 66–87; and C. Higounet, 'Le Milieu social et économique languedocien vers 1200', in *CFan*, II 13–22. P. Wolff, *Commerces et marchands de Toulouse*, and M. A. Mulholland, *Early Gild Records of Toulouse*, although concerned with a period later than ours, have some retrospective comment. The list of late-thirteenth century gilds on p. 56, comes from the latter.

5. M. M. Wood discusses the attitude of the poets in *The Spirit of Protest in Old French Literature*. The strongest argument against an intimate connection of the troubadours and heresy is in R. H. Gere, *The Troubadours, Heresy, and the Albigensian Crusade*; an opposite point of view appears in D. de Rougemont, *Love in the Western World*. See also R. Nelli, 'Le Catharisme vu à travers les troubadours' in *CFan*, III, 177–97; and J. B. Russell, 'Courtly Love as Religious Dissent', *CHR*, LI (1965), 31–44.

6. My debt to Mundy, *Liberty and Political Power in Toulouse*, is apparent in the text. It supplements R. Limouzin-Lamothe, *La Commune de Toulouse et les sources de son histoire*, which publishes archival documents. P. Wolff, *Histoire de Toulouse*, covers a longer span, as does J. Coppolani, *Toulouse, étude de géographie urbaine*. The former is supplemented by *Voix et images de Toulouse* by Wolff and J. Dieuzaide, with translated documents and illustrations. See also C. M. Higounet, 'Le Peuplement de Toulouse au XII siècle', *AM*, LIV–LV (1942–1943), 489–98; and E. Delaruelle, 'La Ville de Toulouse vers 1200 d'après quelques travaux récents', *CFan*, I (1966), 107–22. On Jews, see G. Saige, *Les Juifs en Languedoc anterieurement au XIVe siècle*; and for possible links between the Kabbala in Languedoc and Catharism, E. Delaruelle, 'L'Etat actuel des études sur le Catharisme', *CFan*, III, 38–9.

# IV Churchmen and Heretics

*The Church in Languedoc*

One reason why Languedoc about the year 1200 seemed to be a hotbed of heresy was the tolerance and diversity of Languedocian society. Another and more weighty one was the contrast between the zealous evangelism of the Cathars and Waldenses and the abdication of religious duties by part of the Catholic clergy, the character of whose life and customs was a grave handicap for those priests who did make an effort to keep their parishioners in orthodoxy. Many of the prelates of Languedoc were preoccupied with administration of a wealthy and powerful organization. Bishops were usually important landholders; many monasteries were rich. The Gregorian reforms had increased control of the church livings and tithes by the hierarchy at the expense of lay seigneurs; the substantial endowments administered by bishops, cathedral chapters, and abbots were further augmented by purchase and pious bequest, even in the days when heresy was most prevalent.

Prosperity helped to produce unhappy results for religion when concern for material possessions outweighed the duty of pastoral care and when power was pursued more than humbler Christian virtues. At the beginning of the thirteenth century, most notorious in this respect was the foremost prelate of Languedoc, Archbishop Berengar of Narbonne (1190–1212), a relative of the royal house of Aragon, who devoted himself entirely to the temporal affairs of his see. He was so lax in other matters that his removal became a chief aim of Innocent III's programme for reform of the clergy. The pope's denunciations of Berengar were vitriolic: The Archbishop, Innocent wrote, was the root of evil in his province, where the laws of the church had fallen into disuse and its justice was given only for payment, where the clergy were unworthy, illiterate, and a laughing stock. Berengar, the pope declared, knew only one god, money. He never made visitations in his

E

diocese, demanded large sums for consecrating bishops, left offices vacant so as to appropriate income for himself, allowed monks to marry and the clergy to become usurers, doctors, lawyers, even jongleurs.

The papal language was overstated for effect. It has been suggested that in other circumstances Berengar might have been thought a great bishop because of his success in building the power and prosperity of his see. His activities were by no means unique. Comparable, if less sweeping, charges could have been made against ecclesiastical suzerains in northern France or imperial Germany. Berengar's contemporary, Bishop Hugh of Auxerre (1183–1206), for example, was almost as avaricious and as ruthless in pursuing disputed claims by dubious methods as was Berengar, but his reputation was redeemed, as Berengar's was not, by vigorous prosecution of heretics. The brigand bishop, Matthew of Toul (1198–1210), had not even that merit. Throughout his pontificate Innocent III put great effort into correcting abuses at every clerical level everywhere in Europe; simony, avarice, indolence in office, habits of violence among bishops, marriage, concubinage, illiteracy, non-residence of priests in their parishes, violation of monastic rules, scandalous living and profligacy he deplored everywhere. Yet particularly intolerable in the pope's eyes were prelates like Berengar, 'blind creatures, dumb dogs who no longer bark', in the Midi where the church was so sharply challenged by dissenters. The pope's actions reveal his (or his legates') judgement of the situation.

By 1213 not only Berengar of Narbonne but also the archbishop of Auch, the bishops of Fréjus, Carcassonne, Béziers, Viviers, Toulouse, Valence, and Rodez had been deposed or suspended for reason of age, admitted incapacity, scandalous conduct, simony, or failure to act against heresy. Their replacements were often found in monastic ranks and became willing allies of papal legates and Albigensian crusaders.

There were southern bishops – William Peire of Albi (1185–1227) for example, or William of Roquessel (1199–1204) and Reginald of Montpeyroux (1209–1211), bishops of Béziers – who were zealous in their episcopal duties other than the pursuit of heretics, and the rule of a materialistically minded bishop does not in itself account for heretical success. Archbishop Berengar's cathedral city of Narbonne was less a centre for Catharism than was Toulouse, where bad management by the bishops and invasion of episcopal rights by barons and by other clergy and abbots as well, had reduced the bishop to poverty at the beginning of the century, or Albi, whose good bishop almost blandly ignored heretics beyond an occasional debate. Character and ability had to be reinforced by will for church leaders to function effectively in the contest with heresy.

The wealth and worldliness of prelates made them easy targets for criticism and words almost as sharp as the denunciations by heretics occasionally came from orthodox lips. The council of Avignon (1209) accused some bishops of being money-grubbers rather than shepherds and thus of being responsible for the spread of heresy. Conciliar legislation also provides a list of undesirable habits of bishops. They were forbidden to use rich harness for their mounts, to gamble or follow the hunt, be entertained by musicians at meals, hear matins in bed, or chat inattentively during services in the church. They were not to demand fees for ordaining priests, dispensing with marriage bans, allowing illegal marriages, or breaking legitimate wills. Bishops should faithfully attend to diocesan business, holding at least one synod a year and ought to travel with only a few attendants during their visitations. They must not tolerate concubinage among priests.

The rank and file of the clergy were charged with failings other than incontinence. They were, for the most part, indifferently educated; lay patrons, it was said, often put the children of peasants or serfs into their parishes out of disrespect for the church. The council of Avignon which castigated bishops also reproved priests and curates who were indistinguishable from laymen in conduct and were soiled by debauchery. A chronicler of the time report that to avoid public sneers priests concealed their tonsures and that a popular quip, when confronted by an unpleasant choice, was, 'I'd rather be a priest than do that.'

Such are shocking indictments. Yet it must be recalled that it had become conventional for the clergy assembled in council to deplore their own shortcomings. The defects enumerated for the Languedocian bishops and priests are found equally in conciliar enactments at Paris and elsewhere. Languedoc drew criticism because of the dangers posed by heresy, but the register of Eudes of Rigaud, archbishop of Rouen (1248–1276) has left a record of how hard a good prelate had to work to maintain decent order among his clergy in Normandy half a century later, where heresy was never a problem.

We can accept as only half true at best the complaints of observers that the churches were without worshippers, priests without congregations, and the people without sacraments. The church as a whole was not withering in Languedoc. There were good bishops and good priests; there were devout families in every social class. The late years of the twelfth century were a great period of church building. Pious bequests to religious houses were numerous and continued to be made, even during the Albigensian crusade, even in areas supposed to be saturated with heresy. Hospitals, leper houses, and other institutions of charity were generously supplied. 'If charitable and social work is part of the church, the Toulousan church was blooming before the Albigensian war.' No doubt the newer monastic foundations enjoyed greater popularity than the older and richer establishments; Cistercian abbeys flourished and the new mendicant orders were warmly received in the early thirteenth century.[1]

It is not a paradox but another side of a complex situation to say, however, that the Languedocian church was not in good situation to meet a strong religious challenge. Even if only a portion of its clergy had lost the respect of the people, adequate measures, such as religious instruction, did not develop as a counteraction to dissent. Not from internal resources but from outside came the effort to confront the heretics. The preaching missions of 1206–1208[2] revealed that audiences were ready to give support and sympathy to Catholic spokesmen, but that only points up the problem of the southern church. Those orthodox preachers were ardent missionaries, speaking out for their faith and giving evidence of its vitality in their lives. Their actions were not followed up by the native clergy. The Cathars and Waldenses kept the initiative in religious propaganda, even if they were far fewer in numbers.

## How Many Heretics?

Religious leaders who advocated the Albigensian crusade in 1208–1209 were persuaded that the people of Languedoc were given over to heresy, and the pessimistic forecast was made that unless the wickedness were soon overcome all Europe would be corrupted. That apprehension arose not only from the supposed numbers of heretics and their believers, but also from discouragement at the failure of such measures as had been taken to reduce their influence. The question of how many heretics there actually were and the pervasiveness of their influence needs discussion, then, before recounting the steps taken to suppress them prior to the crusade.

The number of professed heretics, that is, of Cathar Good Men and Waldensian preachers, cannot be stated with assurance,

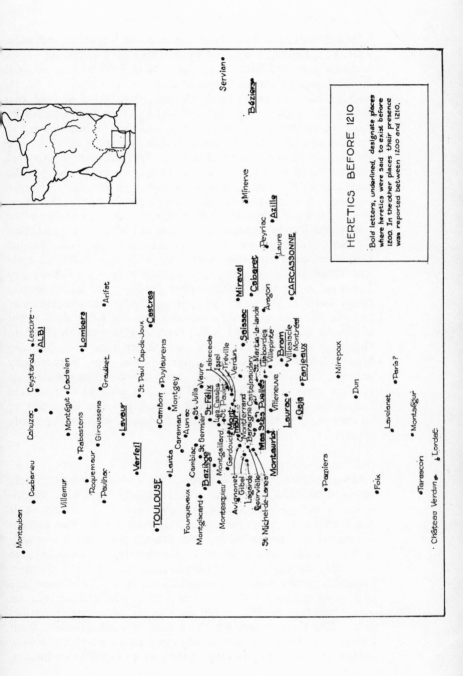

HERETICS BEFORE 1210

Bold letters, underlined, designate places where heretics were said to exist before 1200. In the other places their presence was reported between 1200 and 1210.

Montauban

Carbarieu
Dahuzac
Ceytzarais
Lescure
**ALBI**

Villemur
Montégut
Cadalen

Roquemaur
Giroussens
Graulhet

Paulhac

Arifat

**Laveur**

St Paul Capde-Joux

**Castres**

Cambon
Puylaurens

**TOULOUSE**
Lenta
Caraman
Montgey

St Paul Capde-Joux

Fourquevaux
Cambiac
St Julia
Veure
St Félix
Labecede

Montgiscard
St Germier
Les Casses
Isel
Tréville
Verdun

Montesquieu
Montgaillard
St Paulet
Verdun

Avignonet
Gerdouch
**Mount**
**Soissac**

Gibel
Montferrand
St Martin-la-lande

Lagarde
Baragne
Castelnaudary
Laboardes
**Miraval**

Gourvielle
**Mas Stes Puelles**
Villepinte
Arcgon
**Cabaret**
Peyriac

St Michel-de-Lanes
Villeneuve
**Bram**
Villesiscle
Montréal
Laure
**Azille**

**Montauriol**
**Laurac**
Fanjeaux
**CARCASSONNE**

**Gaja**

Mirepoix

Papiers

Dun

Foix
Lavelanet
Paris?

Montségur

Tarascon
Lordat

Château Verdun

Servian

**Béziers**

Minerve

although attempts have been made to arrive at an estimate. J.J.I. von Döllinger was led by a report of a gathering of six hundred perfected heretics at Mirepoix in 1206 to put the total for all Languedoc at that time at seven to eight hundred. M. H. Vicaire, the biographer of St Dominic, reached a total of two thousand Cathars at the beginning of the thirteenth century by working backward from the number said to have been burned in holocausts during the crusade; perhaps eight hundred to one thousand men and women died thus. (This calculation presumes that the number of victims was accurately reported and that the executioners discriminated between perfected heretics and other prisoners, a nicety that did not always prevail.) Jean Duvernoy states that 1,015 perfected heretics can be known by name in 'the period which ends with the big inquests of 1245', and suggests that the actual number was two or three times as great. Michel Roquebert calculates that there were at least a thousand male and female perfected heretics in the region between Béziers and Toulouse in the years 1200 to 1209. On the other hand, from a recent study of heresy in the diocese of Albi from inquisitorial records, Maurice Bécamel concludes that no more than about ten Good Men were ever active there at one time. In 1250, an inquisitor reported that there were fewer than two hundred heretics left in all the churches north of the Alps. Without any pretence of statistical accuracy, then, it may be suggested that at most there were about 1,000 to 1,500 perfected Cathars in Languedoc as the thirteenth century began. There is no way at all even to guess at a figure for the Waldenses, who were certainly fewer.[3]

*Believers and Sympathizers*
Estimating the number of believers, that is persons who explicitly accepted heretical teaching as true, is equally beset with difficulties. The old generalizations that they were very numerous, if not a majority everywhere, are countered by the few explicit statements that can be made. Yves Dossat, a scholar thoroughly at home in the sources, found that although inquisitors in 1245 and following years took 420 depositions from Le Mas-Saintes-Puelles, a small community notorious for heresy, they were able to discover the names of only seven persons who had received the consolamentum on their death beds in the preceding thirty-five years, plus three others who had been refused baptism; from Fanjeaux, larger and even more ill-famed, they got only twenty-six names. Jean Duvernoy has traced the career of the Cathar bishop,

Guilabert of Castres, from 1193 to about 1240, and that of Bertrand Marty from 1225 to 1244; in the records of their incessant activity not more than forty persons are named as receiving the consolamentum. When the bishop of Béziers drew up a list of those who were defamed for heresy in his city in 1209, some 220 persons out of a total population of 10,000 or more were enumerated.[4]

The impact of heresy ought also to be judged in terms of its geographical distribution and its acceptance in different social groups. For the first there is a fair amount of information. Exact statements about the penetration of heresy in social classes are not possible, but there are certain clues.

*The Geography of Heresy*

In the first decade of the thirteenth century heresy was not diffused evenly throughout southern France. Its heartland lay in the area that would be bounded by lines drawn to connect Toulouse, Albi, Carcassonne, and Foix; nowhere within that region was it concentrated more than along the axis Toulouse–Carcassonne, notably in the plain called the Lauragais. There the fortified towns of Laurac, Montréal, and Fanjeaux were little capitals of heresy and, as was asserted at the time of the Albigensian Crusade, almost all of the knightly families had turned to the heretics. Outside of this area of concentration there were pockets of heresy to the east, around Béziers, to the south in the *pays de Sault* in the Pyrenees, and in the northwest, around Agen. Surprisingly, there seems to have been little infiltration of Gascony, that is, the area south and east of the Garonne. In eastern Languedoc, while the presence of heretics was occasionally noted in later years, they were much less numerous than in the regions just noted.[5]

*Believers among the Nobility*

Many of the greater feudal lords of Languedoc quarrelled with ecclesiastical proprietors over land and income; they invaded the property of monasteries and showed disrespect for the persons of the clergy. Many also admitted Cathars and Waldenses to their households and allowed them to preach freely in their domains. Thus, we hear frequent charges that the aristocracy, great and small, was largely committed to heresy, but we need to ask whether their antagonism to the Catholic clergy in fact sprang primarily from religious disaffection.

Rivalry and hostility between secular and ecclesiastical proprietors was not unique to Languedoc; it was almost a law of society in the Middle Ages. Everywhere in Europe, the lay nobility envied the accumulated capital of the church and its income from tithes and land; everywhere they competed for prestige, property, and power with bishops and abbots, most of whom were drawn from the same social class. The rivalry, perhaps, was less restrained in Languedoc than elsewhere because of the failure of the greater princes to keep a firm hand on their vassals. Moreover, the big feudal powers, unable to call on ecclesiastical leaders for support in political plans, were themselves often trespassers on the rights of the church.

In contemporary narrative sources written by clerics, the prominent families are described as unregenerate aggressors who despoiled bishops, turned monasteries into fortresses, and looted abbey treasures. Count Raymond VI of Toulouse was repeatedly in trouble with the bishops of Carpentras, Vaison, and Agen; the abbots of Moissac and Montauban; and other ecclesiastical lords. For his invasion of the rights of the abbot of St Gilles by building a fortress which dominated monastery and town he was under excommunication from 1196 to 1198; at the end of the crusade in 1229 Raymond VII had to promise reparation for his father's misdeeds to a long list of bishops and abbots.

The Trencavel viscounts were no less ready to look on church property as subject to their will. It was said that the abbot of La Grasse was despoiled of twenty castles by them. An unsavoury incident is reported to have occurred after Roger Trencavel II died, leaving his young son in the tutelage of Bertrand of Saissac, who was on good terms with the Cathars. The monks of St Mary at Alet had the temerity to elect an abbot without consulting Bertrand's wishes, at which he invaded the monastery, imprisoned the abbot-elect, and, propping the exhumed corpse of the predecessor in the chair, had it preside over another election by the cowed remnant of monks. Bertrand's candidate successfully defended his election before Archbishop Berengar of Narbonne, to the latter's profit, but subsequently was accused of dissipating the resources of the monastery and introducing heretics to its precincts. Count Raymond Roger of Foix also was notorious for his maltreatment of monastic houses, allegedly allowing his mercenaries to kill and mutilate monks of St Antonin for their disrespect to the count's aunt, a perfected Cathar. He was also accused of pillaging the monasteries of St Mary and St Volusian and of destroying churches in Cerdanya, despite the remonstrances of King Pedro II of Aragon.

It may be worth note that other offences of which these male-factors were accused often consisted of seeking a share of ecclesiastical income or of building strongholds on church property, aggressions not unknown outside of Languedoc. Behind such acts may have been other motives than heresy. Changes from southern control to that of orthodox princes did not always end the depradations. On capturing Moissac in 1212, Simon of Montfort, leader of the Albigensian crusaders, made an agreement about respective rights with the abbot. A short time later the abbot was complaining to Philip Augustus that Montfort's soldiers had pillaged his abbey and reduced him to near poverty. The legate Arnold Aimery was elected archbishop of Narbonne in 1212 and promptly quarrelled with Montfort over the title of duke. In 1216 the latter's soldiers with drawn swords thrust aside the archbishop standing at the gate to bar their entry and Montfort, ignoring excommunication and interdict, heard Mass in Narbonne, collected tolls, and seized various strong places and sources of revenue claimed by the archbishop.

The great lords who were most seriously accused of hostility to the church insisted stoutly, for what it was worth, on their orthodoxy. Raymond VI, whose enemies reported that he kept Cathars about him to give him baptism if accident befell, repeatedly asserted that he was a good Catholic and unjustly treated. He was promised acceptance as a lay brother in the order of St John of Jerusalem in Toulouse, and he financed enlargement of the cathedral of St Etienne even while he was excommunicate and the town under interdict. Raymond Roger Trencavel, who died a captive of the crusaders in 1209, was defended against the charge of heresy by a contemporary Catholic historian. Raymond Roger of Foix, persecutor of monks, whose wife and sister became Cathars, showed no desire to follow them and refused to make the conventional gestures of veneration to the Good Men. The attitude of these princes was indifference rather than religious partisanship. They allowed heretics to frequent their courts and did not object to their subordinates showing them favour, but they took the moral precepts of the Cathars and Waldenses no more to heart than they responded to the admonitions of the Catholic clergy.

Among the rural nobility in certain areas there is evidence of greater addiction to heresy. It has been suggested that one important reason for this was economic grievance of long standing. During the Gregorian reform parish tithes and other sources of income once usurped by secular lords were reclaimed by the church. The antipathies thus created among the nobility were noticed by members of the party which accompanied Bernard of Clairvaux in 1145. They seem to have long persisted, becoming entrenched family or local traditions.

Very few men of the rural nobility, however, sought the consolamentum until their deathbed. They fought against the Albigensian crusaders, but many of them took service against the Moors in Spain as willingly. Yet, they were in intimate contact with heretical preachers. In the shelter of their crag-perched castles were hospices for heretics to which their daughters could be entrusted for rearing and where their widows could find refuge.

It was often remarked by mevieval observers that women were particularly susceptible to heretical teaching. This was surely true in Languedoc where many women of the feudal class were among the enthusiastic and devoted followers of the Cathars and, in lesser numbers, of the Waldenses. Not only did heretical communities provide old-age security for widows and respectable homes for unmarried daughters, but doctrine also had its appeal. In Catharist teaching, in contrast to a trend of medieval Christian thought, women were not regarded as by nature inferior to men. Physical distinctions were the work of the diabolic maker of bodies and, although to bear children was to do the devil's work, the souls of men and women belonged to the realm of the divine Creator and were indistinguishable in His sight. Women could receive the consolamentum as readily as men. Some female Cathars enjoyed positions of prestige and authority, in which they were active propagandists for their faith, although they did not rise to the rank of deacon or bishop. Philippa, wife of the count of Foix, abandoned marriage to preside over a heretical hospice. When the same count's widowed sister, Esclarmonde, received the consolamentum, together with five other ladies, it was an important social occasion. Blanche, grand dame of the family which held the fortress of Laurac for the Trencavels, directed a popular heretical community there in which one of her daughters also lived as a perfect. A son and a daughter died at the hands of the Albigensian crusaders, another daughter was mother of the Niort brothers, who were prominent as warriors against the invaders and as targets of the Inquisition afterwards. Dame Cavaers, a perfected Cathar, shared the rule of Fanjeaux with the count of Foix.

No wonder that when a knight, Pons Adémar of Rodeille, was induced to admit that the Catholics had had the better of a theological argument with Cathars and was asked by Bishop

Fulk of Toulouse why he did not therefore expel heretics from his land the man replied: 'We cannot. We have been reared in their midst. We have relatives among them and we see them living lives of perfection.' Protected by their men the women preserved and passed on the tradition of heresy in many a family.

It should be added also that heresy divided some families. To cite only certain examples: Bishop Berengar Raymond of Carcassonne (1209–1212) had a brother who was violent against the church. One of the Niort brothers became abbot of Alet while his brothers were protecting the Good Men. The urban branch of the Capdenier clan patronized churches and religious orders in Toulouse; their rural relatives supported the Cathars.[6]

## Heresy and Other Social Classes

Estimates of the penetration of heresy in other social classes are likewise marred by the lack of definiteness in the sources. Narratives of the period of the Albigensian crusade paint a dark picture. Legal or business documents, which are abundant in town archives, are of little help. Records of the Inquisition have been assiduously searched; on pre-war conditions they provide hints but not definitive evidence.

As for the peasantry it is futile to ask about the reception of heresy among them; an answer cannot be given. There certainly was resentment of church tithes and one gathers the impression from reading testimony received by inquisitors later in the century that there had always been rural villagers who willingly revered and sheltered the Good Men and the Waldenses and others who held aloof. The proportions are impossible to estimate.

In the towns it is undeniable that heresy existed. But to what extent? A division, or rather, a confusion of religious loyalties can be seen at every level. The leading families of Toulouse, for example, were often accused of partisanship for the Cathars, and the names of some of them – the Roaix, the Maurands, the Villeneuves – are encountered frequently in inquisitorial documents. Yet other important houses, such as the Guilabert and Capdenier families, were of unimpeachable orthodoxy. Most of the leading citizens of the city joined a White Confraternity which Bishop Fulk organized for vigilante action against usurers and heretics. That an opposing Black Confraternity soon appeared in the bourg might indicate that heresy was present there or only that latent political and economic rivalries were being exploited. In other places the picture is a little clearer. Montpellier was a citadel of orthodoxy. Heresy was not a major problem in Narbonne until some years after the war, although the surrounding countryside had a number of knightly families, believers of the Cathars, with connections in the city. At Béziers in 1209 Bishop Reginald, who accompanied the crusaders, produced a list of some 220 persons accused of heresy. Five of the names are marked *val.*, probably meaning Waldenses; the others presumably were believers of the Cathars. About thirty can be associated with a trade, there were four physicians, and one man of noble status. Even if all had been heads of households, which clearly was not the case, the heretical families that could be identified in Béziers comprised a very small minority.[7]

Much has been said about heresy among artisans and workers, especially in textiles. The reputation of weavers as prone to religious error had been established in the twelfth century, probably less because they furnished easy recruits than that this was a craft which a wandering missionary could practise for subsistence. In some southern towns heretics and their sympathizers did operate textile and other shops and stories circulated about their travelling disguised as merchants or workmen, the better to get a hearing from unsuspecting Christians whom they might convert.

We might attempt to read back into the situation in the towns at the beginning of the thirteenth century evidence of several decades later. There were violent protests against the Inquisition in Toulouse, Albi, and Narbonne in 1234–1235. Yet the record of confessions or convictions of heresy nowhere amounts to more than a fraction of the population and William Pelhisson reveals the support which many townspeople of Toulouse gave to the Dominicans when they were being harassed by the consuls. More evident is the resentment aroused by the methods of prosecution. Fear of arbitrary action in the wake of a vicious war, loss of hard-won judicial rights, disgust at the sight of disinterred bodies dragged through the streets, may explain the outbursts as much as addiction to heresy.

In the light of evidence at best uncertain it seems not unreasonable to conclude that the beginning of the thirteenth century heresy was solidly established in Languedoc, but that this was true only of certain areas. Heretics came from every social class. Yet, with the exception of the rural nobility in the areas where believers were most numerous, it does not seem likely that more than a minority of the populace had turned decisively away from the Roman church. The calculation of numbers, however, takes no account of persons who were willing to tolerate the presence of the Good Men, who themselves did not seriously consider abandoning traditional orthodoxy, yet saw no reason for hostility to men and women of good habits and deeply felt religious convictions, indeed, probably respected them.[8]

### Why Heresy?

In an earlier place the question was posed: Why did the Cathars and Waldenses flourish in Languedoc? An answer was postponed, but now a summing-up may be attempted.

The initial reception of religious reformers and preachers of outright heresy in Languedoc may be ascribed to desires for personal spiritual experience and to discontent with the church, such as was found everywhere. In early years of the twelfth century such sentiments were probably no more prevalent in the south than elsewhere. Peter of Bruys had some success but he was burned by a hostile crowd; despite the tumult caused by Henry no substantial group of disciples survived him, only a general sense of discontent from which later heretics would profit. But as the religious revival gained momentum and new elements of heretical thought were introduced, the missionaries of dissent found ever more receptive audiences among men and women whose consciences were troubled by divisions within the church, who were offended by the indifference of some of the clergy to their needs, and who were deeply concerned and fearful about their own salvation. Such persons heard with enthusiasm the message of a more perfect mode of Christian life.

In these circumstances the signs of piety in the poverty and asceticism of the Cathars and Waldenses were persuasive indications that their words were true. Heresy is not a sign of religious indifference but of intense spiritual concern. The heretics not only profited from the resentment of the church stimulated by their predecessors in dissent, they were advocating in extreme form the most vital elements in religious fervour of the twelfth century: poverty, chastity, personal holiness in a corrupt world. In a simple ecclesiastical structure they drew together the major forces of religious dissent and religious enthusiasm. They read the Scriptures and preached in the vernacular, fostering a sense of participation among their audiences. Their ritual acts were attractive by their simplicity. Thus, for a part of the population, they satisfied pious aspirations better than did the established clergy.

The socio-economic situation in Languedoc in the second half of the twelfth century permitted the spread of heterodoxy. Co-operation of lay and religious officials to check it was not forthcoming. In other parts of Europe, even where church and state did join in repression, heresy yet held on stubbornly; such joint efforts did not occur in Languedoc. Lack of concern and energy at the top discouraged lower ranks of the clergy from action. If great prelates like Berengar of Narbonne were indifferent, if the bishop of Toulouse was too poor and lacklustre, and the bishop of Albi too easy-going to take firm measures, if a prominent family could produce one son who became abbot or bishop and another who was a devoted believer of the Cathars, priests could hardly be expected to do more than shrug at the presence of heretics among their parishioners. And many of the lower clergy in the countryside seem to have been willing to admit that the heretics had much that was right in their teaching.

One reason for the tolerance of religious diversity was a cosmopolitanism in the culture of Languedoc that was encouraged by easy contact with other regions. Heretics also profited from the geographical situation. Connections with older centres of Catharism in the Rhine valley and in northern France, travel between France and Italy, visits of Bogomil missionaries, kept the sectaries in Languedoc from becoming isolated and ingrown. The Poor of Lyon maintained ties with Italian and Burgundian colleagues; they spread across the Pyrenees in advance of the Cathars.

Moreover, transmission of new religious ideas was encouraged by the intimate relationships among citizens of the towns. The close-knit texture of rural life, where peasants were gathered in small defensible villages, had the same consequence. Even if the ability to read the Scriptures by which heretical teaching was authenticated was not commonplace, word of mouth dissemination was easy.

Among certain social groups conditions favoured the acceptance of dissent from the church. The rural aristocracy, disgruntled by loss of control of tithes and ecclesiastical property, made willing audiences for the preachers who disparaged the Catholic clergy for idleness, luxury, and self-seeking. In these families, women had significant influence, and intermarriages created networks of sympathizers with heresy. That feminine influence did not, however, always override political or military necessities. Princes such as the counts of Toulouse and Foix did admit heretics to their company, permitted them free movement, saw their wives and daughters venerate or join them and their subordinates become their protectors, but no good case can be made that they themselves were believers in a real sense. When war came they tried to keep their freedom of political manoeuvre, sacrificing heretics as pawns in their game. The knights of the countryside played for lower stakes and were warmer adherents of the heretics but they too were capable of shifting their religious affections – at least on the surface – to meet changed situations.

It has been suggested, but with less than convincing proof, that heresy was a class phenomenon, with roots in social and economic dissent. We might assume that resentments of the underprivileged in the economic and social sphere would spill over into religious dissent; it would be a hypothesis rather than demonstrable fact. Heretics cannot be shown to have been more numerous among workers and artisans than among merchants, investors, and patricians of the towns. The towns were, however, centres for the propagation of ideas and were never neglected by heretical teachers, although the Cathar bishops made their residences in smaller villages.

We must take account of sympathy which does not become devotion. To acknowledge the merits of men does not necessarily lead to becoming their follower. Heretics won respect from those whom they did not convert when people encountered them in the streets or, out of curiosity, went to hear them preach in the homes of a neighbour. The conformity of Cathars and Waldenses to the ideals of apostolic life, their constant display of piety, could not but elicit admiration. The simplicity of their messages at first hearing would be seductive; so, too, the lightness of the burden laid on believers, who were taught to obey Gospel precepts but were not subjected to regular tithing or requests for more than simple charity. It would not be difficult for casual listeners to conclude that these were good men who taught a good faith, and it is likely that many persons who went no further would bow to the Good Men and Waldensian preachers in courtesy and respect, offer them a meal or a bed, conduct them from place to place when asked to do so, or accept their blessing on the chance that it would confer some benefit. Under existing law, any of these acts made one guilty of complicity in some degree in the crime of heresy.

Clearly, the 'sociology' of heresy, the extent of its acceptance, and the reasons for its spread, cannot now be stated in exact terms. What was important in the thirteenth century, however, was not whether heretics and their believers were a majority or a minority. That heresy existed at all was cause for concern; that it was not effectively restrained seemed to invite disaster. Here the role of prosecution – or persecution – must be weighed. In the fragmented political situation in Languedoc no secular prince could act decisively, even had there been harmony between secular and ecclesiastical lords instead of rivalry for influence and property. Heresy was kept in check in northern France and England because church and state co-operated against it. That was impossible in Languedoc.

Yet the freedom and influence which heretics enjoyed contradicted the ideal of a Christian commonwealth in which one church was arbiter of one faith. Thus it was inevitable that the need for action would be seen at the highest levels and, as the church became centralized, that the papacy would take the lead. Ultimately, all the weapons that could be devised would be used, even though the decision to employ armed force was slowly and hesitantly reached.

# References

1. Again, *HGL*, Vol. VI is basic for individuals and incidents. A. Luchaire discusses the church in Languedoc in the second of his six volumes on Innocent III: *La Croisade des Albigeois*. There is a short survey in Y. Dossat, 'Le Clergé méridional à la veille de la croisade albigeoise', *Revue historique et littéraire de Languedoc*, I (1944), 263–78. For a mild defence of Archbishop Berengar see R. W. Emery, *Heresy and Inquisition in Narbonne*; on Bishop William Peire of Albi, see L. de Lacger, 'L'Albigeois pendant la crise de l'albigéisme', *RHE*, XXIX (1933), 272–315, 586–633, 848–904; and on the episcopacy of Béziers, H. Vidal, *Episcopatus et pouvoir épiscopal à Béziers*. *The Register of Eudes of Rouen* was translated by S. M. Brown and edited by J. F. O'Sullivan. The quotation on p. 68 comes from J. H. Mundy, 'Charity and Social Work in Toulouse', *Traditio*, XXII (1966), 237; and the chronicler mentioned on p. 67 is William of Puylaurens, (edited by Bessyier, 119).
2. See pp. 89–91.
3. Döllinger, *Beiträge zur Sektengeschichte des Mittelalters*, I, 104; Vicaire, *Saint Dominic and His Times*, 464, n. 65; Duvernoy, 'La Liturgie et l'église cathares, Part II', *CEtC*, XVIII, 2nd ser., No. 35 (1967), 25–6; Roquebert, *L'Epopée cathare*, 101; Bécamel, 'Le Catharisme dans le diocèse d'Albi' in *CFan*, III, 251; Rainier Sacconi, *Summa*, A. Dondaine (ed.), in *Un Traité néo-manichéen*, 70. There is no easy way to compare these figures with the number of Catholic clergy, although there were surely many more priests and monks, to say nothing of other clerical ranks, than there were perfected heretics.
4. Dossat, 'Cathares et vaudois à la veille de la croisade albigeoise', *Revue historique et littéraire de Languedoc*, III (1946), 79; Duvernoy, 'Guilhabert de Castres' and 'Bertrand Marty', *CEtC*, XVIII, 2nd ser., No. 34 (1967), 32–42, and XIX, 2nd ser., No. 39 (1968), 19–35, respectively. On the list of Béziers, see p. 76, above.
5. The best evidence of the existence of heresy in particular places comes from the depositions of some three hundred of the witnesses before inquisitors

in the decade of the 1240s who spoke of events of pre-crusading days. They are found in Vols. XXI–XXV of the Collection Doat in Paris and MS 609 of the municipal library of Toulouse. A list of twenty-five places said to harbour heretics in 1209 was in the hands of papal legates; it is printed in J. Roquette and A. Villemagne, *Cartulaire du Maguelonne*, II, 59–60 (No. CCC). Valuable sources also are records of property confiscated for reason of heresy, which have been partially exploited by Y. Dossat, as in his *Les Crises de l'Inquisition toulousaine*, Chs. 12–13. For discussion of specific localities, see M. Roquebert, *L'Epopée cathare, passim*, esp. 525–37; Griffe, *Le Languedoc cathare de 1190 à 1210*, 61–192; and Y. Dossat, 'Catharisme et Gascogne', *Bulletin de la Société archéologique . . . du Gers*, LXXIII (1972), 149–68.

6. On women and heresy, see M. Dmitrevsky, 'Notes sur le catharisme', *AM*, XXXVI (1924), 294–311; E. Werner, 'Die Stellung der Katharer zur Frau', *Studi medievali*, 3rd ser., II (1961), 295–301; and G. Koch, *Frauenfrage und Ketzertum in Mittelalter*. The countess Esclarmonde's reputation has had romantic embroidery, as in Simone Coincy de Saint Palais, *Esclarmonde de Foix, princesse cathare*. Her legend was 'debunked' by J. M. Vidal, 'Esclarmonde de Foix', *Revue de Gascogne*, n.s. XI (1911), 53–79, who was criticized in turn by S. Nelli, 'Esclarmonde de Foix', *CEtC*, VI, No. 24, (1955), 195–204. On Blanche of Niort and her children and grandchildren, see W. L. Wakefield, 'The Family of Niort', *Names*, XVIII (1970), 97–117, 286–303. The words of Pons Adémar were quoted by William of Puylaurens, edited by Bessyier, 127–8. On divided families see M. Mahul, *Cartulaire et archives . . . de Carcassonne*, V, 410; and J. Mundy, *Liberty and Political Power*, 290.

7. Mundy, *Liberty and Political Power*, 76–8, 288–91, nn. 14–19, and Griffe, *Le Languedoc cathare*, 70–5, discuss the situation in Toulouse, the latter concluding that the great majority of Toulousans were orthodox. The list of heretics of Béziers was published by L. Domairon, 'La Rôle des hérétiques de la ville de Béziers', *Le Cabinet historique*, IX (1863), 95–103, who counts 222 names; it was analyzed also by Vidal, *Episcopatus et pouvoir episcopal à Béziers*, 82–3, who finds only 219.

8. Everyone who writes of heresy in southern France must grapple with the problem of numbers and influence. Jean Guiraud based his study in *Cartulaire de Notre Dame de Prouille*, Vol. I (the substance of which appears also in his *Histoire de l'Inquisition*, Vol. I) largely on original sources and his work is often cited as authoritative. I believe, however, that he overstated the extent of diffusion of heresy. Nelli, *La Vie quotidienne des Cathares*, discusses social class and heresy but brings together evidence from sources separated by passage of a century as though there were few changes in that time. Griffe, *Les Débuts de l'aventure cathare*, focuses on the rural nobility. I have consulted these and the works of Dossat, Duvernoy, and Roquebert cited in preceding notes and have also made my own 'soundings' in the sources surviving from the twelfth and thirteenth centuries as a basis for remarks made in the preceding paragraphs.

F

# V The Prosecution of Heresy

The method for dealing with heretics occasioned much uncertainty in the early Middle Ages. St Paul had admonished the faithful to reprove the erring and, if warnings were fruitless, to avoid him. When association of church and state in the later Roman Empire made power available for coercion of dissenters, ideas about toleration or persecution for holy purposes were affected. Constantine and his successors regarded the suppression of heresy as an imperial duty, made it a crime against the state, imposed civil disabilities on heretics, and executed members of certain sects. The reaction of the episcopate was mixed; many were willing to accept the assistance of the state to maintain purity of doctrine, while disagreeing on the extent to which force should be used. Most influential in shaping future thought was St Augustine, whose attitude changed from tolerance to advocacy of 'righteous persecution', conducted with secular assistance, but the penalty of death he disapproved.

## Methods of Prosecution before 1179

There was not much occasion for collaboration of church and state against religious dissenters between the time that imperial authority waned in the West and the medieval revival of heresy. Then, and for some time thereafter, uncertainty about appropriate measures was the rule. Errors that were primarily intellectual would usually be pounced on by intellectuals, debated, corrected, or punished, without raising any great stir among the masses. Heresies of a popular nature which were taken up by groups of laymen were not only more dangerous but hard to detect and eradicate. Normally a bishop who heard reports of unorthodox activity would bring the suspects before a convocation of clergy for questioning, which might lead to debate between the inter-rogators and the accused. If the latter were found guilty from their responses or sometimes by the ordeal of water or hot iron, the question of penalties arose, for there were spokesmen for toleration in the eleventh and twelfth centuries who were dubious about the propriety of harsh measures of coercion.

Sometimes the mob, horrified at the evil that had been unearthed and fearful of divine wrath if it went unpunished, intervened to seize and execute the heretics. Less extreme penalties were gradually introduced in both canon and civil law. The councils of Toulouse (1119), the second Lateran (1139), Reims (1157), and Tours (1163) decreed excommunication of heretics, imprisonment, and confiscation of property, and urged civil officials to take action. They did so swiftly and cruelly in the Rhineland, Flanders, northern France, and England after the middle of the twelfth century, with whipping, branding, and exile. Gradually the idea spread that death by fire, already carried out in certain cases by kings in the eleventh century, was the appropriate penalty for the unrepentant. This the church refused officially to approve and disclaimed responsibility for its use.[1]

Coercion and punishment were not the only tactics. Much effort was put into writing descriptions of the doctrines of various sects and refutations of them, ostensibly in the hope of conversion. The chief effect was to spread knowledge of the heresies and alarm among Catholics. Preaching against heresy was also regarded as a worthy effort and, for a time, was important in Languedoc. There, indeed, violent measures were not attempted until late in the twelfth century.

### A Preaching Mission, 1178

Neither the preaching of Bernard of Clairvaux in 1145 nor the confrontation of heretics and Catholics twenty years later succeeded in checking religious disaffection in Languedoc. In 1178 Count Raymond V of Toulouse took the initiative in another attempt. He was, no doubt, genuinely concerned over the spread of Catharism, but there were also advantages that might follow his taking a stand against it. The contagion was worst in regions controlled directly by his unruly vassal, Roger Trencavel II. A papal schism fostered by Emperor Frederick I was drawing to an end and Raymond, the emperor's ally, wished to extricate himself from the losing side. His citizens in Toulouse were challenging his authority and to embarrass them on the issue of heresy might be a useful move.

The count, therefore, in September 1178 wrote what was in effect an appeal for intervention for the sake of the faith to Louis VII of France, and in another letter to the chapter-general of

Cîteaux he described the doleful ravages of heresy in his lands. Fostered by his chief vassals, he said, it was emptying churches, seducing even clerics, and reducing the Christian religion to naught. The sacraments were scorned and the abominable doctrine of two principles was being preached. Only force could save the church. Henry, abbot of Clairvaux, responded energetically. No doubt recalling the efforts of his saintly predecessor, Bernard, the abbot wrote to the pope for assistance through the papal legate and to the king of France to propose royal action. Louis VII, in consultation with Henry II of England, with whom he had just made peace, decided that a royal visitation would be less useful than a mission of ecclesiastics under a military escort, combining preaching with the threat of force.

Late in 1178 Cardinal Peter of Pavia, papal legate to France, attended by Abbot Henry and several other prelates and escorted by a party of barons and knights, arrived in Toulouse where, according to the abbot, they were jeered in the streets as imposters, hypocrites, and heretics. Nevertheless, with the count's assistance, the legate obtained from the clergy of the city the names of notorious heretics and managed to wring from Peter Maurand, one of the wealthiest citizens who was reputed to be their leader, the confession that he had expressed wrongful views about the Eucharist. This was regarded as proof of the 'Arian heresy', a term the prelates of 1178 found natural because some of Bernard's opponents of 1145 had been so-called and because the Cathars seemed to resemble the ancient Arians in denigrating Christ. The penance imposed on Peter Maurand was severe: flogging, three years exile in the Holy Land during which his property was to be temporarily sequestered, razing of the fortifications of his town house, and a heavy fine to be paid to Raymond V. How thoroughly it was carried out we do not know. Other suspects, terrified into submission, were treated more leniently.

In the meantime Abbot Henry had turned aside in a vain attempt to persuade Roger Trencavel II, viscount of Béziers, Carcassonne, and Albi, to release the bishop of Albi, whom he had captured in a quarrel. The plea failed, but at Castres the abbot did encounter two heretics, Bernard Raymond and Raymond of Baimac, the former probably bishop of the heretical church of Toulouse, who agreed to come to Toulouse under safe conduct to discuss their beliefs. Before a large crowd, the two men produced a document to attest their faith. Questioned in detail on it in the vernacular, for they had little Latin, they seemed to be giving sound replies when they were interrupted by

Count Raymond and others with cries that they lied, that they had been heard to preach publicly the doctrine of two creators and had spoken against matrimony, baptism, and other Christian doctrines. The accused thereupon insisted that they held perfectly orthodox beliefs on all the articles of faith, but they flatly refused to take an oath in confirmation, on the ground that oaths were sinful. It was enough; they were excommunicated but allowed to depart, while the count and leading citizens of the town swore that they would not harbour heretics in the future. With that the mission ended.

### The Third Lateran Council and the Use of Force

The experience of the mission in Toulouse affected the deliberations of the Third Council of the Lateran which convened in March 1179. After making various provisions for improving the state of the episcopacy and clergy, preventing financial abuses, and advancing education, the council condemned in one canon both mercenary soldiers who were such a danger to Languedoc and heretics under various names. The penalties for the crimes of both were to be confiscation and enslavement; all men were urged to hunt down bandits and heretics and were offered the reward of indulgences for doing so. The use of the secular sword against heresy, suggested by the count of Toulouse and urged by the abbot of Cîteaux, was now approved by highest Christian authority.

Henry of Marsiac, abbot of Clairvaux took the lead in the new kind of war which the council had authorized, a crusade within Christian lands. He had been made a cardinal in 1179 and as papal legate had presided at the temporary reconciliation of Waldes with the clergy of Lyon. Then in 1181 he gathered an army – no source tells us who supplied the warriors – for a campaign against heretics and their protectors. Its first and only act was to besiege the castle of Lavaur belonging to Roger Trencavel II and held at that moment by his viscountess, Adelaide. Raymond V of Toulouse, her father, made no move to help either side. Roger II soon sued for peace, promising to renounce heresy and prosecute heretics; the terms of submission included handing over to the cardinal the two heretical spokesmen who had defended themselves at Toulouse three years earlier and had thereafter taken refuge at Lavaur. They were somehow persuaded to convert and before a council at Le Puy acknowledged their former errors, the tenets of the mitigated dualist faction of the Cathars. Confession seems to have spared the converts further penalty, for they became canons in Toulouse, one at St Etienne, the other at St Sernin.[2]

Vigorous action against heresy in Languedoc ceased for nearly two decades after the crusade of 1181 although legislation to encourage it continued to be adopted. Pope Lucius III, after conferring with Emperor Frederick Barbarossa at Verona in 1184, issued an important decretal entitled *Ad abolendam*, in which Cathars, Patarines, the Poor of Lyon, Passagians, Josephines, Arnoldists, Publicans, and any others who denied church doctrine on the Eucharist, baptism, remission of sins, or marriage, together with all persons who protected and defended them, were put under anathema. Clergy convicted of heresy were to be degraded and handed over to secular officials; heretical laymen were to receive 'fitting punishment', the nature of which was not specified, at the same hands. Bishops were instructed annually to visit places suspected of harbouring heretics and to undertake proceedings against any persons who were denounced by sworn witnesses. There was no subsequent action under this decretal in Languedoc. King Alphonse II of Aragon did issue statutes ordering heretics out of his realm and declaring their supporters guilty of lese-majesty; these were republished by his son, Pedro II, specifically naming the Waldenses and decreeing death by fire for the guilty, but since Aragonese authority was only indirect in Languedoc they had little relevance there. At Montpellier a council presided over by a papal legate repeated the legislation of the Lateran council of 1179 and Count William VIII encouraged the clergy to vigilance, with results unknown. After Roger Trencavel II died his heir was entrusted to the tutelage of Bertrand of Saissac, who was known to have heretical sympathies. However, Bertrand promised the bishop of Béziers, perhaps with tongue in cheek, that he would expel and keep out heretics. Years later the consuls of Toulouse would declare that in the days of Raymond V they had burned many heretics. No document attesting the validity of their statement has come to light.

Such was the situation when a new and energetic pope in 1198 began one of the most momentous pontificates of the Middle Ages and set in motion events fateful to the Albigensian heretics, to Languedoc, and to the church itself.

## Innocent III and Languedoc

On 8 January 1198, at the age of thirty-seven, Lothar of Segni, Roman aristocrat, former student in canon and civil law at Paris and Bologna, and cardinal since 1190, was elected pope on the day of his predecessor's death. For eighteen years, dynamic and indefatigable, Innocent III directed the complex institution of the church, dealing with kings and emperors with the assurance of supreme authority, summoning crusades, pressing the cause of church reform, formulating significant definitions of dogma, and adding important statutes to canon law. Of great events in Europe there were few in which he did not have a hand. Nothing had his more constant interest than bolstering the Christian faith wherever it was challenged by heresy, against which in 1199 he justified the penalties already existing in canon law by likening it to lese-majesty against God. It is to Innocent's programme in Languedoc that our attention must be confined, even though that was only one strand in the web of papal policies.

For the first five years of his pontificate Innocent III directed his efforts in southern France at three goals which the church might achieve with its own resources: reform of the clergy by removing the indolent or scandalous from high places, persuading the nobility to lend their aid against heresy, and re-animation of the faith by preaching. The first results in all respects were discouraging, and in 1204 the pope began to urge on King Philip Augustus of France the need for forceful intervention. Soon thereafter, however, the programme of preaching found important advocates so that between 1206 and 1208 Languedoc was the scene of peaceful missionary activities. Then events conspired to alter papal policies again toward the use of force.

## Diplomacy and Persuasion

Execution of the papal programme in Languedoc was entrusted at the outset to members of the Cistercian order. In April 1198 Innocent sent his own confessor, Rainier of Ponza, with a fellow Cistercian, Brother Guy, as his representatives. They were commissioned as preachers, but also were empowered to excommunicate heretics, to place under interdict lands that were infested, and to order the confiscation of property of believers or protectors of heretics. A few months later the legates were given full authority also to correct clerical abuses. In 1203 Rainer and Guy were succeeded by two other Cistercians, Peter of Castelnau, a recent entrant to the order, and Master Ralph of Fontfroide. The involvement of the Cistercians increased with the appointment of Arnold Aimery, abbot of Cîteaux, as a third legate, while the order at large was instructed to provide monks to supplement the public preaching of the legates.

Few prelates of the region welcomed the visitors or failed to resent the extraordinary powers conferred on them. Archbishop Berengar of Narbonne was openly hostile, while the bishop of Béziers refused to excommunicate the consuls of his town at the legates' command and was suspended. The archbishop escaped the same penalty only because Innocent III temporized on the matter of his appeal, thereby discouraging his legates, and the case dragged on until 1212, when Berengar was deposed. Meanwhile, proceedings against other unwanted prelates moved more quickly and bishops of better repute and more responsive to papal direction, were found to replace them.

Secular co-operation with Innocent's plans was even more difficult to obtain. Simultaneously with the appointment of his first representatives, Innocent III had admonished the nobility to assist them and to take up arms against heretics, promising the reward of an indulgence equal to that earned by pilgrims to Compostella or Rome. Those who refused to respond were threatened with excommunication and interdict. Neither promise nor threat obtained any significant action from feudal rulers, although Montpellier, Carcassonne, and Arles did adopt statutes excluding from public office anyone who was defamed as a heretic. The legates also persuaded the consuls of Toulouse in 1203 to swear to maintain the Catholic faith, but only in exchange for a guarantee of civic liberties and immunity from certain pending charges of heresy. Two years later Count Raymond VI took an oath to expel heretics and mercenaries from his lands. These successes were illusory, for the consuls of Toulouse blocked an important procedure by forbidding prosecution of a deceased person unless he had been charged with heresy during his lifetime or was known to have been baptized in heresy at death, and the count refused to join an armed league against heretics organized among some of his vassals by Peter of Castelnau. As a result the legate excommunicated him in 1207, an act confirmed by Innocent III in a scathing letter to the count.

Pedro II of Aragon seemed to be more co-operative. In February 1204, he arranged for Catholics and heretics to appear before him at Carcassonne so that he could be informed about the nature of the latter's errors. Waldensian spokesmen came to debate with the legates one day; on the next the Catharist bishop of Carcassonne with a dozen colleagues argued with a similar number of Catholics. In each case Pedro was persuaded by the legates that what he had heard from both Cathars and Waldenses was heresy. No prosecutions followed. Innocent III, however, treated the king as a valuable ally and applauded a foray that he made soon thereafter against a castle which was legally a fief of the pope but had been occupied by heretical sympathizers in the region of Albi.

## The Preaching Campaign of 1206–1208

Innocent III did not lose sight of the fact that neither clerical reform nor the threat of force struck at the root of the problem of religious disaffection and that instruction through preaching was a primary necessity. In the first years, however, evangelism among the people to challenge heretics on their own ground had remained incidental to the reform of the episcopate and to diplomatic negotiations with secular powers. The appointment of Arnold Aimery in 1204, with instructions to emphasize preaching, gave the missionary aspects of Innocent's plans new life. A greater stimulus came from the arrival in Languedoc in 1206 of two inspired travellers. Bishop Diego of the Spanish see of Osma had already journeyed widely on affairs of the king of Castile, accompanied by the subprior of his cathedral, Dominic of Guzman or of Caleruega. Both had some acquaintance with the situation in Languedoc, and Dominic is credited with the conversion from Catharism of the host with whom he had lodged on an earlier trip. They were returning now from an interview with the pope, who had refused Diego's request to be allowed to give up his office in order to become a missionary to the pagans; instead, Innocent entrusted to him some advice for the legates in Languedoc.

When Diego and Dominic met the three Cistercians at Montpellier the bishop of Osma proposed to the legates the full execution of the project which the pope had put forward when he appointed Arnold Aimery – incessant preaching to instruct the multitudes who were ignorant of the faith – to which Diego added another prescription, teaching 'by example and word'. Let the preachers travel barefoot like the apostles, avoiding every appearance of the pomp and luxury which were the scandal of the church, in effect, turning the weapons of the heretics against them. Let the adversaries be sought out in the field and the value of the true faith be proved in controversy.

The inspiration for the proposal may have come from Innocent III; the fulfilment fell to the bishop, whom the legates agreed to follow, somewhat reluctantly because of the novelty of the method. It was difficult to drop from the level of papal plenipotentiaries to that of itinerant evangelists; furthermore, preaching to the people had always been an episcopal prerogative. Diego's proposal for confronting the heretics in free debate was also unusual, for in the discussions that had taken place at Lombers, Toulouse, and Carcassonne condemnation of the dissenters had always been virtually certain unless they recanted. Not until Innocent proclaimed to the whole Cistercian order the need for men who would redeem the heretics through 'the example of their action and the doctrine they preach', thus explicitly endorsing the methods advocated by Bishop Diego, were the legates' doubts entirely resolved.

In the summer of 1206 the Cistercian legates and their new allies began the preaching campaign. At the outset Diego and Dominic carried the chief burden, for Arnold Aimery was sometimes absent on the business of his order and Peter of Castelnau was not only occupied with other legatine affairs but also was so unpopular that his presence in a meeting with heretics in public debate was a dubious asset. Even after Innocent III summoned twelve Cistercian abbots and companion monks to participate in the holy preaching in the spring of 1207 Diego remained the unofficial leader and it was he who bore most of the expenses of the mission.

How greatly the new mode of preaching impressed Catholic contemporaries is shown by admiring comment in chronicles of the time, although they say little about the day-to-day evangelism and put the emphasis on more spectacular incidents, when heretics accepted the challenge to open debate before an audience. Thus occurred a series of theological tournaments in which the weapons were biblical texts and the prize the allegiance of the people. The setting was in towns, large and small: Servian, Béziers, Carcassonne, Verfeil, Lavaur, Montréal. The Cathars put forward their best champions. At Servian in eight days of debate there was Bernard of Simorre, heretical bishop of Carcassonne, accompanied by Theodoric, who, as canon of Nevers had fled from prosecution, changed his name, and became an important Catharist theologian. At Montréal for fifteen days a group composed of Arnold Otto, a heretical deacon, Guilabert of Castres, elder son and soon to be bishop of the Cathars of Toulouse, Benedict, future heretical bishop of Termes, and the veteran disputant Pons Jordan gathered to debate with Diego, Dominic, Peter of Castelnau, and Ralph.

The themes of the disputes are imperfectly known. At Verfeil the human nature of Christ was discussed; at Montréal the character of the Roman church which the heretics impugned as the devil's agent and as Babylon, mother of fornications. The exchanges were not free from rancour. When a heretic charged Diego with appearing in the wrathful spirit of Elijah, the bishop replied, 'And you come in the spirit of Antichrist!' Sometimes a panel of judges, including both Catholics and heretical sympathizers, presided, and in some disputations each side was asked to submit to the arbiters a brief which summarized their arguments. An instance of this gave rise to the famous legend that when a page on which Dominic had recorded the texts used to prove his points had been handed to heretics they attempted to burn it, only three times to see the fire cast the document out unharmed. The heretics, however, refused to be converted even by this miraculous event.

There was some profit for the church in this devoted labour. At Servian Diego and Dominic won over the audience, although the seigneur of the place gave the heretics protection against reprisals from the people. One hundred and fifty persons, it is said, returned to the church at Montréal. At Pamiers Bishop Diego was so persuasive that he converted his Waldensian opponents as well as the judge presiding. Among the former was Durand of Huesca, whose reconciliation with the church has already been mentioned.

Despite these successes the rewards of the preaching campaign seemed discouragingly small and the pull of the monastery was strong on the Cistercians. Most of the abbots and monks left the field at the end of the summer of 1207. Bishop Diego returned to Osma to arrange financing for a continued mission and died there in December of the same year. Within a few weeks the murder of Peter of Castelnau would abruptly change the climate and lead to a storm of violence in Languedoc in which only Dominic continued to carry on the mission of conversion by preaching.[3]

### The Call for a Crusade
Under the best of circumstances the campaigns of preaching and reform of the clergy could only slowly have shown results in an area where indifference or hostility to the church was deep rooted. It is not surprising that in the face of the refusal of the political powers in Languedoc to support him that Innocent's thoughts would have intermittently turned to recruitment of assistance from outside. His recourse could be either to persuade King Philip Augustus to intervene as suzerain – an appeal to another monarch, such as Pedro of Aragon, would have been an affront to the Capetian – or to lay the county of Toulouse open as prey to Christian warriors because of its ruler's crimes. Writing to the

king in 1204 the pope had combined these proposals by urging that the lands of those who protected heretics be confiscated and added to the royal domain, offering to the warriors who would be needed the same indulgence as could be earned by crusade to the Holy Land.

Philip Augustus, however, engrossed in a conflict with England and anticipating further troubles from the strife over the German crown, replied coolly that he could find no justification in human law for the pope's proposal and that, in fact, the affairs of kings were outside papal jurisdiction. Nor was there a royal response to similar pleas from Innocent in the following year. In 1207, however, as the Cistercian preaching mission was collapsing, the pope turned again to the project of forceful measures. Writing to Philip Augustus in November that every effort against heresy had been foiled by stubbornness he declared it necessary to use the iron of secular power to force advocates of heretical depravity to appreciate the truth by suffering the miseries of war. This time the king saw the prospect of some diplomatic advantage. Replying to the pope indirectly in a letter addressed to the bishop of Paris Philip said that he had not the resources to maintain one army against England and another in Languedoc. To make action in the south possible the pope must arrange a two-year truce with King John and allow the cost of an expedition southward to be met by financial levy on the clergy and baronage of France. The king's conditions were not met, but two months later the murder of Peter of Castelnau led Innocent III to commit himself irrevocably to the use of force.

Since 1203 Peter of Castelnau's execution of papal directives had won him the hatred of heretics and the resentment of the prelates and princes whom he denounced and threatened in virtue of his legatine authority. In 1207 came his excommunication of Raymond VI and Innocent's renewed appeal to Philip Augustus. The count of Toulouse attempted to avert the obvious danger of intervention by seeking an interview with the legate at St Gilles in January 1208. Apparently Raymond both promised to obey Peter of Castelnau's commands and at the same time sought to excuse himself in advance if they were not carried out. The discussion became a quarrel and ended, according to the report which the pope later broadcast, with Raymond's threat that go where Peter would, he would be under the count's menacing surveillance. Soon afterwards, on 14 January 1208, a knight approached Peter of Castelnau as he was preparing to cross the Rhône and killed him. Innocent, relying on the reports of the legates, leaped to the conclusion that the assassination was instigated by Raymond VI, although he later reduced the charge to suspicion of complicity. Even that seems hardly credible. Raymond was vacillating and wily but not stupid; even he could have foreseen the dangers raised by such an act. Perhaps, like Henry II with Becket, he was the victim of a subject who sought to serve him; perhaps the assassin was revenging a personal grievance; in any case Raymond made the mistakes of neither searching out the murderer nor mollifying the pope by expressions of regret and thus laid himself open to the suspicion and condemnation which promptly came upon him.

The murder of Peter of Castelnau, not only a crime but a direct affront to papal authority, turned Innocent's negotiations for a crusade into demands. Letters that were now addressed to the king, barons, and people of France were peremptory exhortations to take up the sword, confiscate the lands infested with heresy, and people them with faithful Catholics under Philip's rule. The legates were ordered to preach a crusade against the heretics and their protectors – hopefully not at the risk of reducing support for the war in the Holy Land – and the Cistercian order mobilized itself for that task. Philip Augustus was disturbed at the possibility of papal interference with his right to choose his vassals and protested that it was beyond the pope's authority to deprive Raymond VI of his lands until he had been convicted of heresy; let that be done, he said, and he would act. Nevertheless, he gave reluctant permission for not more than 500 knights to take the cross for the Albigensian crusade. He refused to allow his son to do so or to lead the expedition himself. 'I have two strong and fierce lions at my flanks, Otto of Germany and John of England,' he declared, in arguing that only after a guaranteed truce with John would he dare to become embroiled in the south. The refusal cost him the power to control events, and during the remainder of the year preparations for the crusade moved forward. Its conditions were defined by the pope: those who took the cross were granted a moratorium on debts and release from usurious interest, vassals were encouraged to contribute to the expenses of a lord, and the clergy authorized to use their funds to support warriors. The spiritual reward was to be a plenary indulgence for serving forty days. There was much to recommend the crusade to northerners. All the spiritual and material benefits of the arduous voyage to Palestine were now proffered for war against men of their own habits and military tactics in a country reputed to be rich. Taking the cross could also be a release from troubles;

more than one knight went on crusade as a penance for his sins.

Thus the struggle against heresy approached a climax in Languedoc. The business of the faith had not been conducted there in isolation from similar affairs elsewhere. Innocent III had also pressed it in Italian cities by suggesting new legal procedures and, using bishops, legates, or his own direct intervention to insert legislation against heresy in municipal statutes. In France he had interested himself in the prosecutions in Nevers and at La Charité-sur-Loire. He had written letters of warning and correction and sent commissioners to investigate incidents of religious unrest in the Rhineland. But the task in Languedoc was the heaviest and the measures taken there were of the greatest importance for the future.

There had been no insincerity in Innocent's encouragement of preaching and persuasion as countermeasures to heresy. His inclination to show mercy was strong; moderate policies and generous treatment had already won back some Humiliati and a group of Waldenses. Preaching was the method of choice, if one assumed that heresy had been encouraged by clerical negligence or by lack of instruction and saw the success of the Cathars and Waldenses as a result of their direct response to popular aspirations. In retrospect it seems possible that a combination of programmes to rehabilitate the clergy and to win back the dissidents by example and instruction might eventually have had some success, but only slowly, for alienation so long-standing, existing in some families for three or four generations could not easily be overcome.

Nor was there inconsistency in the papal call for a crusade. Both persuasion and force had been integral to Innocent III's grand design of preserving the unity of the Christian world and bringing peace to the church. Behind his summons to war within Christian lands lay a complex of concepts and institutions evolved over more than two centuries: associations of clergy and people to establish the Peace of God and suppress disorders in society; crusades of the eleventh and twelfth centuries, uniting people and clergy under spiritual jurisdiction in enterprises for Christ; the extension of the concept of papal duty to supervision of justice and order everywhere. For Innocent the situation of southern France was 'an affair of peace and faith'. If peace had to be attained by righteous use of the secular sword, that was lawful by long tradition. No more than most men was the pope able to foresee the ultimate results of his decision.[4]

# References

1. The development of repressive measures is discussed in all the histories of the Inquisition. On the general theme see E. W. Nelson, 'The Theory of Persecution' in *Persecution and Liberty*; and M. Bévenot, 'The Inquisition and Its Antecedents', *Heythrop Journal*, VII (1966), 257–68, 381–93; VIII (1967), 52–69, 152–68. H. Maisonneuve, *Études sur les origines de l'Inquisition* (2nd ed.) Ch. 1, discusses the imperial and canonical traditions. Actions of the twelfth century are described most fully in H. Theloe, *Die Ketzerverfolgungen im 11. und 12. Jahrhundert*; and J. Havet, 'L'Hérésie et le bras séculier', *Bibliothèque de l'école des chartes*, XLI (1880), 488–517, 570–607, 670; and are briefly resumed by R. Foreville, in Ch. 10 of Fliche and Martin, *Histoire de l'église*, Vol. IX. R. Manselli, 'De la "persuasio" à la "coercitio" ', *CFan*, VI, 175–9, sees the decisive shift from reluctant tolerance to prosecution occurring between 1163 and 1184. H. Maillet, *L'Église et la répression sanglante de l'hérésie*, presents the actions of the church in the most favourable light.

2. The leaders of the preaching mission of 1178 and the crusade of 1181 are the subjects of H. Delehaye, 'Pierre de Pavie', *RQH*, XLIX (1891), 5–61; and Y. M. J. Congar, 'Henri de Marcy, abbé de Clairvaux', *Studia Anselmiana*, XLIII: *Analecta monastica*, V (1958), 1–90. See also Griffe, *Les Débuts de l'aventure cathare*, 84–132. One narrative of the mission of 1178 is translated in Wakefield and Evans, *Heresies*, No. 29.

3. A. Luchaire, *Innocent III: La Croisade des albigeois*, was the most useful to me of numerous studies of the pope. Other important recent biographies are S. Sibilia, *Innocenzo III, 1198–1216*; and H. Tillman, *Papst Innocenz III*. Papal legations are the subject of H. Zimmerman, *Die päpstlichen Legation in der ersten Hälfte des 13. Jahrhunderts*, and the themes emphasized by the pope are discussed in O. Olíver, *Tactica de propaganda y motivos literarios en las cartas antihereticas de Innocencio III*. C. Thouzellier gives a succinct summary of the pope's attitude and actions in the matter of heresy in *Catharisme et valdéisme*, 139–68, 183–212. I have relied on the definitive biography by M. H. Vicaire, *Saint Dominic*, with reference also to P. Mandonnet, *Saint Dominic and His Work*. Vicaire's study gives the best account of the preaching campaign of 1206–1208; see also C. Thouzellier, 'La Pauvreté, arme contre l'albigéisme en 1206' in *Hérésie et hérétiques*, Ch. 6. The history of the Waldensian converts of Pamiers was studied by J. B. Pierron, *Die katholischen Armen*. On their leader, Durand of Huesca, see pp. 45–6, above, and the works of Thouzellier and Selge, cited on p. 49, n. 15.

4. R. Foreville, 'Innocent III et la croisade des Albigeois' in *CFan*, IV, 184–217, analyses the attitude and policies of the pope.

# VI The Albigensian Crusade
## invasion and conquest 1209–1215

A French army gathered late in June 1209 to answer the summons from Innocent III. The refusal of Philip Augustus to participate left the command to Arnold Aimery as legate of the pope. Among the military chieftains were the duke of Burgundy, counts of Nevers, St Pol, and many others. The archbishops of Rouen, Reims, and Sens brought contingents, as did a number of bishops; and there were many lesser lords and individual knights. Squires, sergeants, cooks, smiths, carpenters, camp followers, and ordinary men and women lured by the chance of adventure or the promise of indulgence accompanied them, to make it, as the legate proudly wrote to the pope, the greatest army Christendom had seen assembled.[1]

*Manoeuvres of the Count of Toulouse*
While the host was assembling, Raymond VI searched for ways to meet or divert its onslaught. Old political rivalries dissuaded Raymond Roger Trencavel, viscount of Béziers, Carcassonne, and Albi, from agreeing with the count on plans for a common defence; perhaps Raymond Roger counted on protection by the king of Aragon, perhaps he believed that the attack would fall first on the count. Neither proved to be true. Whatever the reason – and the count of Toulouse himself may not have been eager – the failure to make common cause led Raymond VI to seek whatever peace he could. His messengers to Innocent III brought back the demand that seven important castles be handed over to the custody of various bishops and abbots as surety for the count's good faith in promising to submit. The pope also heeded Raymond's complaint that discussions with Arnold Aimery would be

difficult because of the abbot's animosity for him, sending the papal secretary Milon with commission to negotiate. But the pope privately instructed Milon to rely on Arnold Aimery's advice and to pursue a policy that would divide the princes of Languedoc.

In June, a few days before the crusaders began to march southward, Milon summoned Raymond before a council of prelates and notables at St Gilles, where the count was required to demonstrate his repentance by accepting the charges laid against him. They may be summarized as violations of the peace by employing mercenaries, ignoring holy days during campaigns, and refusing offers of truce; attacks on the church in the persons and property of bishops and abbots; affronts to the faith by harbouring heretics and employing Jews in public office; injustice in tolls; and above all, suspicion of involvement in the murder of Peter of Castelnau. Having promised to purge himself of guilt in the last-named point, to make reparation to the clergy, and to guarantee their privileges, Raymond was led to the altar of the church to be scourged by the legate. This done, and the interdict on his lands rescinded, he asked and received permission to join the crusaders, hoping, no doubt, to divert them from his county and to direct them against Trencavel possessions. That, at least, is what happened. But the count, for all his craftiness, did not foresee that his own troubles had only begun.

The campaigns of the next twenty years cannot be described in detail here. The plan will be to sketch the general character of warfare and then to survey the military actions and accompanying diplomacy in each of three periods: (1) from 1209 to 1215, years in which most of Languedoc passed into the hands of the invaders and the Fourth Lateran Council confirmed Simon of Montfort in possession of the former territories of the Trencavels and the count of Toulouse; (2) from 1216 to 1225, when, after a southern resurgence and the death of Montfort, the southerners seemed near success; and (3) from 1226 to 1229, when the Capetians intervened decisively and won the victory.[2]

*Warfare in Languedoc*
There was nothing to choose between warriors of North and South as to individual bravery or prowess. The crusaders usually had far better discipline and organization, and Montfort was a better general than Raymond VI, although, perhaps, no more capable a tactician than Raymond Roger of Foix. Military operations of the crusade were shaped by the normal conditions of

medieval warfare: the prevalence of fortifications and the superiority of heavy cavalry in the field. The first was more significant; of battlefield encounters only that at Muret had decisive results, for mastery of a region required possession of its chief castles and towns. Simon of Montfort spent his years conquering and garrisoning them, often having to repeat the process when they were retaken by the other side.

Attack on a fortified place began with encircling it if possible, erecting stone-throwing machines to harass the defenders, and attempting to mine and sap the walls until they could be stormed. The defenders might sally out against the besiegers' camp or their machines. The problem of supplies worried both sides; short rations or starvation could be the fate of a castle garrison under long attack, but assailants abandoned more than one siege for want of provisions. To reduce a castle well-sited on the heights, such as the fortresses of Termes or Lavaur, called for great exertions to bring in timber for catapaults, to prepare their platforms by digging into the slopes or filling gullies with rubble, and to manhandle the stone ammunition to the emplacement. The work of siege machines was entrusted to professionals or skilled amateurs, such as William, an archdeacon of Paris, one of the most talented of Montfort's aides in siegecraft, who was apparently so devoted to it that he refused the bishopric of Béziers when it was offered to him in 1212. Working parties protected by movable barriers were set to undercut the walls or constructed towers called 'cats', armoured with hides, which could be pushed forward for an assault. Inventive minds occasionally produced a new strategem. In one siege within a siege, when a crusader garrison in Beaucaire was shut up in the castle inside the town by troops of the younger Count Raymond, the defenders of the castle improvised a form of gas warfare by letting down on chains bundles of burning tow and sulphur, the fumes of which dispersed the miners at the foot of the walls.[3]

Not all sieges had to be pressed to a final assault, for discouraged defenders might ask for parleys to discuss terms of surrender or might merely slip away in darkness. The terms of capitulation usually allowed knights of the garrison to go free or be held for exchange for prisoners of the other side. They never covered heretics who were captured. The unrepentant were disposed of on pyres, to which they were often accompanied by those who were thought to have recanted only out of fear. One hundred and forty were burned at Minerve in 1210, three or four hundred after the fall of Lavaur, and there were many lesser holocausts. In Lea's phrase: 'Lavaur, Minerve, Cassès, Termes are names that suggest all that man can inflict and man can suffer for the glory of God.' Mercenaries could expect nothing but death if captured, and if a place had to be taken by storm even its knightly garrison could expect a harsh fate, especially those individuals who had a reputation for cruelty or deceit. After Lavaur was captured, its commander, Aimery of Montréal, died on a makeshift gallows and eighty of his knights were butchered because Aimery had already twice defected after making peace with Simon of Montfort. Baldwin, half-brother of Raymond VI, went over to the crusaders; when captured in a surprise attack, he was hanged by his brother's order. Hardly more happy were prisoners who were thrown into dungeons to rot, unless lucky enough to be exchanged. Massacre of inhabitants of a captured town marked the invaders' first victory at Béziers, and in 1219 French troops are said to have slaughtered five thousand people of Marmande after the garrison had surrendered.

The second basic factor in warfare was the heavy cavalry, composed of knights in chain mail and iron helmets, carrying shields rounded at the top and tapering down to a point, wielding lance, sword, mace, or battle axe; some southern horsemen threw javelins at close quarters. Sergeants, more lightly armed, accompanied and usually outnumbered the knights in a cavalcade. When parties of mounted warriors met, most often in small numbers – the battle of Muret, an ambuscade at Montgey and a fight at Baziège in 1219 are the chief exceptions – a charge might kill a few and unhorse others who would be made prisoners. The losers would scatter unless reinforcements were at hand and there was opportunity to regroup. Militia or auxiliary foot soldiers could not stand against horsemen and when convoys were ambushed the cooks, servants, muleteers and camp followers were easy prey for the mounted.

Crusaders normally came to serve only the forty days necessary to win an indulgence, although they might return another year. Some, especially in the first campaigns, hoped in win fiefs and were rewarded with confiscated property. Simon of Montfort, however, could count for continuous service only on a handful of veteran companions, his counsellors and commanders, who stood with him in triumphant and in difficult days. Each spring, or in emergencies when the crusade was preached with special fervour, fresh contingents rode south. On the other side the looser feudal military obligations prevalent in Languedoc and defections under Montfort's hammering made reliance on mercenaries imperative, yet there were always dispossessed knights to fight where they could and to take their opportunities for revenge. Moreover, few of the southern lords who had come to terms with the crusaders in order to keep part of their lands were reluctant to go to war again when the southern cause seemed to prosper.

Both sides employed mercenary troops. Some knights and sergeants fought for hire, but most mercenaries were professionals, recruited in Spain or the Low Countries, serving under their own captains as auxiliary troops and castle garrisons. The wars of the twelfth century had raised many bands of these *routiers*, with such dreadful results for any region where they campaigned or lived off the land in intervals of peace that they were outlawed by the Third Lateran Council, whose decree called the roll of their victims: 'Churches, monasteries, widows, orphans, old men, children'. They would fight when there was prospect of victory but, knowing that it was death to be captured, they ran rather than face heavy odds and readily changed sides for sufficient reward. Yet some mercenary captains acquired a certain prominence. Two examples among several: Martin Algai had already served Richard I and John of England so well that he became a seneschal in Gascony and Perigord. Montfort recruited him in 1211, but the troops the veteran mercenary brought did not fight well and Martin defected. A year later Montfort spared time to attack Martin Algai's stronghold at Biron, persuaded the garrison to hand over their commander to save their own lives, and made his execution a public spectacle. A Navarese captain, Hugh of Alfaro, fought steadfastly for Raymond VI and married the count's illegitimate daughter. His son served Raymond VII also, and the family name is memorialized in Toulouse by the Rue Pharaon.

Small honour can be awarded either side for their conduct in the war. Hatred and cruelty were fanned by religious zeal, antipathy for strangers, greed for land and power, and the bitterness of the dispossessed. Combat erodes pity; this war was more ruthless than most.

### Béziers and Carcassonne

Having moved its baggage down the Rhône, the crusading army left the river and marched westward through Nîmes and Montpellier toward Béziers. A source of much later date records that the Trencavel viscount requested but was refused a parley with the legates. He then encouraged Béziers to prepare its defences, while he, accompanied by Jews of the town and other non-

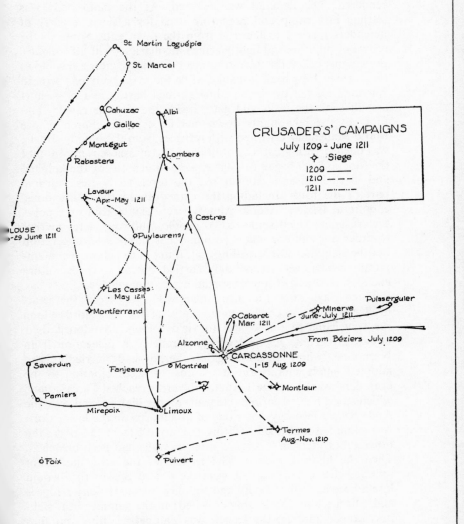

CRUSADERS' CAMPAIGNS
July 1209 – June 1211
◇ Siege
1209 ————
1210 ————
1211 ————·—·

St Martin Laguépie
St Marcel
Cahuzac
Gaillac
Albi
Montégut
Rabastens
Lombers
Lavaur
Apr.–May 1211
Castres
TOULOUSE
-29 June 1211
Puylaurens
Les Casses
May 1211
Montferrand
Puisserguier
Minerve
June–July 1211
Cabaret
Mar. 1211
Alzonne
From Béziers July 1209
Saverdun
Fanjeaux
Montréal
CARCASSONNE
1–15 Aug. 1209
Pamiers
Montlaur
Mirepoix
Limoux
Termes
Aug.–Nov. 1210
Foix
Puivert

combatants, retired to Carcassonne. On 22 July the army appeared before the walls of Béziers and sent in an ultimatum that the heretics named on a list drawn up by Bishop Reginald be surrendered. The demand was rejected. As the main body was settling into camp and preparing itself for a siege, a party of defenders made a rash sortie from the town gate. Some of the crowd of pilgrims and lightly armed auxiliaries – 'riffraff (*ribaldi*)' the knights called them – ran to meet the foray; after a few blows the citizens drew back in panic, while the main body of northern warriors, alerted by the squabble, armed hastily and in a short assault took the walls and gate. Inside the city the cavalry and foot cut the inhabitants down mercilessly. The church of Ste Marie-Madeleine, crowded with refugees from the bloody streets, was burned with great loss of life and the massacre went on until the foot soldiers began to pillage, were driven out by the knights, and in their disappointment put the torch to houses, burning part of the town, including the cathedral. In the 'miraculous' capture of Béziers, Arnold Aimery wrote exultantly to the pope, the crusaders killed some 15,000 people, 'showing mercy neither to order nor age nor sex'. The number is surely an exaggeration but the slaughter was appalling and, if one is to believe a contemporary report, was deliberately carried out to terrorize future enemies. A shock of horror spread across Languedoc.[4]

Three days later the army marched away from the ruins of Béziers toward Carcassonne. Many of the local lords along the way came to the legates to yield; others abandoned their homes to become *faidits* (exiles and rebels). A delegation from Narbonne, where statutes against heresy had hurriedly been adopted, made submission at the cost of a contribution to the crusaders' war chest. On 1 August the army reached Carcassonne, which stood behind formidable walls on the high ground over the Aude River. Two days later one of its suburbs on the lower slope was assaulted and taken, cutting the city off from the river; the other suburb fell on 8 August, after its walls had been breached. Then the fighting paused. The leaders of the army no doubt reflected that if Carcassonne went the way of Béziers they would lose a base as well as booty and supplies. Inside the city refugees and citizens were intolerably crowded; in the summer heat sickness sapped morale, the stench was nauseating, filth and flies multiplied, and the wells ran dry. Parleys were called for. One report says that Pedro II of Aragon sought to use his good offices on behalf of Viscount Raymond Roger, but that the latter indignantly refused the offer of safe conduct for himself and eleven companions at the price of surrendering all others in the city. Yet the defenders had no heart for prolonged resistance and negotiations were resumed. Although the sources do not agree on the final terms reached on 15 August, Raymond Roger did become a prisoner. When he died a few months later, probably of dysentery, common report said that it was murder by his captors. The inhabitants of Carcassonne were expelled from the city empty-handed, 'bearing with them only their sins'. Many filtered back in later days to take up life with what possessions remained after methodical confiscations by the victors.

## Simon of Montfort

The immediate concern of the victors was to choose a lord of the conquests and a leader to continue the crusade. After courtesy offers to the leading French barons had been declined a committee of knights and clerics recommended Simon, lord of Montfort l'Amaury, a member of a respected family which controlled a group of castles in the region between the Ile de France and Normandy and had marriage alliances in both Norman and Capetian areas. Through his mother Simon also claimed the English earldom of Leicester.[5] Now in his mid-forties he had a reputation for piety, bravery, and seriousness of purpose. In 1204, when the Fourth Crusade was diverted to Zara, he had left it and gone to the Holy Land, saying, 'I did not take the cross to kill Christians.' Command in Languedoc now gave him scope for his military ability and energy, proved his courage in adversity and his willingness to serve the church, and offered him opportunity to win power and wealth. No ordinary adventurer, Montfort was, nonetheless, as ambitious as any feudal lord to increase his possessions and prestige. For the time being he shared the overall direction of affairs with Arnold Aimery.[6]

## Conquest of Trencavel Lands: Attack on Toulouse

The shock of the fall of Béziers and Carcassonne brought other places to quick submission: Fanjeaux, Montréal, and Mirepoix were occupied without a fight; Limoux and Pamiers voluntarily yielded, as did Castres, Lombers, and Albi. Although Montfort's forces dwindled to a handful during the winter, so that many places that had rushed to surrender repudiated their act, fresh contingents in the campaigning seasons of the next two years allowed him to regain the initiative. Fortresses and towns which had rebelled were retaken. In 1210, by enormous effort, the crusaders succeeded in reducing the powerful strongholds of Minerve and Termes. Cabaret yielded in the following year, then Lavaur and Les Cassès were assaulted and taken. With most of the towns from Albi to Pamiers again submissive and the most redoubtable fortresses of the Trencavels in the crusaders' hands, the stage was set for drawing the count of Toulouse and his capital city into the war.

*Attack on Toulouse*

Raymond VI had been with the crusaders until the fall of Carcassonne. Then, having discussed arrangements for peace between himself and Simon of Montfort, he departed, believing that the worst danger had passed. Disillusionment came quickly with a peremptory order sent after him by the legates that any of his subjects whom they might name as suspect of heresy must appear before them for examination. When prompt compliance was not forthcoming Raymond VI was excommunicated and Toulouse was put under interdict. The count and his citizens appealed to the pope, the former going in person to Rome in January 1210. Innocent III received him fairly and heard his protests that although he had never been convicted of the worst charges against him he nevertheless had done penance and aided the crusaders, that he had done all possible in the circumstances of war to keep the promises made at St Gilles. The pope was a lawyer and priest who wished to see legality observed and justice done. He was also committed to ridding Languedoc of heretics through the efforts of a resolute military commander guided by legates who were equally stubborn in their hostility to the count of Toulouse. Thus, events took a tortuous course.

Innocent granted Raymond three months in which he could use formal canonical procedures to purge himself of the charge of complicity in Peter of Castelnau's murder. The count visited Emperor Otto and King Philip Augustus, finding scant comfort from either, before pursuing the matter of purgation. But Arnold Aimery and his colleagues were convinced, not without reason, that Raymond VI was shifty and unreliable. Their responses to him give reason to think them also guilty of duplicity. In councils, which were at the same time conferences on crusading strategy, at St Gilles (1210) and Narbonne and Montpellier (1211), assembled prelates and legates rejected Raymond's requests that he be allowed to clear himself. They responded that because he had failed to drive out heretics and mercenaries and had not recompensed churches for damages, as promised at St Gilles, he could have no hearing on graver matters. The council at Montpellier completely dashed any hopes Raymond had for a negotiated settlement. One report is that the count was handed an ultimatum: not only must all the old demands be met but he must dismantle his fortresses, allow crusaders free passage through his lands and himself depart for Palestine; his subjects were to be restricted to simple clothing and diet, and the nobles among them must keep away from the towns. It is not assured that these, in fact, were the terms presented, but Raymond did leave the conference abruptly, and his sentence of excommunication was reaffirmed.

During these events Philip Augustus, although concerned about the possibility of infringement on his claim to suzerainty by the acts of Simon of Montfort and the legates, remained aloof. Pedro II of Aragon was ambivalent in policy. Early in 1211, when he finally accepted Montfort's homage for the viscounties taken from the Trencavels, the king also attested his sympathy for Raymond VI by giving his sister in marriage to the count's son.

Meanwhile, the town of Toulouse had its troubles. Innocent III had agreed to lift the interdict, but in announcing this Arnold Aimery provoked a quarrel with the consuls by his demand for a substantial indemnity. Thereafter, Bishop Fulk, through his White Confraternity, led a campaign against usurers and heretics, to which opposition, chiefly among inhabitants of the bourg, brought on 'not a bad peace but a good war' between factions in the town. When Simon of Montfort attacked Lavaur, near Albi, in March 1211, Fulk, over Raymond's protests, sent contingents of the White Confraternity to aid. A final break between bishop and count came when the former, wishing to consecrate some priests and unable to do so because interdict lay on any place where the excommunicated Raymond was, asked him to leave Toulouse. In a fury the count ordered the bishop out instead. Fulk chose to depart rather than risk the martyrdom which would have ruined Raymond completely.

After the fall of Lavaur in May 1211 Montfort moved his army into the county of Toulouse, brushing aside an offer from Raymond VI to negotiate. A delegation of Toulousans visited the army to protest. The legates blandly replied to them that the enemy was the count; the citizens might save themselves by expelling him. The consuls staunchly reiterated their sworn loyalty to Raymond and returned to prepare for attack. Although strengthened by German crusaders, Simon was yet not strong enough to invest Toulouse completely and camped in front of its southeastern walls (17 July 1211), proposing to batter a way in.

Toulouse, however, was not Béziers or Carcassonne. Not only were the walls held, but the defenders harassed the besiegers' camp and raided their supply trains, an important tactic, for harvest had not yet begun and the crusaders could not live off the land. If Simon of Montfort had counted on the quarrel of confraternities weakening the defence, he was disappointed; there was no lack of unity. Raymond VI showed his unconcern by continuing the construction of the nave of the cathedral which he was financing. Two weeks after the siege began Montfort lifted it and marched away to raid in the county of Foix. Excommunication fell on Toulouse's citizens for their resistance, and from that moment on the town was wholly committed to the war against the invaders.

The Toulousan resistance stimulated a spurt of activity among the southerners, allowing Raymond VI to gather a sizeable army of mercenaries. Montfort, weak at the moment because of the departure of troops who had served their forty days, elected to take a defensive stand at Castelnaudary. It was not a strong position, but Raymond soon proved his inability in military command, and, after losing a skirmish due to his own inaction, gave up the siege. A few months later the balance swung again with northern reinforcements. Assiduous preaching of the crusade was now bringing warriors from the Rhineland, Frisia, Saxony, Westphalia, even the Balkans, as well as from France. Places lost during the counter-attack were regained, the area north and east of the county of Toulouse was subjugated, and by the summer of 1212 the Toulousan region was practically encircled. Simon of Montfort in December of that year proceeded to organize his conquests under statutes drawn up at a meeting of nobles, clergy, and commoners at Pamiers, establishing a feudal regime similar to that which prevailed in the Ile de France.

## The King of Aragon Intervenes

Between 1212 and 1215 the first stage of invasion grew to its crisis and climax. The crisis was precipitated by the intervention of Pedro II of Aragon. He had at first followed a middle course, acting as go-between at Béziers, negotiating with Simon of Montfort about homage, and arranging a marriage agreement for their children, while at the same time keeping up his ties with Raymond VI. The attack on Toulouse must have led him to believe that Montfort's ambition was unlimited, an impression the consuls sought to strengthen by a fervent letter to Pedro. When Raymond VI also appealed to him for aid the king took the

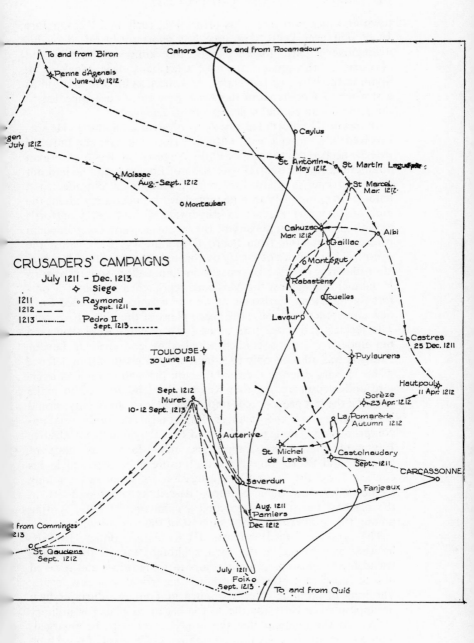

CRUSADERS' CAMPAIGNS

July 1211 – Dec. 1213
◇ Siege

| 1211 | ——— | ○ Raymond |
| 1212 | ——— | Sept. 1211 ———— |
| 1213 | ——·—— | Pedro II |
| | | Sept. 1213 ········· |

To and from Biron

✦ Penne d'Agenais
June-July 1212

gen
July 1212

○ Caylus

✦ St Antonin
May 1212

St Martin Lagu

○ Moissac
Aug.-Sept. 1212

✦ St Marcel
Mar. 1212

○ Montauban

Cahuzac
Mar. 1212

○ Gaillac

○ Albi

○ Montégut

✦ Rabastens

○ Touelles

Lavaur ○

○ Castres
25 Dec. 1211

TOULOUSE ◇
30 June 1211

✦ Puylaurens

Sept. 1212
Muret
10-12 Sept. 1213

Hautpouly
11 Apr. 1212

Sorèze
✦ 23 Apr. 1212

La Pomarède
Autumn 1212

○ Auterive

St. Michel
de Lanès

Castelnaudary
◇ Sept. 1211

CARCASSONNE ○

✦ Saverdun

○ Fanjeaux

Aug. 1211
Pamiers
Dec. 1212

from Comminges
213

○
St Gaudens
Sept. 1212

July 1211
Foix ○
Sept. 1213

To and from Quié

Cahors ○

To and from Rocamadour

town and its count under his protection, early in 1212. On July 16 of that year Pedro's prestige was enormously raised by his distinguished part, together with the kings of Castile and Navarre, in the great victory of Christians over Moslems in Spain in the battle of Las Navas de Tolosa. With a reputation as a saviour of Christendom the Aragonese ruler now appealed to the pope for an equitable settlement in Languedoc.

Innocent III confronted problems of great complexity. He was involved in a struggle with Otto of Brunswick over the imperial title, he needed the support of Philip Augustus no less for German affairs than for his quarrel with John of England, and he had not ceased to cherish plans for another Palestinian crusade. In a letter to the king of France he hinted at his uncertainty about the guilt of Raymond VI; he was fully aware of Simon of Montfort's ambitions and the animosity of the legates toward Languedocian princes. Complaints from Pedro II in January 1213 against the overreaching policies of the legates brought the pope to a decision. He ordered a halt to the crusade in Languedoc, sought to turn its momentum against the Moslems, reproached Simon of Montfort for attacking Christians as well as heretics, and called for a new conference to discuss the peace plans of the king of Aragon. The legates and extremists among the prelates were dismayed but undeterred. At a council which they convened at Lavaur Pedro II was allowed only to submit written proposals in defence of his vassals, offering their submission through himself as overlord and recommending that Raymond VI be allowed to make peace; if the last proved to be impossible at least the county should be guaranteed to the younger Raymond. The reply was uncompromising. The legates declared that they could not absolve Raymond, that Foix, Comminges, and Béarn were nests of heretics, and Pedro himself risked censure if he persisted in his course. They also sent off a delegation to Rome with a long memorandum on their position, describing Raymond VI in the blackest terms, and instigated a campaign of letter writing among the southern clergy in support of their position.

The pressure forced Innocent III to change policy. In June he went over to the legates' side, scolding Pedro II for abusing friendship by misrepresenting affairs in Languedoc, and ordered him to interfere no further, pending the arrival of a new legate. The king of Aragon, after a sojourn in Toulouse during which he appointed a vicar for the town, began to plan for military action. At the moment that the war was about to be enlarged, Simon of Montfort's position seemed weak. Renewal of preaching the crusade for the Holy Land had diverted reinforcements from Languedoc, and the plans of Prince Louis of France to join Montfort had been cancelled because of troubles looming in Flanders and the continuing tension with England.

## The Battle of Muret

In August 1213 Pedro II assembled his vassals to cross the Pyrenees while knights of Toulouse, Foix, and Comminges moved to join him at Muret, a small walled town twelve miles from Toulouse, an important point on the lines of communication to the south. At the news, Simon, who had been ravaging the area around Toulouse, also hastened toward Muret, while his urgent calls went out for reinforcements.

Muret stands at the junction of the Loude River with the Garonne. It was lightly held by one of Simon of Montfort's detachments and already under siege by Toulousan militia, whom Pedro II withdrew, allowing Montfort to enter, for his plan was to destroy the whole crusading force by one assault. The crusaders' chances seemed slim. In an ill-provisioned town eight or nine hundred mounted warriors, two-thirds of them sergeants, confronted at least twice their number commanded by a hero of the war in Spain. Simon of Montfort was well aware that defeat would jeopardize the gains of four years' hard fighting, yet he professed utter confidence; neither he nor the king paid much attention to the offers of the clergy to mediate. The crusaders were well led, while disagreements broke out among the besiegers when Raymond VI, with habitual caution, urged a delay to bring Simon out to attack a well-defended position and the Spaniards sneered at the plan.

The battle of Muret has been much discussed but the details are still in dispute. The Aragonese camp was north of Muret, probably not far from the Garonne; Raymond VI occupied an adjacent position; and the militia of Toulouse had camped nearer the town. On the morning of September 13 an exploratory attack by militia failed to penetrate the gates of the town. They had just fallen back when Simon of Montfort struck. He led his men through a gate on the river side, out of sight of the enemy, as the prayers of the clergy rose to howls in their ears. Debouched on the plain, two squadrons charged the knights of Foix screening the Aragonese position where battle lines were hastily being formed. The impetus carried them full into the main body. Some made for the king who had rashly taken his position in the second line. Pedro had changed armour with a vassal, but as the charge closed was roaring out his identity as a rallying cry. In a furious flurry the attackers struck Pedro down at the moment that Simon of Montfort at the head of a third division hit the flank. Gascon and Catalan troops had already begun to give way and now fled; the Aragonese were in disarray. It is said that five hundred of their knights fell with the king, while the crusaders' casualties amounted to only one knight and a few sergeants. The battle was over so quickly that Raymond VI never formed his troops to join it.

Meanwhile the Toulousan militia had begun another advance toward Muret and were unaware of the outcome of the cavalry charge until Montfort's knights turned and caught them in the open. Fifteen to twenty thousand, the sources say with obvious exaggeration, were ridden down as they fled or were drowned in the Garonne as they sought to scramble abroad the barges which had brought them to the scene. Raymond VI rode away without striking a blow.[7]

Although not one of the great decisive battles of history, Muret was a triumph of daring leadership which broke Aragon's power to intervene. With reinforcements in the spring of 1214 Simon of Montfort exploited the victory in a brisk campaign which reduced most points of resistance in northern parts of the county. Full possession, however, and the title which would legitimate the conquest were not yet his. A new papal legate, Peter of Benevento, received the submission of southern nobles and the important towns, which kept their gates closed to Montfort. Perhaps Innocent III was reluctant to upset normal feudal succession without the support of a general council of the church which he had already summoned for 1215; no doubt the political advantages to the papacy of keeping Languedoc from too close dependence on any one ruler also suggested themselves. Once more there were attempts to force the pope's hand. Robert of Curson, who was legate to France, visited Languedoc briefly with a party of crusaders in July 1214 and, apparently without consulting Innocent III, confirmed Simon of Montfort in possession of all the lands in upper Languedoc confiscated from heretics or their supporters. In January 1215 a council at Montpellier recommended that Montfort replace Raymond VI as 'prince and sole ruler'. The most that the pope would agree to was temporary custody of the conquests.

The victors in Languedoc were uncertain also of the attitude of Philip Augustus. The old king had shown little interest in aiding Montfort directly and had refused to let his son join the crusade in 1213. But the French victory at Bouvines (1214)

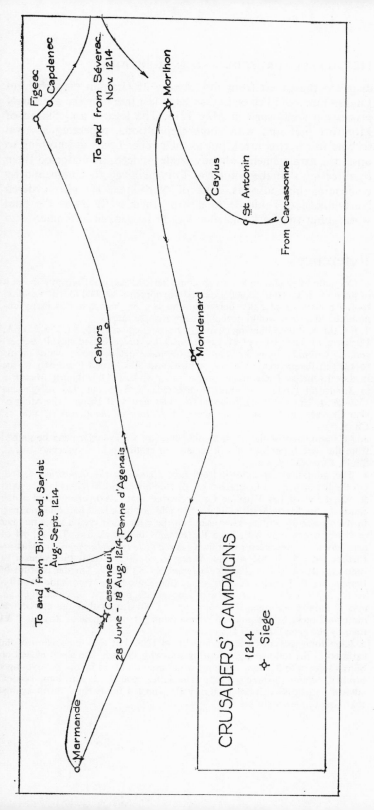

CRUSADERS' CAMPAIGNS
1214
✦ Siege

dispelled the threat from the alliance of German emperor and English king, and Prince Louis was at last free to make a leisurely procession southward in May 1215. The legates and Simon of Montfort met him with some trepidation, suspecting a royal scheme to assert control, but to their relief Louis did nothing to upset the arrangements already made; indeed, he endorsed them by directing that the county of Foix be given to Simon and by confirming him also as duke of Narbonne. He also ordered Narbonne and Toulouse to destroy their walls. Now the final word about title to Languedoc had to be spoken in Rome.

# References

1. Contemporary chroniclers, with characteristic exaggeration, put the size of the host at 20,000 to 50,000 mounted warriors and 200,000 to half a million foot. An estimate of 5,000 horsemen and two or three times as many unmounted 'pilgrims' would probably be nearer the mark.
2. For this and the following chapter, I have relied on *HGL*, VI, 275–751; A. Luchaire, *Innocent III*, Vol. II: *La Croisade des Albigeois* (3rd ed.); P. Belperron, *La Croisade contre les Albigeois*; the more detailed narrative of events to 1212 in Roquebert, *L'Epopée cathare*; and also turned frequently to the medieval sources. There are accounts in English in Z. Oldenbourg, *Massacre at Montségur* (vivid, but southern-oriented); J. Madaule, *The Albigensian Crusade*; J. Strayer, *The Albigensian Crusades*, and A. P. Evans, 'The Albigensian Crusade' in Setton *et al.* (eds.), *A History of the Crusades*, Vol. II, Ch. 8.
3. An impression of the physical difficulties of siege warfare can be gained from the superb photographs of remains of castles in M. Roquebert and C. Soula, *Citadelles du vertige*.
4. The quotation on p. 99 is from Lea, *History of the Inquisition*, I, 162. On the list of heretics in Béziers, see p. 76, above. In his *Hystoria albigensis* (I, 92), Peter of Les Vaux de Cernay wrote that 7,000 persons died in the church of Ste Marie-Madeleine, which could not have held half that number. In the nineteenth century excavations of the floor uncovered a large number of bones which may have been the remains of the victims. The report of massacre to produce terror is in the *Chanson de la croisade albigeoise* (Martin-Chabot [ed.], I, 56–8); Arnold Aimery's words are from the *Regesta* of Innocent III in Migne, *Patrologia latina*, CCXVI, 139: On the capture of Béziers, see P. Tamizey de Larroque, 'Une Épisode de la croisade des albigeois', *RQH*, I (1866), 168–91; also Appendix I, p. 197, n. 6. Vidal (*Episcopatus et pouvoir épiscopal à Béziers*, pp. 89–90) argues that the attack was motivated more by the political schemes and persuasiveness of Raymond VI than by the expectation of killing heretics.
5. King John recognized Simon's rights in 1206, but took possession of the earldom in the following year during war with France. The claim passed on Simon's death to his son, Amaury, who renounced it in favour of a younger brother, Simon (born *ca.* 1208). The latter gained the earldom, became advisor and brother-in-law to Henry III, and led the barons' revolt against that king in mid-century.

6. Detailed accounts of these and other episodes of the war to 1212 are in Roquebert, *L'Epopée cathare*. On the siege of Carcassonne, see J. Poux, *La Cité de Carcassonne*, II, 43–65. Peter of Les Vaux de Cernay (I, 128); *La Chanson de la croisade albigeoise* (I, 110), and William of Puylaurens (131) all attribute the death of the viscount to natural causes and the last two explicitly deny the charge of murder which, however, was still being voiced in 1215 (*Chanson*, II, 56). There are biographical sketches of Simon of Montfort in Yves Renouard, 'La Famille féodale la plus marquante de l'Occident au XIIIe siècle: les Montfort' in his *Études d'histoire médiévale*, II, 959–76; and Y. Dossat, 'Simon de Montfort', *CFan*, IV, 281–302; and a longer unpublished study by R. J. Kovarik, 'Simon de Montfort' (microfilm, St Louis University, 1962). A Varagnac, 'Croisade et marchandise', *Annales: économies, sociétés, civilisations*, I (1946), 209–18, speculates that the warrior leader was moved by the desire to control southern trade routes.

7. The terms supposedly offered to Raymond VI at Montpellier in 1211 are stated only in William of Tudela, *Chanson de la croisade albigeoise* (Martin-Chabot [ed.], I, 149–54, although Peter of Les Vaux de Cernay admits (I, 166–9) that the aim of the legate Thedisius was to prevent the count from obtaining absolution. On the siege of Lavaur, see Appendix II, and on the ambuscade at Montgey at that time, R. Toulouse-Lautrec, 'Siège de Lavaur', *Revue historique . . . du Tarn*, IV (1885), 344–8. Muret has received more attention than any other battle of the war. Belperron's account (*La Croisade des albigeois*, 290–304) is adequate but does not dispose of all questions about the numbers engaged and the tactics. Other significant works are listed in Evans, 'The Albigensian Crusade' in Setton *et al.*, *History of the Crusades*, II, 301, n. 34.

H

# The Albigensian Crusade

## counter-offensive and defeat, 1216–1229

A magnificent assembly including three patriarchs, more than four hundred bishops, and twice that many abbots and priors, attended by the representatives of emperors, kings, and princes, gathered in Rome on 11 November 1215 to open the ecumenical council for which Innocent III had long planned. The legislation incorporating papal ideas and policies which was already prepared for the council's ratification covered a wide range: restatement of a Christian creed, the extirpation of heresy, definitions in moral and dogmatic theology, changes in canon law and criminal procedure, education, religious orders and clerical reform. There were troublesome problems to be discussed such as the fate of the archbishop of Canterbury under King John, the choice of a German emperor, and a new crusade in the East. Albigensian affairs were debated in a series of small but not quiet meetings with the pope. The counts of Toulouse and Comminges were there in person and one source depicts Count Raymond Roger of Foix speaking vigorously in his own behalf. They found a few allies: an archdeacon of Lyon who was rash enough to defend Raymond VI as a good Christian and to sneer at Bishop Fulk of Toulouse[1] and, most unexpectedly, Arnold Aimery, now archbishop of Narbonne, who had quarrelled so bitterly with Simon of Montfort over the title of duke that he now swung to the other side. Simon himself had not come to Rome, but Bishop Fulk and other prelates pressed the arguments in his behalf and there is no doubt that they reflected the opinion of the great majority of participants in the council.

Any scruples in the pope's mind about dispossession of Count Raymond before his guilt had been formally proved or about annulling the rights of his heir, who was charged with no offence, had to give way before the reality of Simon of Montfort's victories and the attitude of most of the clergy toward the losers. In its last session, on 30 November, the council announced its decision which Innocent III confirmed two weeks later: Raymond VI was to lose his county because he had harboured heretics and routiers. He was guaranteed a small annual income, his wife's dower rights were to be respected, and his lands east of the Rhône were to be held in trust by the church for the younger Raymond. To Montfort went the title of count. The case of Raymond Roger of Foix was reserved for further inquiry. If the county of Comminges was also given to Montfort – the decision in its case is not clear – it was soon regained by Count Bernard IV.

Before approaching the king of France for formal recognition of his lordship, Simon of Montfort made sure of his grasp on his new possessions. He visited Narbonne where Archbishop Arnold Aimery who was rebuilding the walls sought to deny him entry but was brushed aside. From there he went on to Toulouse to demand and receive oaths of fidelity from the townsmen and to hasten their half-hearted demolition of walls and towers. As a precaution the Château Narbonnais, which housed the French garrison, was separated from the walls of the city by a new ditch and a gate was cut to allow entrance to the fortress on the side away from the town. Then Simon travelled to the French court at Melun. Whatever his opinion of his new vassal, Philip Augustus accepted his homage as count of Toulouse, duke of Narbonne, and viscount of Béziers and Carcassonne. Yet, even at this moment of success, Simon of Montfort surely realized his altered position. The king of France was occupied with plans for invading England, the crusade was now being preached for the Holy Land, and it was clear that the new count had to depend on his own resources. Proof of the difficulties came almost at once.[2]

### Rebellion

When Raymond VI left Rome his son remained behind for private talks with the pope, then joined his father at Marseille. The city welcomed them as heroes rather than outcasts. Their reception was even warmer at Avignon, whose citizens offered the town to their governance, while proffers of support came also from nobles in the marquisate of Provence. Raymond VI was encouraged at the prospect of renewing the struggle and departed to recruit

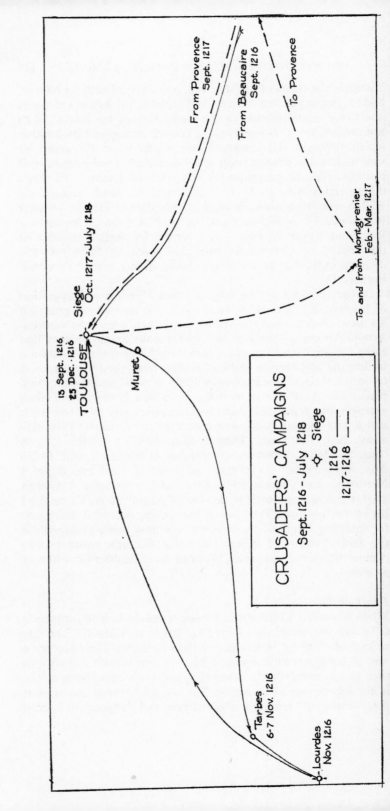

CRUSADERS' CAMPAIGNS
Sept. 1216 - July 1218
◇ Siege
———— 1216
– – – 1217-1218

From Provence
Sept. 1217

From Beaucaire
Sept. 1216

To Provence

Siege
Oct. 1217-July 1218

15 Sept. 1216
25 Dec. 1216
TOULOUSE

To and from Montgrenier
Feb. - Mar. 1217

Muret

Tarbes
6-7 Nov. 1216

Lourdes
Nov. 1216

soldiers in Spain, while his son rallied the eastern region. In June 1216 the town of Beaucaire, birthplace of the young count, invited him in, despite the presence of a French garrison. Avignon and Marseille sent militia. Young Raymond and the citizens promptly put the French troops in the castle of Beaucaire under siege, but very soon had also to defend the town walls against the brother and son of Simon of Montfort who himself was hurrying south to deal with the revolt.

A new phase of the war began with the fighting at Beaucaire, for all Languedoc took heart at Simon of Montfort's difficulties. The French garrison in the castle held out in starvation and suffering but the relatively small forces outside the town were unable to relieve them. On 24 August, Montfort had to negotiate a truce and safe conduct for the troops in the castle in order to march westward whence had come disquieting reports that Raymond VI had crossed the Pyrenees and was moving toward Toulouse. Raymond prudently avoided battle. However, a French detachment which entered Toulouse was captured by the towns-people and Montfort rode there, determined to break the resistance. Delegations of citizens who came to meet and parley with him were roughly treated, and when the count reached Toulouse he found the inhabitants arming against him. He promptly charged into the streets, despite hasty barricades of beams and barrels. Fires were set in several places but the citizens fought back stoutly, driving some of the attackers to shelter in the cathedral, the episcopal palace, or towers, and eventually forcing Montfort to withdraw to the Château. His threats to kill prisoners and the all-night mediation of Bishop Fulk persuaded the consuls to accept a truce in terms that gave Simon of Montfort the victory and raised suspicions among citizens that their bishop had betrayed them: Montfort kept as hostages the prisoners he already had and demanded more; an indemnity of thirty thousand marks was exacted; French soldiers roamed the city to pillage and to supervise destruction of towers of houses and other strong points. The harshness of the acts betrays Simon's estimate of the danger of his situation and his need of money to pay mercenaries who were now his chief reliance. It lost him any chance of peace with the town he governed.

From that uneasy base the new count did what he could during the winter to consolidate his position, arranging the marriage of his son to the heiress of the county of Bigorre and marching out to demolish a newly built castle in the county of Foix. But support for the younger Raymond was growing in the east, and Montfort spent the summer of 1217 campaigning in Provence with only moderate success. He was still there in September when a messenger reached him with news that Toulouse had again risen in revolt.

The consuls of Toulouse, furious at the heavy financial indemnity, loss of municipal independence, destruction of the walls, and indignities from the occupying troops, had been in touch with Raymond VI and now judged the time right for his return. The old count led an army of knights and mercenaries toward Toulouse, beat off one small outlying French detachment, and entered the town under cover of a fog on 13 September to an excited welcome. Some of the French garrison were caught and slaughtered in the streets, others got back to the Château; there also or to sanctuary in churches fled certain townsmen who had become too closely identified with the occupation. From Countess Alice, holding the Château Narbonnais for her husband, messengers rushed eastward to summon Simon of Montfort. Nearer at hand were his brother and uncles who marched from Carcassonne and attempted to storm through the southern gates of Toulouse. They were bloodily repulsed. So, too, was Simon of Montfort when he came up and repeated the attack.

*The Siege of Toulouse*
Both sides now mustered resources for a struggle all knew would be of the utmost importance. Toulouse could not expect anything but savage reprisals if the rising failed; for Simon of Montfort defeat would be disastrous; all the gains for the church would be thrown in doubt.

Innocent III, the instigator of the crusade which had now reached a crucial point, was dead. He had succumbed suddenly on 16 July 1216, aware that Beaucaire was in revolt but spared knowledge of the collapse of the Lateran settlement. Perhaps it would not have surprised that pope who had so keen an awareness of how plans could go awry. To a certain extent the weaknesses in the political arrangements for Languedoc were his responsibility. After the refusal of the king of France to take command of the crusade the pope had done what he could from a distance, sometimes hampered by the intemperate conduct of his legates, to subordinate his secular agents to the great plan of restoring the unity of the church, to prevent the crusade against heretics from being transformed into a land-grabbing expedition. His successors, who had to deal with the new situation, would soon show themselves unwilling or incapable of applying similar restraints.

The French could not encircle Toulouse with their limited force. Therefore they camped on the southern side in order to keep open the line of communications with Carcassonne, building 'a new Toulouse' of tents and shacks for the army and the sutlers, peddlers, money-changers, clergy, and camp followers. Countess Alice and Bishop Fulk were sent north to raise reinforcements. Pope Honorius III (1216–1227) did what he could by a shower of letters which ordered the preaching of a new Albigensian crusade, begged Philip Augustus to intervene, commanded the southern cities to aid Simon of Montfort, and warned the younger Raymond of the perils of his course.

Toulouse faced the battle in good heart. It was open to reinforcement and supply through its northern and western gates. An emotion very near to patriotism surged up throughout Languedoc. Mercenaries were hired. Dispossessed knights came in to join the defence. The walls that had been partly destroyed were hastily rebuilt. Outside them ran a moat which broadened into marshy ground near the Montoulieu gate where the hardest fighting would develop, and beyond the moat were wooden barricades and another ditch. The area between these outermost works and the walls comprised the lists (*lices*), an expanse cut by trenches and barriers designed to slow and channel an attack so that enfilade fire from archers and crossbowmen could be delivered from the ramparts into this 'killing ground'. Stone-throwing machines were emplaced on platforms behind the walls to harass the Château and to shower assault parties with stones hauled from the bank of the Garonne.

Together, count and consuls organized the defensive works and raised funds for the mercenaries and supplies. Property of citizens who had fled rather than join the revolt was confiscated; a forced levy was made on others who were slow to contribute voluntarily. Mercenaries and militia sent from other towns were quartered on church property, although we are told that all were sworn to do no harm to the clergy. Neither religious sentiments nor patriotism drew a clear line of loyalties. Members of the order of St John of Jerusalem in the city seem to have remained on good terms with Count Raymond, while a number of southern lords joined Simon of Montfort in anticipation of his eventual victory.

An advance by the crusaders that autumn through the suburb of St Cyprien toward the bridges was repulsed at the city's outposts on the west bank. Most of the fighting of the following months took place along the southern walls, where the Montoulieu gate was the main target. One attack at dawn broke through the outer works there but was checked by fire from the walls and hand-to-hand fighting at the gate. Of that battlefield the anonymous poet of the *Chanson de la croisade albigeois* wrote:

In the field of Montoulieu was planted a garden which every day sprouted and put forth shoots. It was sown with lilies, but the white and red which budded and flowered were of flesh and blood, of weapons and of the brains which were spilled there. Thence went spirits and souls, sinners and redeemed, to people hell and paradise anew.

Quarter was neither asked nor given. Prisoners expected no mercy. They were mutilated, blinded, dragged at the heels of horses, used for target practice, and their dismembered bodies were thrown back to their comrades. These atrocities are reported of the defenders. There is no reason to believe that the attackers were less ruthless.

Morale within the town, never severely diminished in the first months, grew higher with reinforcements in the spring, while the crusaders wearied of fighting without result, the legates ungratefully reproached the count for his lack of success, and even Simon of Montfort's confidence was shaken by a Toulousan sortie which almost penetrated his camp. More crusaders arrived in May 1218, however, to raise his hopes. With knights from Flanders he made another attempt through St Cyprien against the bridges that was checked only in savage fighting at the outposts on the river bank. He made camp in the suburb, with one of its hospitals as his base. Then a sudden flood of the Garonne struck the defence, washing away their works on the west bank, destroying part of the bridges, and leaving the garrisons in the bridge towers isolated. Simon attacked again. Brave work by an Aragonese squire carried a line from the city to the outer towers of the New Bridge and a sling was devised by which its supplies were replenished. The towers were battered with projectiles until one was taken, but the others held, and after some inconclusive skirmishing from boats on the river Montfort ceased to press the attack.

At the end of May and in early June both sides welcomed fresh troops. Montfort and his advisers, incessantly nagged by the legate, had already decided to construct a 'cat', a large movable tower, with which to shelter the warriors as they filled ditches and worked at the walls in preparation for another assault near the Montoulieu gate. While it was being built a party of crusaders marched around the town to the east, destroying vines and attacking the walls, but were beaten off at the outer barricades. A few days later, Simon's base in St Cyprien was harassed by attacks across the river from the city. The cat now seemed the only hope for Montfort's funds were running low, the Toulousans had cleared enough of St Cyprien to receive supplies from the countryside, and the arrival of young Count Raymond in Toulouse raised enthusiasm in Toulouse.

When the tower, shielded with fresh hides and provided with a second story for archers, was first levered toward its position, projectiles damaged it severely. It was ready again by 25 June, as were the barricades to protect the troops who would move it forward. Early that morning, however, a two-pronged attack was launched from the town against the machine and the camp. It seems to have been a complete surprise. Simon of Montfort was hearing Mass in the chapel of the Château Narbonnais. He ignored the sounds of combat and the messages that his men were in grave difficulties until the Host had been elevated, then led a counterattack which carried to the ditches in front of the walls. In the mêlée, with the cries of 'Toulouse!', 'Montfort!' from the warriors, the screams of the wounded, the blare of trumphets, and the crash of swords on armour, came the thuds of stones, falling so thickly, says the *Chanson*, that the ground shook with their impact. At the moat the Toulousans were able to bring their full defensive fire to bear. Darts, arrows, stones flew with a sound 'like the wind or the rain or a rapids in flood', and the French had to fall back to the barricades around the cat. An arbalest bolt wounded Guy of Montfort. Simon ran to his brother. And, in the words of the anonymous poet:

There was in the town a catapault constructed by a carpenter of Saint Sernin, which had been dragged from Saint Sernin to the platform. Dames and girls and married women were serving it. And the stone came straight to its mark. It struck the count on the steel of his helm, so mighty a blow that it crushed his eyes and his brain, his teeth, his brow, and his jaws. And the count fell to the ground, dead, bloodied, and pallid.

So sudden was the death of Simon of Montfort, so shocking to one side and exhilarating to the other, that the combat paused. The French abandoned St Cyprien in dismay, leaving the camp there as booty for the enemy. Wild excitement seized the town, candles were lighted in thanksgiving at every altar, bells rang, trumpets blew. A party dashed out from the town to burn the cat, but there was little thought of other fighting that day.

Simon of Montfort's son, Amaury, was at once acclaimed by legates and barons as his father's successor. The energy of the besieging force, however, fell sharply. One more assault was attempted on 1 July, when wagons loaded with straw and vines were set afire and pushed toward the wooden barricades, bringing on an inconclusive fight. Then, after three weeks of inaction, the army burned its camp and departed. Amaury took his father's body to Carcassonne for funeral services. Toulouse set about repairing damage and strengthening its fortifications, while Count Bernard of Comminges cleared a French expedition out of his county, the younger Raymond took the lead in recovering upper Languedoc, and Amaury of Montfort did what he could to hold his father's conquest.[3]

*The Second Siege of Toulouse*
Amaury of Montfort had neither his father's military reputation to attract warriors nor the funds to hire them. Although Pope Honorius III accepted Amaury's succession and ordered a new crusade to be preached, he saw the need of greater force. His policy, thus, had to be to obtain the intervention of Philip Augustus whom the two Raymonds were also seeking to win to their side. The old king had no more enthusiasm for the war in the south than before, yet the promise of financial contributions from the church and the threat that one of his potentially rebellious barons, Thibald of Champagne, might have the prestige of leading a new crusade were considerations not to be dismissed. Therefore, in May 1219, after a year of preparation, Prince Louis was allowed to make his second expedition to Languedoc.

The younger Raymond of Toulouse, now the actual commander in the field, had recovered much of the northern and eastern parts of the county. Amaury of Montfort, at the same time, was determined to keep a hold on Albi and Moissac, and in 1219 was attempting to drive the count's garrison out of Marmande. There he was joined in May by Prince Louis and a host, including bishops and barons gathered by royal command and some genuine crusaders. The fate of Languedoc seemed to hang on the acts of this royal army, for the war had changed now from a crusade against the protectors of heretics to an attempt at territorial conquest by the French crown.

The dispiriting effect on the southerners of the royal intervention was alleviated by a minor victory of knights from Foix, Comminges, and Toulouse over a party of French knights near Baziège, in which the younger Raymond distinguished himself. Even the fate of Marmande did not have the demoralizing effect of Béziers a decade earlier. The outer works of the town were quickly taken, at which the garrison capitulated. Despite the proposal of the bishop of Saintes to execute all prisoners, the nobles were spared for exchange. Not so the townspeople. Amaury's troops massacred them to the reported number of five thousand. Prince Louis is said to have been displeased, but he did not halt the slaughter.

From Marmande the royal army marched to Toulouse which it was able to encircle completely. The defence, however, had the benefit of new works, notably barbicans or redoubts protecting each of its seventeen gates, in addition to a mobile reserve which could move quickly to any danger point. There was no lack of fighting men; the consuls had promised food and quarters for all who rallied to Toulouse; the relics of St Exupéry, their traditional protector, were exhibited at St Sernin to hearten the people. We have few details of the ensuing siege, for the history of Peter of Les Vaux de Cernay stops with Montfort's death, and the verses of the *Chanson* with the preparations for defence. The investment began on 16 June 1219. On 1 August, Louis abruptly broke camp, abandoned his siege machines, and went home. The reason officially given was that, his forty days having been completed, he could spare no more time for the war. Rumour supplied other explanations: discovery of plots between some of Louis's followers and the count of Toulouse, or the prince's decision to wait until Amaury of Montfort should be forced by defeat to relinquish his claims to the crown, when royal power could be used for its own benefit entirely.

Toulouse had endured and won by the tenacity of its citizens, the stubbornness of its consuls, loyalty to the count, readiness to pour blood and resources into the fight, and its example which rallied southern warriors in patriotic support of their land. The older generation of leaders was now passing; among the new, Raymond VII stood in the foreground. His father died in August 1222, the doughty old warrior counts of Foix and Comminges in 1223 and 1225 respectively. Philip Augustus died in 1223 also, and Archbishop Arnold Aimery in 1225. The young Jaime of Aragon showed no desire to pursue his father's plans for expansion in Languedoc, Amaury of Montfort was weak, and whatever plans Louis VIII of France might contemplate had to wait on coronation and a firm grasp of power.

*The Royal Conquest*

With Toulouse as his base, Raymond VII moved to virtual mastery of his county by 1225 and threatened to possess the viscounties of Béziers and Albi as well. Many of the French who had acquired lands in the time of the elder Montfort now abandoned them; others hung on, living sometimes by banditry and extortion. William of Puylaurens, a chronicler favourably disposed to the crusaders, denounced their behaviour of earlier years as shameless concubinage, rape, and other excesses. In a desperate situation it would hardly improve. Amaury of Montfort had garrisons in several castles and towns and made his headquarters in Carcassonne with a score of his father's old companions and some hired knights. When the latter's pay fell into arrears they used strong measures, virtually a kidnapping, to extort their wages. Amaury tried in vain to pawn his northern inheritance; his offer to cede his claims in Languedoc to the crown was unheeded; appeals from Honorius III to the king and French prelates on Amaury's behalf were not answered.

In 1223, therefore, Amaury arranged a truce with Raymond VII and a personal meeting, which seems to have gone along with much amiability and led to discussion of a marriage alliance between Amaury's sister and Raymond. The prospect of a larger peace settlement was bruited, but Philip Augustus died on the eve of the council which was to discuss it. Troops of Toulouse and Foix thereupon advanced on Carcassonne. Many of the French knightly garrison fled the city and Amaury had no choice but to ask for another truce in January 1224. It was agreed that for two months, during which he would discuss the question of the war with 'friends' in the North, his garrisons outside Carcassonne would be spared attack, no reprisals on his supporters would be made, and church property would be unmolested. As soon as he departed the counts of Toulouse and Foix recalled young Raymond Trencavel to Carcassonne and installed him as 'by grace of God viscount of Béziers, Carcassonne, Razès, and Albi'. After fifteen years of war, Languedoc was nearly restored to the rule of its own princes – but neither the pope in Rome nor Louis VIII in Paris had accepted the fact.

For two years diplomacy and discussion took precedence over military operations. Honorius III pressed Louis VIII to a more active role, for which the king demanded a high price: all the safeguards and rewards usually offered to crusaders, a truce with England, sixty thousand pounds a year from church funds for a decade, his own candidate to be made legate, and papal confirmation of the cession to the crown of Simon of Montfort's inheritance. The pope refused, and in irritation Louis washed his hands of the project. A conference in Montpellier heard Raymond VII repeat the promises his father had made at St Gilles in 1209 and the count sent envoys to press his case with Honorius III, to no avail, for Guy of Montfort went to Rome also, as did a delegation from Louis VIII, while the clergy of Languedoc made clear to the pope their apprehensions about a revival of heresy and the threats to their own security if Raymond were successful in his suit.

Again the party opposing compromise won. A new legate of ability and unwavering purpose was delegated to France. He was Romanus, of the prominent Frangipani family, cardinal-deacon of St Angelo. His consultations with Louis VIII were accompanied by a series of church councils, notably one convened at Bourges on 30 November 1225, which ratified the decision of the legate and king to renew the war. Raymond VII had come there and was allowed to make an offer to submit. Not until he had departed was the answer given; it was renewed excommunication for him, the count of Foix, and Raymond Trencavel.

Under the eye of Cardinal Romanus preparations now began for the royal enterprise. Papal influence on the crusade was virtually renounced and Louis VIII was able to plan his expedition as a march of conquest. Financial aid from the church, with the other concessions which had been refused two years earlier, was now forthcoming. Aimery of Montfort ceded his rights to the king and was recompensed with the post of constable of France.[4] Royal officials laboured to enlist the barons so that the army which presently assembled at Lyon in June 1226 was at least twice the size of that of 1209. Dismay at the prospect of renewed war against such might caused men to hasten from all over Languedoc to make their peace with the king. Raymond VII was a more able and attractive leader than his father had been, but who could resist the king of France?

Nevertheless, a check to the royal army occurred at Avignon. The town had negotiated for an end of the excommunication it had endured for twelve years in return for submission to the king and safe passage for his troops through the city. Some mis-understanding occurred, the town closed its gates, and the king vowed that the citizens must yield, even though Avignon belonged nominally to the German emperor. The fortifications were strong, and for some weeks the siege, which began on 10 June, seemed apt to be another affair like that of Toulouse. Both sides suffered: Avignon from a shortage of provisions; the besiegers from disease, quarrels among the barons who had little taste for the king's ambitions, and harassment of their outlying detachments by the count of Toulouse. It was Avignon's will that broke. Surrender was negotiated on 9 September, with hostages given and the citizens' agreement to destroy their fortifications, pay an indemnity, and acquiesce in the occupation of neighbouring Beaucaire by the crown. There followed the usual slaughter of captured mercenaries.

Louis VIII was now free to move directly against Raymond VII and Toulouse. More and more of the nobility of Provence and Languedoc had sought peace with him during the siege. Even Roger Bernard, count of Foix, and Bernard V of Comminges had made their offers, although the former was refused at the instigation of the legate Romanus. Toulouse waited, while the king passed through Béziers, Carcassonne, and Pamiers, whose citizens vied in protestations of loyalty, then turned north to Castelnaudary and Puylaurens. But instead of moving to attack Toulouse, he continued on to Albi and from there in October led his army toward home. Its ranks were depleted from disease that had beset it at Avignon and the season was too far advanced to begin a siege. Perhaps the king was already aware of his own illness. He died on 8 November at Montpensier, leaving the throne to an adolescent son under the regency of his mother.

What relief the death of Louis VIII brought to the count of Toulouse and his city was short-lived. The king had installed seneschals and *baillis* in all the places he passed through and had reorganized the possessions ceded to him by Amaury of Montfort. His cousin, Humbert of Beaujeu, was governor of the newly acquired domain, with 500 knights at his command and behind them not the sporadic assistance of crusaders but the prestige and power of the French crown. All the troubles which Queen Blanche as regent experienced with truculent barons and bishops who wished to discontinue the crusading tithe could not diminish the odds against Raymond VII. Desultory fighting during 1227 gave neither side much advantage, although Guy of Montfort was killed. Atrocities were now too commonplace to remark. Early in 1228, Humbert of Beaujeu began methodically to ravage the fields around Toulouse. Protected by squads of bowmen, his soldiers destroyed the crops, uprooted vines, burned houses, and overran poorly defended strongpoints, while armed knights in reserve deterred their enemy from venturing out to oppose them.

*The Peace of Paris*
The policy of a scorched earth was more terrifying than armed

clashes. Raymond VII, almost at the end of his financial resources, heavily in debt to his richer subjects, his eastern lands in pawn to their towns, heard hints of negotiation and, late in 1228, discussed through mediators the terms of peace which might be arranged. As the first proposals were being revised, accepted by a council at Meaux in January 1229, and approved by the crown, the atmosphere changed from that of a conference among princes to that of surrender of a defeated foe, for Cardinal Romanus spoke not only as papal legate but as the constant adviser of the queen mother. On Holy Thursday, 12 April 1229, the count of Toulouse joined King Louis IX – Raymond was thirty-one, Louis in two weeks would be fifteen – the papal legates to France and England, and numerous other prelates and nobles in the square in front of the cathedral of Notre Dame of Paris, and there the treaty of Meaux was ratified. Raymond swore submission to the king and church and was led to the altar to be relieved of excommunication. He and a delegation of citizens from Toulouse were required to surrender themselves as prisoners in the Louvre until the first stages of disarmament set forth in the treaty were accomplished.

In twenty-one articles, the Peace of Paris dealt with three major consequences of the war:

(1) *The royal victory*: Raymond forfeited approximately two-thirds of the lands once held by his father in order to retain the remainder during his lifetime. As vassal of the king he was allowed to keep substantially all of the diocese of Toulouse, the Albigeois north of the Tarn, the Rouergue, Quercy (except Cahors), and the Agenais – the areas were defined by their ecclesiastical boundaries. The marquisate of Provence, east of the Rhône, was surrendered to the church.[5] A vital qualification was added. Raymond's nine-year-old daughter, Jeanne, was given into the king's custody, to be married to one of his brothers. (The choice fell on Alphonse of Poitiers and the marriage took place in 1236 or 1237.) At Raymond's death Jeanne and her husband would inherit the town and diocese of Toulouse; if they were childless the lands would pass to the crown. Since southern and eastern portions of Languedoc were already in royal hands the Capetians were assured of eventually bringing the whole into the royal domain.

As security the king was to hold the Château Narbonnais for ten years and Raymond VII was to pay 6,000 marks toward the cost of occupation. Thirty castles or walled towns were to lose their fortifications and nine more were to be garrisoned by the king at the count's expense. No new castles were to be built.

The town of Toulouse would receive an amnesty when it accepted the treaty; its walls were to be dismantled and the ditches filled. On the other hand, throughout Languedoc generally grants made by Simon of Montfort or Louis VIII were annulled, and exiles could regain their property under amnesty, provided that they were not heretics. Raymond VII would take the cross for the Holy Land and serve there for five years.

(2) *The victory of the church*: In addition to acquiring Provence and receiving Raymond's oath to obey its will, the church had assurance of further support from the count. He would expel routiers, dismiss Jews from his employ, and confiscate the property of any subject who remained under excommunication for a year. As a general indemnity he was to pay 10,000 marks, in addition to sums totalling another 4,100 marks to specified churches and abbeys. Also 4,000 marks would be given over ten years for the salaries of professors of theology, law, and the arts in a university to be established at Toulouse.

(3) *The attack on heresy*: Raymond VII promised his aid and that of his officials in tracking down heretics. (The clause relative to confiscations from excommunicated persons mentioned above was aimed at them.) All his subjects would be required to take an oath to aid in this pursuit, which the count would encourage by paying a bounty of two marks for each heretic seized in the next two years; after that the reward would be one mark. These arrangements were paralleled by a royal ordinance of Louis IX which promised the same bounty in royal territories.[6]

The terms were harsh, but they did not, in fact, clearly resolve any of the major issues. While many lords who favoured heresy had been dispossessed, other rebels against the king were restored, and the verdict of the Lateran Council against the count of Toulouse was partly reversed. Raymond VII was young and no more ready to accept his losses than were the exiles from the Trencavel lands now in the king's hands. The character of the episcopate had been improved, but the hope of recalling dissenters by evangelization had been one of the casualties of the war. Nor had techniques for consistent and effective legal prosecution of heresy yet been devised. Adjustment to peace in Languedoc was thus to be hindered by a continuation of the conflict in other forms; smoldering resentment against changes in the political structure left tensions which were heightened when the new tribunal of

Inquisition was created to pursue heresy. In 1229 the crown and church seemed to have the victory. Over the next two decades, however, their success was thrown in doubt.

# References

1. The outspoken archdeacon was excommunicated and deprived of his post in 1218 for having defended heretics.

2. A. Luchaire, *Innocent III*, Vol. VI: *Le concile de Latran et la réforme de l'église*, describes the work of the council. E. Boutaric, 'La Guerre des Albigeois et Alphonse de Poitiers', *RQH*, II (1867), 155–80, offers comments on the political astuteness of Philip Augustus.

3. The battle for Toulouse has been studied in detail in J. de Malafosse, 'Le Siège de Toulouse par Simon de Montfort', *Revue des Pyrénées*, IV (1892), 497–522, 725–56. Some of the hardships of its inhabitants are illustrated in E. Martin-Chabot, 'Mésaventures d'un Toulousain "donat" de Saint-Sernin', *Mélanges . . . dediés à la memoire de Louis Halphen*, 501–5. The quotations from the *Chanson* on pp. 120 and 121 are from the edition by Martin-Chabot, III, 87, 205, 207–9, respectively.

4. Amaury of Montfort took no further part in Languedocian affairs. He went on crusade in 1240, was captured at Gaza but released, and died in Rome in 1241.

5. There was an invasion of feudal rights in these clauses, since the Agenais had previously been held by Raymond from the king of England and Provence from the emperor. Provence was returned to Raymond in 1234, and in 1259 Louis IX recognized the English claim to the Agenais.

6. The royal crusade of 1226 is described in C. Petit-Dutaillis, *Étude sur la règne de Louis VIII (1187–1226)*, 297–328. Papal archivists brought together in one collection most of the documents on the peace negotiations. They are printed in Auvray, *Registres de Grégoire IX*, Vol. II, Nos 1265–92. The text of the final agreement is also in *HGL*, VIII, 883–94.

I

# VIII The First Decade of Peace

What damage the war had done to the economy of Languedoc was speedily repaired and the growth of population and commerce, so evident in the twelfth century, continued. The evidence is the establishment of new villages (*bastides*) by secular and ecclesiastical proprietors; increased production of textiles (a start was made on silk manufacture some years later); the appearance of southern merchants at the fairs of Champagne and more numerously in trade centres of the eastern Mediterranean. Building a breakwater in the Garonne at the Bazacle in Toulouse to channel the water to mills along the bank employed much capital and engineering skill. Amenities of life were restored. Of Toulouse, Professor John Mundy has written: 'It is obvious that ... its citizens were richer, more numerous, better serviced by charitable agencies, and better educated by mid-thirteenth century than they had been in 1200.'

There were readjustments, of course. Beaucaire replaced St Gilles as the site of the largest southern fair. Ecclesiastical proprietors prospered, sometimes at the expense of lay lords. The see of Toulouse, poverty-stricken at the beginning of the century, was now well endowed; the archbishop of Narbonne vigorously pressed claims to property in the southwest; with the ousting of the Trencavels, the bishop of Albi had become lord of that city and adjacent areas.

There was political restiveness, however, in areas that had come to the French crown. Royal officials in the seneschalsies of Beaucaire and Carcassonne – as in Provence during its temporary administration by the French – were not averse from lining their own pockets, even at the expense of the church, evoking so many complaints that Pope Gregory IX (1227–1241) begged Louis IX to restrain them. Humbler persons had few advocates and their protests at confiscation and extortion sometimes led to worse exactions. Greatly to the credit of Louis IX, he ordered investigation of the administration of his seneschals in 1247 and again in 1255 and some restitutions were made, but not before resentment had led to revolt in 1240.

Controversy also attended Count Raymond VII's attempts to recover property as he was authorized to do by the treaty of 1229. The bishops and abbots to whom Montfort had given confiscations not unnaturally resisted and the count more than once had to ask the support of his cousins, the king and queen-mother, in quarrels with the bishop of Cahors or the abbots of Gaillac and Montauban. With the prior of Le Mas d'Agenais he had a ten-year struggle over property rights. He also tightened his control in lands left to him by the treaty by buying rights to castles, acquiring a share in their control through *pariage* (shared jurisdiction and income) or converting allods into fiefs.

Raymond sought also to recover the marquisate of Provence which had been given to the church in 1229 and was administered by French officials. Neither Emperor Frederick from whom the marquisate depended nor Louis IX was content with that situation. Gregory IX resisted their recommendations for its return to Raymond until 1234, then relinquished it to the count, who renewed his vassalage to Frederick II. In the meantime, in the adjacent county of Provence, Marseille had rebelled against Count Raymond Berengar. Raymond VII's aid to the townsmen began a decade of intermittent war which would become an international issue in 1240.

Raymond VII's activities deepened the mistrust of him by prelates who, like Bishop Fulk, were old enemies of his father or who had come into office during the war and were suspicious of the count as representative of the old bad order. Gregory IX, however, was aware of the value of detaching the count from allegiance to Emperor Frederick II; perhaps he also toyed with the project of fostering in Toulouse a counterweight to Capetian power. Thus, papal policies combined sternness with moderation. Repeatedly, delay was allowed for Raymond's promised departure for the Holy Land or for payment of reparations to the church. One often-made request was never granted, and the body of Raymond VI, refused interment in consecrated ground, decayed in its unburied coffin.[1]

## The Prosecution of Heretics

Such were the conditions in which the task of extirpating heresy was undertaken. Massacre, hardships and exile had reduced the number of perfected heretics and hurt their organization but the survivors, no doubt, profited from the common hatred of invaders who persecuted them. After 1215 Cathars and Waldenses who had fled to Lombardy or Spain or retreated to mountain refuges began to return, and preaching was heard again in the old centres of disaffection. A Catharist council summoned by Bernard of La Mothe, heretical bishop of Toulouse, in 1225 created a new church of Razès and installed Benedict of Termes as its bishop. It was said that about a hundred Good Men attended, about one-sixth of the number that had gathered at a conference in 1206; thus, the new church may have been less a sign of vitality than recognition of the difficulties of the lessened numbers of Good Men in serving their believers.

Waldenses were also to be found, more numerous in the northern parts of Languedoc and in the valley of the Rhône than in the region around Toulouse, and always fewer than the Cathars. The conversion of Durand of Huesca in 1207 had, no doubt, reduced their number. Sometimes the Poor Catholics were mistaken for the unreconciled Poor of Lyon.

Persecution was sporadic. In Toulouse, Dominican friars preached and encouraged vigilante action against heretics and their devotees; in Narbonne, the archbishop commissioned a friar as inquisitor and rewarded a certain Master Ralph of Narbonne with an annual income of grain in 1233 for his work as 'persecutor of heretics'. For the moment the count of Toulouse found it expedient to join the pursuit and in 1232 he co-operated with the bishop of Toulouse to seize nearly a score of heretics and believers at Labécède, while some of his men also captured John Cambiare, elder son of the heretics of Toulouse, Vigoros of La Bacone, famous figure among heretics of Agen, and several others. All were burned. In 1233, the count also published his own statutes on the prosecution of heresy.

The persecution met with resistance. When, in 1230, the bishop of Toulouse tried to take possession of Verfeil, granted to him by the treaty of 1229, he was opposed by armed force. Bernard Oth of Niort, lord of Laurac, protected heretics and repulsed servants of the count and of the archbishop of Narbonne who wished to arrest them; when one of the Good Men who attended him in illness was captured by a French knight, the captor was ambushed and killed. Other members of the Niort family, who were quarrelling with the archbishop of Narbonne over property rights, raided that prelate's lands in 1232, even wounding the archbishop. He, in turn, investigated reports that the Niorts were sheltering heretics and induced Gregory IX to order an inquiry, which resulted several years later in their condemnation as believers of heretics.

The situation was dangerous for heretics but not intolerable. There was no reign of terror and heretics could count on protectors, even among *baillis* of the count of Toulouse, but the halcyon days of freedom were gone, and caution became their rule. They travelled under escort, often at night, from the shelter of one castle to another or from village to village. Some worked in the textile and leather crafts for livelihood and disguise. Passwords and signs were used to identify among strangers persons of their faith.[2]

When the Albigensian Crusade ended no well-informed person would have minimized the difficulties of eradicating heresy. Cathars and Waldenses were too selflessly devoted, too confident of the righteousness of their mission to be dissuaded by personal danger. Pope Gregory IX was well aware of conditions in Languedoc. Nor was it the only area in which heresy seemed to be increasing. Hence, in 1230, when there was a temporary lull in papal-imperial controversy and he was able to return to Rome after two years of exile, the pope took the steps which led to the creation of a special tribunal 'to make inquisition of heretical depravity'.[3]

## Precedents for the Inquisition

In the Middle Ages inquest or inquisition (*inquisitio*) was a method of inquiry to ascertain facts in all kinds of affairs. It also designated one of several procedures in civil and canon law for detecting and punishing violations. The others were 'accusation,' in which a charge was laid by an accuser at his own peril if it proved false, and 'denunciation,' in which an official with knowledge of the crime began the action. In an inquisition, one who was suspect could be summoned and interrogated under oath, his answers making him, in effect, his own accuser, while other testimony could also be taken against him. This was relatively more efficient than other procedures when the crime, as often was the case with heresy, was difficult to discover and prove unless suspicion alone was cause for action and the witness could be required to inculpate himself.

In 1184, as we have seen, Pope Lucius III, attempting to regularize hitherto inconsistent forms of prosecution, had authorized inquisition by bishops. Their actions over the next three decades, although not markedly successful, were encouraged by more legislation, notably bulls of Innocent III in 1199 and action by the Lateran Council in 1215. Supplementary procedures were later devised, such as the appointment in 1227 of 'synodal witnesses', persons who were charged with reporting incidents of heresy to the bishops. The council of Toulouse in 1229 also provided for teams of two laymen and a priest in each parish, who were to search houses, outbuildings, even caves, and to denounce to the bishop heretics they discovered.

At the conclusion of the council of Toulouse also occurred a legatine inquisition, an earlier form of which we have seen at work in Toulouse in 1178. Cardinal Romanus produced before the assembled clerics a converted Cathar, William of Solier, who was willing to talk freely about his former associates. Men of good repute also testified, then suspects were called to do the same. Some of the latter confessed, while others stood stubbornly silent. All the prelates at the council were pressed into service to conduct interrogations and record the depositions, on the basis of which the legate subsequently handed down his verdicts, many of them requiring the accused to go on crusade to the Holy Land, a penance which most of them seem to have avoided for nearly a decade, if not entirely. In this instance Romanus set an important precedent by refusing, for fear of reprisals against witnesses, to identify for the accused the names of those who had testified against them.

The actions of the legate and clergy in Languedoc did not give Gregory IX the assurance that the machinery of suppression was adequate to the task nor that its operation by the episcopate would be efficient. Moreover, reports continued to reach him of dangerous manifestations of dissent all over Europe. In Germany, the bishop of Bremen persuaded the pope to proclaim a crusade against the Stedingers, peasants in the region at the mouth of the Weser River, who were called heretics because of their stubborn refusal to pay tithes and because of their violent resistance to ecclesiastical overlordship and exploitation. Excited accounts came from Trier of the discovery of devil-worshipping 'Luciferans' and other sects. The imperial-papal controversy distorted the question of religious dissent in Italian cities where the Cathars were thought to profit by the discord. In Reims and La Charité heretics were again discovered. The pope saw the need not only to codify existing legislation in canon and civil law but to regularize the procedure by which it was applied.

*Legislation against Heresy before 1233*
Legislation on heresy had accumulated in papal decrees and the

action of church councils over two centuries, which were supplemented by acts of various rulers. To some extent it had been codified by the Fourth Lateran Council and more enactments came from councils during the Albigensian Crusade. What follows here is a summary of the legislation on heresy in canon and civil law at the time that the Inquisition began to take shape.

The need of assistance from the secular government in the extirpation of heresy was not only explicit in ancient tradition and in Roman law but had been emphasized by councils since early in the twelfth century. The co-operation already offered by the kings of England and Aragon and Emperor Frederick I was extended by imperial laws of Frederick II between 1220 and 1230, as well as by the ordinances of Louis VIII in 1226 and Louis IX in 1229. Town governments were induced to include laws against heresy in their statutes and Raymond VII of Toulouse added his own edicts in 1233. In general this legislation required secular officials to drive out heretics or seize them for trial in church courts, established penalties, and bound the civil government to execute the death sentence on the incorrigible.

Heretics of every sort and their protectors and followers were under anathema. Every faithful Christian was under obligation to reveal those known to him and to assist in their capture, but otherwise to avoid any association with them. Believers and sympathizers were classified according to the extent of their commitment. They too could fall under excommunication and, if they failed to purge themselves within a year, were treated as heretics.

When a suspect was apprehended, his examination was normally before an ecclesiastical court. One whose guilt was admitted or proved by witnesses, yet who refused to abandon his errors or one who had relapsed into heresy after once abjuring it was handed over to secular officials. The holocausts of the Albigensian crusade and the harsh penalties decreed by Emperor Frederick II show how readily orthodox officialdom now accepted that the 'fitting punishment' proposed by Lucius III in 1184 meant death by fire. By 1231 Gregory IX had fully agreed with that interpretation.

Persons who died in heresy were denied burial in consecrated ground; if their guilt was proved only after death, the bones must be disinterred and cast out of the cemetery or burned. Property of anyone convicted of heresy or of permitting heretics to dwell under his protection was to be confiscated; any house which heretics had frequented should be destroyed and the site made into a refuse pit. Children of heretics, even if themselves innocent, could not inherit, nor could they, to the second generation, hold any ecclesiastical benefice or church office unless they first demonstrated their fidelity by denouncing anyone they knew to be contaminated in faith. No heretic could act as advocate, notary, physician, be a witness, or hold public office.

The treatment of heretics or believers who recanted and asked for reconciliation to the church was regarded as penance. Imprisonment had been decreed, probably with clerics in mind, as early as 1157. The council of Toulouse in 1229 required life imprisonment for anyone who was converted in fear of death. However, heretics who gave proof of their repentance by freely confessing their former beliefs and revealing the names of other heretics or of their defenders and believers, might receive shorter prison terms or escape confinement altogether, on condition of residing in an area free from heresy. Acts of sympathy or favour for heretics were punishable by prison or by pilgrimages to sacred shrines in Europe or to the Holy Land. Another penalty for repentant believers, devised by Dominic or Bishop Fulk during the crusade and approved by the Council of Toulouse, was the wearing of cloth crosses sewn conspicuously on outer garments. Fines and flogging were sometimes decreed. Penance in some form was required even of those who had come into contact with heretics unknowingly.

It was not difficult to fall under suspicion. The council of Toulouse required from every person in Languedoc an oath, renewable every two years, to remain a good Catholic and to denounce heretics. Young men took it at fourteen, girls at twelve. Failure to do so or failure to confess and receive communion at least three times a year made one suspect. After 1229 possession of either the Old or New Testament in any language or of breviaries, psalters, and books of hours in the vernacular was forbidden. Anyone defamed by public report or through evidence received in court was to be treated as suspect of heresy.

During the proceedings in an episcopal court certain disabilities hampered the defence. Legal or notarial assistance was difficult or impossible to obtain. Appeal from the sentence was forbidden, although on occasion a plea to the pope in the course of the hearing was permissible.[4]

In 1231 Gregory IX summed up the various provisions in the matter of heresy in his 'new statutes' which, together with secular legislation by the senator of Rome, he circulated to various prelates as encouragement to them to act. To legislate, however, was one thing; to apply the laws effectively another. Of three conditions needed for consistent prosecution of heresy, two existed by 1233: the body of laws just described and, in most areas of Europe, assurance of support by the state. The third need, officials endowed with special powers who could act with perseverance and skill, was then met by the appointment of friars of the mendicant orders to the task. In Languedoc they were the members of the Order of Preachers, founded by Dominic.

## The Order of Friars Preachers

When the crusade began Dominic had been left almost alone to continue the holy preaching with its double purpose of evangelization and attack on heresy. By then he had a solid tie with the region for in 1206, under the guidance of Bishop Diego and with the aid of Bishop Fulk, he had founded a hospice at Prouille to provide a shelter for daughters of the impoverished nobility and to draw them away from the Cathars. About a dozen nuns had been installed there in 1207, some of them perhaps converts from heresy.

During the early years of the war Dominic was sometimes with the army and was on friendly terms with Simon of Montfort, but for the most part he continued to preach in Toulouse, Carcassonne, and throughout lower Languedoc. He obtained a number of conversions and surely witnessed some executions of heretics, but he was not the first inquisitor, as his order later proclaimed. In 1215, came a decisive step when Dominic returned to Toulouse with Bishop Fulk. There his preaching drew others to join him. One of them, a prosperous citizen named Peter Seila, gave Dominic three houses near the Narbonne gate, of which the principal one still stands. At about the same time Bishop Fulk gave a charter to the group, establishing them as preachers in the town.

Thus endowed with a home, officially commissioned to preach, and committed to the apostolic evangelism of its founder, the Dominican order was born. At the Lateran Council of 1215, Dominic and Bishop Fulk discussed with Innocent III plans to perpetuate the preaching. To circumvent the council's ban on new religious orders, Dominic was instructed to select an existing rule. The one chosen was that of Saint Augustine, with certain modifications to combine the austerity of the monastery with opportunity for study and preaching. Fulk provided the group in Toulouse with a grant of tithes and the chapel of St Romain for their preaching.

In the first months of 1217 Toulouse was hot with resentment against Montfort and uncomfortable for the friars, who numbered about twenty. Dominic decided on dispersal. The world-wide apostolate, which in his own lifetime would carry the friars to northern France, Spain, Germany, Denmark, Poland, Hungary, Sweden, and England, began when seven were sent to Paris, four to Spain, to preach and found new houses. A few native Toulousans, including Peter Seila, were left in Toulouse. Dominic himself was outside the town when it was under siege and travelled widely in the next four years. Nowhere did his followers increase more rapidly than in the university city of Bologna; there in 1220 and 1221 were held the first general chapters and there Dominic died on 6 August 1221.

After the founder's death the head of the 'Order of Friars Preachers' – the name was a happy choice of Honorius III in 1216 – was its elected Master, who governed in conjunction with annual general chapters. There were about twenty houses or convents in 1221, nearly a hundred by 1234, which were divided into provinces. Each province had its provincial prior and chapter; individual houses elected their own conventual priors. Communities of nuns, the earliest of which were at Prouille and St Sixtus at Rome, were also under guidance of the friars.

Dominic's indefatigable evangelism was at the heart of his programme for the order. Personal poverty was fundamental and, although the order could possess dwellings and places of worship, acquiring anything beyond the needs of conventual existence was forbidden. That provision before long was often circumvented. Friars were licensed to preach only after study and an examination by the general chapter. To that end each conventual prior could dispense his brothers from ordinary regulations and by 1224 there were 120 studying theology at Paris. With increase in numbers and pursuit of learning, the order moved away from the wandering evangelism of its founder, but equipped itself better to combat heresy.[5]

For that purpose the discipline and training of the friars and their obedience to the papacy made them apt instruments. Gregory IX began to call on individuals as early as 1227. In Toulouse in 1230 the Preachers began impromptu actions which demonstrated their readiness to take a hand in 'the business of the faith'.[6]

### Dominicans against Heretics in Toulouse

The friars who remained in Toulouse in 1217 apparently had

no unusual difficulties, even during the siege. Peter Seila, who, to judge from his later attitude, had developed a personal animosity toward Raymond VI and his son, went to found a convent in Limoges in 1219. Dominic came for a last visit in May 1219, just before the siege by Prince Louis.

New members came to the order during the war years, more after the peace of 1229, so that the premises at St Romain became crowded. Thanks to the generosity of certain citizens the friars were able to move to a new home at the end of 1230. The site lay partly in the city, partly in the bourg, athwart the old Saracen wall. Raymond of Le Fauga, bishop of Toulouse from 1232 to 1270, was a former provincial prior. Preaching again took the friars into the streets and the celebrated theologian Roland of Cremona, who had joined Dominic at Bologna in 1219, came to lecture in the newly established university.

It is not surprising that the friars interested themselves in heresy among the citizens of Toulouse nor that their actions aroused resentment. When a friar declared in a public sermon in 1231 that heretics were active in the town, the consuls protested to the prior that it was an insult. Roland of Cremona advised even more preaching and led a party of friars and clergy to exhume from a cemetery in the bourg the body of a man reported to have died in heresy. He did the same for the bones of a prominent Waldensian. Perhaps Roland's departure from Toulouse soon thereafter was hastened by the town's resentment and the consuls' protest at acts which seem to have been undertaken without any kind of judicial procedure.

Even before the Dominicans in Toulouse had begun to act on their own initiative Gregory IX had utilized their colleagues elsewhere for similar purposes. The prior of the convent in Florence was instructed to prosecute a prominent heretic in that city in 1227. In Germany a priest named Conrad of Marburg who had been commissioned to act against heretics in 1227, with the assistance of a Dominican friar and a layman who claimed special knowledge of heresy, in 1231 began prosecutions and condemnations which make fanatical too mild a word to apply to him and caused his murder in 1233. Dominican priors in Germany had also received instructions to pursue heretics in 1231. In France a Dominican friar, Robert le Petit, nicknamed 'the Bulgar' (le bougre) because he had once been a Cathar, who had been investigating heresy in its old centre at La Charité-sur-Loire, was given a papal commission early in 1233. His actions were no less arbitrary and brutal than those of Conrad of Marburg, but with a brief interruption in 1234–1235, he was allowed to continue for several years.[7]

## Establishment of the Inquisition in Toulouse

Although the events in Germany and France allow the statement that inquisitors with special power to act against heresy had already been commissioned by 1231,[8] it cannot be disputed that the creation of a permanent tribunal, staffed by Dominican friars who worked from a fixed base in conjunction with the episcopate and were endowed with generous authority, occurred first in Languedoc in 1233–1234. It was part of postwar history there. The procedures it developed were models for operations elsewhere, and it was in Languedoc that the institution survived the most serious crises of its early history.

The establishment of the Inquisition in Languedoc was specifically authorized by Gregory IX in bulls of 20 and 22 April 1233. On the first of these dates the pope wrote to the archbishops of Bourges, Bordeaux, Narbonne, and Auch that because it seemed desirable to assist bishops with their onerous duties he was sending Friars Preachers to aid them in combating heresy. The bishops were not supplanted; the friars would work in co-operation with them and bear the major responsibility. In the second letter instructions were given to the provincial priors of the order to select qualified persons for the task. Thus was confirmed the association between the order Dominic had founded to win back by preaching and example those who had strayed from the faith and the tribunal which, deservedly or not, was to acquire a reputation for stern and inflexible prosecution of religious dissenters.

To implement his plans Gregory IX appointed a new legate, John of Bernin, archbishop of Arles, who had a good reputation as administrator, diplomat and preacher. Inquisitors were to be established in the diocese of Valence, at Montpellier and at Toulouse. There is not much information about activities in the first two of these places in the early years but for Toulouse we have a lively, if sometimes carelessly written, account in the chronicle of William Pelhisson, and, for Albi, an anonymous tale of the first inquisitorial activities there.

When John of Bernin reached Toulouse in January 1234 the provincial prior of the Dominicans was ready with the names of those who were to be the judges. For the dioceses of Toulouse and Cahors they were Pons of Saint Gilles, prior of the Toulousan convent; Peter Seila, Dominic's old companion; and William

Arnold, a former legist from Montpellier. Arnold Catalan was named for the diocese of Albi, where William of Pelhisson joined him as associate.

The first inquisitors no doubt devised day-to-day procedures as circumstances required. The process began with a public sermon and call for confessions; by early 1235 the legate had authorized a 'period of grace' after this first announcement, during which voluntary confessions could win more lenient treatment than if the suspects waited to be summoned. Perhaps some evidence had already been gathered by episcopal officials and, no doubt, there were plenty of informants among the local clergy, although the fate of Hugh, a priest of Cahors, who seized three heretical women for his bishop and was harried out of his parish in retaliation, would be discouraging. It may be supposed that from the outset the testimony, confessions, and sentences would be entered in special registers, but we are not told by what hands, except that in April 1235 various canons and priests had to be pressed into service to deal with an unusually large number of voluntary confessions and not long thereafter William Pelhisson speaks of inquisitors compiling confessions in books. The tribunal soon developed its own staff of notaries.

Arnold Catalan began his work in Albi accompanied by William Pelhisson. Peter Seila and William Arnold were in Cahors and Moissac at the same time, and Pons of St Gilles in Toulouse. There is no certainty about the number of persons called before them. At Albi corpses were exhumed and burned despite tumultuous popular protest, two heretics were taken alive and handed to secular officials, a dozen other persons received penances of pilgrimage to the Holy Land. In Cahors and Moissac the first victims also were the defunct, while three men who fled prosecution were condemned *in absentia* and another suspect was ordered to Palestine for twenty years, a sentence subsequently reduced by Gregory IX. Many persons, says William Pelhisson, were questioned at Toulouse, but only two seem to have been burned as a result of the investigations of the friars. The inquisitors, however, intervened in a civil suit for slander, in which a citizen having the reputation of a good Catholic was fined by the consuls for calling another man a heretic. The friars encouraged the man who had been fined to appeal to the bishop's court and helped him to prove that his accusation was justified, to the great discomfiture of the consular faction. The bishop continued to have a hand in prosecutions: it was he who sentenced a man converted to heresy while in prison, condemned other heretics apprehended by the vicar, and sent to the fire an unfortunate old woman whom he trapped into confession on her deathbed. At about the same time in Narbonne another Dominican, Friar Ferrier, acting under orders of the archbishop, undertook prosecutions in the bourg of that town, causing an uprising of the citizens.

### Resistance to the Inquisition

However fragmentary the information on the first investigations and penalties there is no doubt of the hostile reaction to the Inquisition. Already there were conspiracies of witnesses to keep silent, either out of self-interest or in fear of retaliation from those whom they might incriminate; there were also agreements to give false evidence. A few persons dared to interrupt their hearings before Peter Seila and William Arnold by appeals to the pope, as did two widows of Cahors whom the inquisitors, allegedly without justification, coerced into entering a convent. One man spirited away the body of his condemned father before it could be burned. Bolder was the action of crowds which pummelled Arnold Catalan in Albi, thwarted an arrest in Narbonne, and temporarily prevented an execution in Toulouse. Nothing caused more public disgust and resentment than the sight of exhumed corpses dragged through the streets to the fire. Toulouse was full of complaints against the inquisitors by the end of the summer of 1234 and the agitations were egged on by a number of individuals who had so far successfully delayed the pilgrimages to which they had been sentenced by Cardinal Romanus in 1229.

Quite apart from the danger to persons tainted by heresy it was impossible for the Inquisition to act in any Languedocian town without trampling on cherished customs. Where a bishop had seigneurial rights he might be tempted to encourage prosecutions to increase his authority; even if he were innocent of that ambition the accusation would probably be made by his opponents. Confiscation, disinheritance, and destruction of houses invaded property rights painstakingly guarded in municipal law; the secrecy of inquisitorial investigations, withholding of witnesses' names, and denial of appeal contravened the privileges of citizens established in town charters.

It was on the score of illegal procedure that Raymond VII voiced a strong complaint to the pope in 1234. The friars, he charged, heard testimony in secret, welcomed wrongful accusations against men of good repute, allowed no advocates and no defence, accepted the accusations of personal enemies against the innocent and harassed anyone who dared to appeal. They acted, Raymond concluded, as though they were intent on driving the faithful into error. It was a harsh indictment, not dissimilar in tone to what the pope had already heard against Robert the Bulgar. Gregory IX's reply in November 1234 was to order Languedocian prelates to correct any abuses they discovered and to ask the legate to assure Raymond of the papal good will. The legate also listened to the count's contention that Peter Seila was motivated by enmity and at the end of 1234 or early in 1235 limited that friar's jurisdiction to Quercy. Some Toulousans seem to have interpreted these occurrences to mean that the Inquisition was suspended in their town.[9]

## Revolt in Narbonne

Violent popular reaction to the pursuit of heretics had already broken out in Narbonne in 1234. That town, founded by the Romans, was not only the seat of an archbishop but a major commercial centre. Its city and bourg, divided by the Aude, had each its own consulate, which had acquired important roles only two or three decades earlier. In their respective areas each consulate controlled police, levied taxes, maintained the walls and streets, and represented the inhabitants against the archbishop and viscount who shared overlordship of Narbonne. They had, however, no municipal courts, for in the city the rights of justice were divided between archbishop and viscount, in the bourg between the viscount and the abbey church of St Paul. Rivalries between these legal jurisdictions had given the citizens an opportunity to play archbishop, viscount, and abbot against each other and to acquire important benefits: the right of every citizen to be tried in a criminal case before a jury of 'honest men'; the privilege of selecting the court in which his case would be heard; and other customs such as freedom from both corporal and financial punishment for the same offence and exemption of heirs of criminals from penalty for their parents' crimes. Not one of these rights but was threatened by the Inquisition.

Archbishop Peter Amiel of Narbonne was an ambitious man. He quarrelled with his own cathedral chapter over property rights until the canons denounced him in terms reminiscent of Innocent III's attacks on Berengar, his predecessor, and accused him of senility as well. By a shrewd bargain struck with King Louis VIII in 1226 he was authorized to acquire all property confiscated for heresy in his domain and his rights as the viscount's overlord were safeguarded in case the viscount were prosecuted for heresy. Peter Amiel was also a most resolute enemy of the nobility of his see who were partisans of the heretics.

By his own authority the archbishop had appointed a Dominican, Friar Ferrier, as inquisitor for Narbonne about 1229 and assisted him to establish a convent of Preachers outside the walls of the bourg and to become its first prior. Narbonne had not been much defamed for heresy. Indeed, although there had been some anti-French riots in 1212, the citizens had been praised for their steadfastness in the faith when they supported Amaury of Montfort in his dark days and fought some skirmishes with neighbours who opposed the crusaders. Yet there were heretics in Narbonne. We know that in 1225 the consolamentum was offered to an invalid and refused by him because of some question of the proper faith of the ministrants. It would be most surprising if fugitives from persecution elsewhere had not drifted into the town after the peace of 1229 or if heretical teachers were not at work among the burghers, artisans, and labourers of a flourishing commercial centre. In 1229 Ferrier prosecuted three cases in the archbishop's court and in February 1234 occurred the first recorded confiscation for heresy in the bourg. Since there was rather more activity by the inquisitor in those years in the countryside these fragments of information justify the assumption that Ferrier had been busy but not that he had focused on the bourg. It was, however, an attempted arrest there that precipitated Narbonne's troubles.

In March 1234 Friar Ferrier, probably acting under the archbishop's mandate, although by this time he may have been commissioned by the papal legate, went into the bourg to arrest a suspect. As he did so guards were posted on the prisoner's house in anticipation of its confiscation. A crowd at once gathered and freed the captive and the next day, when the archbishop and viscount together tried to repeat the arrest, a mob thwarted them again. An interdict was at once issued against the bourg, whose consuls retaliated by seizing the property of the archbishop and of the abbot of St Paul. This was followed by some fighting when inhabitants of the bourg sought to invade the city.

A major factor in prolonging the strife was Archbishop Peter Amiel's dislike of a confraternity in the bourg known as the *Amistance*. It comprised a group of citizens – drapers, weavers, and other artisans, as well as merchants – presumably joined together to support the consuls in their defence of rights of the bourg. The archbishop, however, declared that the purpose of the *Amistance* was to defend heretics and, after the incident just described, he excommunicated its members and anyone who had any connection with them. When a peace was negotiated in October, stipulating observance of the statutes of the Council of Toulouse against heretics, release of prisoners by both sides, and compensation for damages, the accord soon broke down because the archbishop interpreted the terms to call for dissolution of the *Amistance* and to require from the consuls an oath of fealty to himself. Both were refused by the bourg.

Tension rose further in 1235, leading to more bloodshed. Ferrier tried to resume inquests in the bourg but was blocked by its consuls; when he denounced them for heresy a mob sacked the Dominican convent. The archbishop meanwhile had purchased the allegiance of the city by promising that there would be no inquisition there. Both sectors of Narbonne armed, and skirmishes took place.

The consuls of the bourg turned for assistance to prominent men such as Oliver of Termes and Gerald of Niort, well-known for their truculence toward church and crown, as well as to some of the country nobles in the vicinity. They also hoped to gain support from other towns of Languedoc by raising the issue of municipal liberties, as is shown by a letter they sent to the consuls of Nîmes. There was no heresy in the bourg of Narbonne, they declared, and they were ready to permit the prosecution of heretics, if it were done according to the rules of the council of Toulouse; the archbishop was actually seeking to destroy the consulate and was applying an unusually cruel interdict which he would lift only for a substantial payment of money. The Inquisition under Ferrier, they added, abused its powers, arrested the innocent, ignored legal safeguards for the accused, imprisoned persons and confiscated property without trial, and, in fact, was conducted with tactics which trapped the unwary rather than gave a fair hearing.[10]

The archbishop's side of the controversy, reported by him to King Louis IX in August 1236, was the outright accusation that all but a few persons in the bourg were heretics. They defended heretics, used violence against their prelate, and had seized his property. They had broken promises made in the earlier agreement and had ransacked the Dominican convent. By appealing to the count of Toulouse and the notorious brigands, Olivier of Termes and Gerald of Niort, the archbishop asserted, they were seeking to remove Narbonne from the jurisdiction of the king.

A truce was patched up through intermediaries in 1236, with

K

the agreement that the king's seneschal would make a final arbitration of the conflict. Meanwhile, at the consuls' invitation, Count Raymond VII had established a seneschal in the bourg. Armed clashes continued and a new truce had to be negotiated after which the seneschal issued his decision in 1237. Although preserved only in part, it indicates that he apportioned the blame quite evenly, for there was to be mutual restoration of property and only eleven persons from the bourg were punished. They got off rather lightly: nine, charged with murder, were to serve for a year with the crusade in Spain or in the Holy Land; two other men were exiled. Of heresy or the Inquisition the seneschal said nothing.

By this time Friar Ferrier had withdrawn from Narbonne to other regions where he acquired a considerable reputation for his pursuit of heretics. Apparently he did not act again in Narbonne, although there is a letter of his, dated October 1237, in which he says that he had been repeatedly invited by the consuls of the city to make inquisition there. He contented himself, however, with announcing a period of grace for any who would come to him to confess. There is scant evidence, in fact, of further prosecutions of heretics either in the bourg or the city before 1250. How small an issue heresy had really been in the conflict is shown not only by the failure to mention it in the truce and peace documents of 1236–1237 but also by what is known of the later careers of individuals who had participated in the rising of the bourg. None of them were prosecuted as heretics.[11]

*Expulsion of the Dominicans from Toulouse*
There had probably been a lull in the investigations in Toulouse during the winter of 1234–1235. William Pelhisson, on whom we depend for details, is seldom precise about the chronology of events, but it may be supposed that during those months occurred the institution of a period of grace to allow voluntary confessions, a few exhumations, and Count Raymond's personal protest to the friars. At any rate there was renewed activity when a spate of confessions came on Good Friday, 1235. No doubt the inquisitors followed up leads from these during the summer. The count's vicar and the abbot of St Sernin also captured seven heretics in a raid on a hiding place outside the town, but tried in vain to seize a citizen of the bourg. Thus, the town was already restive when William Arnold undertook the prosecutions which precipitated the first major crisis of the Toulousan Inquisition. Most of the citizens who had hitherto been investigated or

condemned by the inquisitors had been of the working or artisan classes. Cases had now been prepared, however, against more prominent individuals. At an uncertain date, probably mid-September, citations were suddenly issued for twelve citizens; eight whose names are preserved were of consular families and the aftermath makes it appear that the consular group in the town at once felt itself seriously threatened. The suspects, relying on the count's support, refused to appear and demanded that the processes be dropped or that Friar William Arnold leave the town. The friars urged the inquisitor to stand fast. He did so, and on 15 October the consuls intervened and forcibly expelled him.

The struggle of the town, or at least of the consuls, against the Inquisition was now joined. Further summons ordered by William Arnold from his exile in Carcassonne resulted in the consuls expelling the clergy who attempted to deliver them and declaring a boycott on the Order of Preachers. According to reports reaching Gregory IX this was accompanied by an invasion of the episcopal palace and the cloister of the canons of St Etienne, where property was stolen and the canons were beaten. The situation was serious enough to force Bishop Raymond, who was ill of a fever, to leave the town for want of provisions; the friars in the convent, however, endured it as a siege for some three weeks. Then William Arnold again demanded service of the summons, this time by the friars themselves. Convinced that they were going to martyrdom, four member of the convent, among whom was William Pelhisson, delivered the citations fearlessly, suffering no worse harm than a scuffle in one house. This took place on 3 or 4 November 1235.

The consuls, egged on by the open partisans of heretics, now decided that all the Dominicans must go. On 5 or 6 November, accompanied by a crowd, they invaded the convent. Forewarned, the friars had entrusted their valuables to friends and gathered in the cloister, answering the consuls' orders with passive resistance. One by one they were hauled outside, then firmly but without brutality herded through the streets and across the bridge to St Cyprien. Only one aged and seven sick friars were allowed to remain in the convent with a lay brother to attend them; even the invalids were expelled a few days later. The prior dispersed the exiles to various convents; among them were two members who had just then joined the order out of a wish to share its tribulations.

The reaction to the expulsion of the Dominicans was immediate. From Carcassonne William Arnold excommunicated the count

and the consuls. Some priests who published the sentence in
Toulouse were driven from the town in retaliation, and Franciscan
friars who did the same were jostled and struck. Meanwhile the
prior of Toulouse and Bishop Raymond hastened to inform
Gregory IX of the outrage.

The first response of the pope was to order Count Raymond
to see the friars restored to Toulouse. The count did not demur,
although later he protested against the excommunication of his
vicar and consuls on the grounds that they had reason to believe
the Inquisition had been suspended; moreover, he pointed out,
the convent had been brought back again 'not many days' after
the expulsion. The date given by William Pelhisson for that return
is 'the octave of the feast day of St Augustine', that is, 28 August
1236, ten months after the incident. It has been cogently argued
by Professor Yves Dossat, however, that William was inexact in
his recollection or in his statement of the date and that he meant
to refer to the feast day of the translation of St Augustine, which
is 28 February. This would mean an exile of four instead of ten
months. Whether the return was in February or, as is more likely,
August a sense of caution seems to have attended the renewal
of the Inquisition. Because of the reputation of the Franciscans
for mildness a member of that order, Stephen of St Thibéry,
was named as co-inquisitor with William Arnold. The friars also
began to travel out to various localities for their investigations
instead of summoning witnesses to some central point, and the
penance imposed by Peter Seila and two other inquisitors at
Castelsarrasin on 29 March 1236 on a seneschal of Raymond VII
was light, in view of his offences.

Then in April occurred a notable event, dismaying to heretics;
after twenty-two years as a Good Man Raymond Gros came
voluntarily to the friars in Toulouse to ask for reconciliation. His
revelations led to the summons of persons of every social class
whom had he named as guilty of heresy; others who were sure
that they would be incriminated made a virtue of coming voluntarily. Many were so eager to confess that they asked the ex-heretic
to supply details they might have forgotten. The harvest of names
of persons who had died in heresy was rich, and bodies were dug
up from cemeteries in city and bourg to be dragged to the flames,
while the town herald proclaimed their names with the cry
'Those who behave thus shall perish thus.' Even more numerous
were the living who were convicted in 1237 and early 1238.

The triumphant note on which William Pelhisson ended his
chronicle with a list of persons condemned as heretics does not

ring quite true. Very many of the persons implicated by Raymond Gros's confession were already dead or were condemned only after they had fled. In July 1237 the consuls were excommunicated for failing to seize certain condemned persons, without apparent results. In February 1238 more than a score of persons were sentenced to imprisonment but, because prison space was not available, could only be ordered to remain in the bishop's palace. And already events were occurring which would cause serious prosecutions to halt for many months.[12]

### The Inquisition is Suspended

In 1236 Emperor Frederick II had begun a campaign against north Italian cities which was an obvious threat to the papacy although not yet open war against it. One goal of Gregory IX's diplomacy was to detach allies from the emperor. Raymond VII was linked to Frederick II by long acquaintance and by homage for the marquisate of Provence. That tie might be weakened or cut, and one step toward the goal could be to accept the count's suggestion of discussing the Languedocian situation.

Raymond's envoys had informed the pope of the count's requests: the most important were for release from the excommunications that had fallen on him during disputes over property with ecclesiastics and because of the expulsion of the Dominicans from Toulouse, for permission to bury his father in consecrated ground, and for such dispensation from his crusading vow as would allow him the appearance of going voluntarily; as for the Inquisition, he asked that the friars, whom he believed to be motivated by personal animosity toward him, be withdrawn so that the pursuit of heresy would again be entrusted to the bishops. The pope's reply was conciliatory. He approved Raymond's postponement of a crusade, agreed to have the quarrels over property rights of churchmen investigated, promised that the excommunication of count and consuls would be lifted, and hinted at greater leniency toward persons charged with heresy. Gregory refused, however, to remove the friars from the Inquisition or to permit Christian burial for the body of Raymond VI.

The exchange between the count and the pope in 1237 helped pave the way for the subsequent slackening of inquisitorial activity in Toulouse. The pope's desire for further negotiations with Raymond VII led him, in May 1238, to suspend the Inquisition, pending the arrival of a new legate in Languedoc. But James, cardinal-bishop of Palestrina, who was designated, dared not leave Rome out of fear of his personal enemy, Frederick II. Little was accomplished by the bishop of Sora who came as his temporary replacement, beyond persuading Raymond to agree to favour the pope against the emperor, a promise the count probably had no intention of keeping at that time. Thus, the three-months suspension of the prosecution of heresy in Toulouse which Gregory IX had ordered stretched to nearly three years.

While the Inquisition was in abeyance at Toulouse it was not abandoned elsewhere. Between 1237 and 1239 Friar Ferrier sentenced to prison about a score of persons from the area between Carcassonne and Narbonne. In the Spanish territories of the count of Foix there were investigations in 1237 from which that count himself was not exempt, primarily because of his parentage and his feud with the bishop of Urghel.[13] However, changes in the situation were to afford opportunity for the tribunal to take up its duties again in the northern parts of the county of Toulouse in 1241 and political disaster for Raymond VII soon thereafter opened the way for its renewal of its unimpeded operations everywhere in Languedoc.

# References

1. On economic recovery, see Wolff, *Histoire du Languedoc*, 212–18; and for somewhat later developments the same author's *Commerces et marchands de Toulouse*, and E. Le Roy Ladurie, *Les Paysans de Languedoc*. Construction of the breakwater at Toulouse is described in a note to C. Higounet, 'Les Villes et l'urbanisme' in *Le Siècle de Saint Louis*, 38–41. For political conditions I have relied chiefly on *HGL*, VI, 649–808, and Dognon, *Les institutions politiques et administratives du pays de Languedoc*. R. Michel, *L'Administration royale dans le sénéchassée de Beaucaire*, supplements the study by A. Molinier on administration under Louis IX and Alphonse of Poitiers in *HGL*, VII, Part 1, 462–570. Records of the royal inquests are published in part in the same volume, Part 2; in full by L. Delisle, in *Recueil des historiens des Gaules et de la France*, Vol. XXIV. The affair of Marseilles is studied in L. de Santi, 'Relations du comte de Toulouse Raimond VII avec la ville de Marseille', *AM*, XI (1899), 200–7. Useful sources for Raymond VII's activities are the acts catalogued by A. Molinier, *HGL*, VIII, 1940–2008. The quotation on p. 130 is from Mundy, 'Charity and Social Work', *Traditio*, XXII (1966), 236.
2. For the situation in the years 1229 to 1233 see Y. Dossat, 'La Répression de l'hérésie', *CFan*, VI, 217–51; and W. L. Wakefield, 'The Family of Niort', *Names*, XVIII (1970), 107–14. Evidence about heretical activities is abundant in inquisitorial records in the Collection Doat of the Bibliothèque nationale Paris, Vols. XXII–XXIV, and in MS 609 of the Municipal library of Toulouse. See also Guiraud, *Histoire de l'Inquisition*, Vol. II, Ch. 3, but with caution. Y. Dossat summarizes what is known of Waldensian activities in 'Les Vaudois méridionaux d'après les documents de l'Inquisition', *CFan*, II, 207–26.

3. T. Walsh, *Characters of the Inquisition*, Ch. 2, summarizes Gregory's career; a longer account is by H. K. Mann, *Lives of the Popes in the Middle Ages*, XIII, 174–436.

4. For all the preceding paragraphs see the works listed on p. 95, n. 1, especially those of Foreville and Maisonneuve; also Thouzellier, 'La Répression de l'hérésie et les débuts de l'Inquisition' in Fliche and Martin, *Histoire de l'église*, Vol. X, Ch. 3, esp. 291–315.

5. I have relied heavily on Vicaire, *Saint Dominic and His Times*; G. R. Galbraith, *The Constitution of the Dominican Order, 1216 to 1360*; and on the essays in Vol. I of *Cahiers de Fanjeaux*. On Dominic's activities against heresy, see the exchange of views between C. Thouzellier and M. H. Vicaire in *AM*, LXXX (1968), 121–38.

6. Foundation of the Friars Minor by Francis of Assisi is not discussed here because they were little involved in the Inquisition in Languedoc in the period covered in this book. For the attitude of Francis himself, see K. Esser, 'Franziskus von Assisi und die Katharer seiner Zeit', *Archivum franciscanum historicum*, LI (1958), 225–64. Anthony of Padua acquired a great reputation but achieved little in a visit to the region around Toulouse in 1225; others preached against heresy in Burgundy. Franciscans also assisted Robert the Bulgar and Conrad of Marburg in northern France and Germany (see pp. 139–40), and members of the order who became bishops in Italy took their inquisitorial duties seriously. One Franciscan of Toulouse, Stephen of St Thibéry, was appointed inquisitor in 1235 and died at the hands of heretics (see pp. 169–71). In the second half of the thirteenth century, the Inquisition in lands east of the Rhône ruled by Charles of Anjou was entrusted to the Franciscans. A convenient history of the order is R. M. Huber, *A Documented History of the Franciscan Order*, Vol. I.

7. Actions of the friars in Toulouse are recounted in the chronicle of William Pelhisson, translated in Appendix III. The indispensable study is Y. Dossat, *Les Crises de l'Inquisition toulousaine (1233–1273)*. On Conrad of Marburg, see B. Kaltner, *Konrad von Marburg*; and L. Förg, *Die Ketzerverfolgung in Deutschland unter Gregor IX*. On Robert the Bulgar, see E. Chénon, 'L'Hérésie à la Charité sur Loire et les débuts de l'Inquisition monastique', *Nouvelle Revue historique de droit français et étranger*, XLI (1917), 299–345; and C. H. Haskins, 'Robert le Bougre and the Beginnings of the Inquisition' in *Studies in Mediaeval Culture*, 193–244.

8. For various views on the date when the tribunal was constituted see Dossat, *Les Crises de l'Inquisition toulousaine*, 111–18; Lea, *History of the Inquisition*, II, 326–36; Maisonneuve, *Études sur les Origines de l'Inquisition*, 243–66; Thouzellier, 'La Répression de l'hérésie' in Fliche and Martin, *Histoire de l'église*, X, 309–17.

9. For events in Toulouse see Appendix III; also Dossat, *Les Crises de l'Inquisition toulousaine*, 118–27. The contemporary setting up of tribunals in Montpellier and Provence is noted in Dossat, 'Les Débuts de l'Inquisition à Montpellier et en Provence', *BPH*, 1961, 561–79. On the case of the priest Hugh, see E. Albe, 'L'Hérésie albigeoise et l'Inquisition en Quercy', *Revue de l'histoire de l'église de France*, V (1910), 278–9. The legend of murder of three inquisitors at Cordes is disproved in C. Portal, *Histoire de la ville de Cordes*, 21–2.

10. Ferrier was accused of using loaded questions. It was alleged that he would ask a prisoner whether a woman conceived through the act of God or of man. If the answer were 'Man' it showed heresy by denying God's power;

to say that conception came through God made one a heretic for asserting that God had carnal relations with women. Again: 'Does the Host consecrated by a priest become the actual body of God?' 'Yes.' 'If four priests consecrate the host at the same time, is each wafer the body of God?' An affirmative answer was taken as proof of the heresy of believing in four gods.

11. All the foregoing is based on R. W. Emery, *Heresy and Inquisition in Narbonne*, Chs. 3–4.

12. For the events described in these paragraphs see Appendix III; also Dossat, *Les Crises de l'Inquisition toulousaine*, 130–7.

13. Dossat, *Les Crises de l'Inquisition toulousaine*, 139–45. Operations of Friar Ferrier are discussed in W. L. Wakefield, 'Friar Ferrier, Inquisition at Caunes, and Escapes from Prison at Carcassonne', *CHR*, LVIII (1972), 220–37.

# IX The Last Resistance

In 1240 and 1242 occurred two final acts of military defiance of the French power which had intruded into Languedoc. The first was an invasion led from Spain by the heir of the dispossessed Trencavel viscounts, which beat in vain against a stubborn defence at Carcassonne and was scattered by a royal relief force. The second was a poorly planned and badly managed little war against the French king, in which Raymond VII had a part and for which he was humbled. These events, with a postscript on the county of Toulouse after Raymond's death form the subject of this chapter. The political situation worked to the benefit of the Inquisition, for reprisals after 1240 badly hurt the rural nobility who had joined Trencavel, and it was among them that the heretics had found their staunchest protectors. Raymond VII himself adopted a policy of persecution after 1242. Thus, as will be seen in the following chapter, the inquisitors were able to resume their work, establishing the routines and procedures which would thereafter be generally accepted by tribunals elsewhere. They also became so devoted to their office and its powers as to be impatient with attempts, even by a pope, to restrain them. The result was that, just as the Inquisition reached maturity, a crisis occurred which, for a time, threatened to change its character and sever the connection of the Friars Preachers with the prosecution of heresy in Languedoc.

## The Revolt of Raymond Trencavel

Raymond Trencavel had been an infant when his father died in the hands of the crusaders in 1209 and his mother fled with her young son to Foix and then to Aragon. He must have regarded his disinheritance as unjustified conquest, for his father had neither been formally charged with heresy nor brought to trial before his overlords. When Raymond came of age he took service with Jaime I, 'the Conqueror' of Aragon, fighting well against the

Moslems in Majorca and Valencia. During the southern resurgence of 1224 he had been briefly restored as viscount in Carcassonne, only to be expelled by Louis VIII in 1226.

Trencavel had long had refugee nobles around him in Aragon; he could rely as well on the loyalty of former vassals in Languedoc who were existing sullenly under French rule. Why he decided on war in 1240 is not clear; perhaps he counted on the French being embroiled with Raymond VII and Frederick II in Provence.[1] In August of that year, at the head of a small group of knights and some Aragonese and Catalan mercenaries, Trencavel marched from Roussillon into southern Languedoc. His reception was enthusiastic: Alet, Limoux, and Montréal welcomed him joyously; when admitted to Montoulieu his troops showed their temper by pillaging its abbey; a general uprising of the petty nobility occurred; and by the time the expedition approached Carcassonne, early in September, it had some two hundred knights, many of them veterans of crusading days. French lords prudently retired to Carcassonne, whither also hastened the bishop of Toulouse, the archbishop of Narbonne, and other ecclesiastics. Raymond VII, returning from Provence about the time Trencavel was marching from the west, was summoned by the French seneschal in Carcassonne to give the aid required by his vassalage. The count, however, replied that he must first confer with his counsellors, proceeded to Toulouse, and held aloof from the subsequent fighting.

On 7 September the invaders reached Carcassonne. The gates of the bourg of Granoillant, at the foot of the bluff on which the city stood, were opened to them on the following night, and the ruthlessness of the rebels was demonstrated by the massacre of thirty-three priests who had been promised safe-conduct to leave. Soon afterwards the siege of the strongly garrisoned and well-provisioned city began in earnest. Miners tunnelled at the fortifications but were harassed by sorties and frustrated by countermining or new barricades thrown up inside the walls under which they dug. Assaults on every angle of the walls led to hard fighting without penetration of the defences until the approach of a relief force under the royal chamberlain, John of Beaumont, was signalled on 11 October. Thereupon the attackers withdrew, after destroying the Franciscan convent and another monastery and setting fire to houses. Most of the bourg's inhabitants fled with them. Trencavel and some hardened companions retired to Montréal, where they in turn came under siege by the royal army. At that point, the counts of Toulouse and Foix intervened as negotiators and obtained safe conduct for Raymond Trencavel and his companions to retire to Catalonia.

Reprisals on those who did not flee to exile were prompt and severe. John of Beaumont hanged some knights taken prisoner as he reduced rebel refuges; others died in the dungeons of Carcassonne. The destruction of the native lesser feudality in the region between Carcassonne and the Pyrenees by methodical reprisals after 1240 completed what had begun in the crusade. A few of the stronger families were able to bargain. The Niorts, for example, surrendered their mountain castles to the king and, although forbidden ever to live there again, were allowed a certain income. Apparently by the king's intercession the condemnation for heresy under which they had existed since 1236 was quietly ignored. Olivier of Termes, who had fought on the side of the bourg of Narbonne in 1235 and with Trencavel in 1240, also surrendered, only to rebel again with Raymond VII in 1242. When at last he capitulated in 1246 he took the cross and fought with distinction in the Egyptian crusade of Louis IX in 1248. He continued to serve the king faithfully and joined him at Tunis in 1270. After Louis died the fierce old warrior took a force of knights and crossbowmen to Palestine in 1273 where he died.

Raymond Trencavel also accepted his lot in 1246. After some haggling his submission was received with the agreement that the king award him a modest estate in the seneschalsy of Beaucaire. Something of a ceremony was then made of his procession through his father's one-time lands in April 1247 to renounce his claims publicly and to release the inhabitants from all ties to himself. He, too, joined the crusade of 1248 and afterwards managed to exchange his small holding for one nearer the ancestral home. By 1267 he was dead. His son, known only as Roger of Béziers, followed Louis IX on crusade in 1270.

The treatment of towns which had welcomed the invaders or driven out their French lords was severe. Montréal was ransacked by the seneschal's troops, Montoulieu was almost destroyed, the inhabitants of Limoux were required to pay fines and transfer their habitations from defensible heights to lower ground. At Carcassonne the seneschal completed the destruction of the bourg begun by the besiegers. Not until 1247 did the king allow the inhabitants to be recalled and permit them to construct a new suburb in a different location, and this was done only at considerable cost in fines and indemnities for damage to church property during the revolt.[2]

## Raymond VII Changes His Policy

We can only guess at the reasons why Raymond VII had held aloof from Trencavel's rash invasion. Perhaps he had not enough troops at hand to make a decisive impact in the fighting, perhaps he wished to see the direction of events before acting, probably he thought it a foolhardy venture, and almost certainly he was reluctant to jeopardize plans for a shift of policy which he was contemplating. His war against Count Raymond Berengar of Provence had just ended. Raymond had resumed it in 1239, with the approval of Frederick II, and in 1240 had such success that he seemed about to claim Beaucaire again, despite the usual excommunication which fell on him. Then French troops moved toward the area of the fighting in response to appeals from the count of Provence to his son-in-law, Louis IX. Raymond VII met and scattered them. This the king could not ignore, and he wrote to Frederick II to inquire if it was by the emperor's will that Raymond made war on him. Frederick had quite enough difficulties at that moment for Gregory IX had excommunicated him and Rome and the Lombard towns were yet unconquered; hence his reply was conciliatory. He proposed peace, with mutual restoration of conquests, to which Count Raymond and the king agreed. Raymond then moved to place himself in Avignon as podesta for the emperor but was forestalled by Frederick's vicar for the kingdom of Arles. It was from that scene that the count was returning, late in August 1240, as Trencavel was approaching Carcassonne.

A number of points had, no doubt, entered Raymond's reflections. Recent events had showed that little help could be expected from the emperor for any military venture against France, while the count's present alignment with Frederick II was proving a hindrance to re-establishment of good relations with the pope and to a solution of the problems created by the Inquisition. The good will of Gregory IX, moreover, was essential to a scheme Raymond was now considering. Its elements were these: by the peace of Paris, succession to the county of Toulouse was limited to Raymond's only child, Jeanne, and her husband or to their children or, if they had none, to the crown. Married since 1236 or 1237 Jeanne had as yet no child. If she failed to produce an heir and if Raymond himself could have a son the custom of male inheritance might override the treaty and preserve the county for his line. The count's wife, Sanchia had lived apart from him in Provence for years, yet another marriage was possible. The count of Provence, he on whom Raymond had recently been making war, after marrying one daughter to Louis IX and another to Henry III, had two more girls to provide for. If Raymond's divorce from Sanchia could be arranged, if a papal dispensation to allow him to marry a princess of Provence (who was his niece by marriage) could be obtained, and if he had a son, the count might keep Toulouse out of French hands. It was thus important to come to terms with Gregory IX in order to clear the obstacles to these matrimonial plans.

The failure of Trencavel's revolt and the arrival in Languedoc of the cardinal of Palestrina as papal legate gave Raymond VII the opportunity to abandon the imperial party. Since he had been widely suspected of encouraging the revolt of 1240 Louis IX demanded new assurances of the count's loyalty. En route to the king Raymond met the legate and on 1 March 1241 concluded an agreement by which he swore to support the pope against 'Frederick, so-called emperor'. Going on then to the French court he renewed his oath to Louis IX. The promises which he also made to oppose the king's enemies and to reduce the heretical fortress of Montségur had to be guaranteed by leaving in royal hands for two more years the castles that had been surrendered in 1229, as well as by a pledge to destroy strongholds built since that time. Then, having readily assented to Louis IX's suggestion that he make peace with the count of Provence, Raymond rode southward, intending to take ship for Rome, where Gregory IX was convening a council, in order to confirm with the pope the plans for his divorce and marriage. However, before embarking from Marseilles in company with the bishop of Toulouse, he heard that news that Frederick II had captured the Genoese ships carrying a great array of prelates to Rome, thus effectively cancelling the council.

Even without an opportunity to discuss matters with the pope Raymond VII proceeded with his plans. In a treaty of 1 April 1241 Jaime I of Aragon proved himself a willing accomplice by promising to use his influence at Rome in Raymond's favour and by recommending the match to the count of Provence. The latter saw no objection to marrying off another daughter. Since he and Jaime I were nephews of Sanchia, Raymond's countess,[2] they agreed to urge their aunt to agree to dissolution of her marriage. She was reluctant but helpless and kept dignified silence while witnesses proved before the bishop of Albi that Count Raymond VI had been her godfather, which placed her marriage with his son within the prohibited limits of consanguinity. It was therefore dissolved, and in August the king of Aragon stood proxy for Raymond VII in a wedding ceremony with the princess of Provence – whose name also was Sanchia – which was provisional, pending the dispensation which all were sure would result from an embassy to Rome sent jointly by the counts of Toulouse and Provence and the king of Aragon.

The plans were in vain. The envoys had only reached Pisa when they heard that Gregory IX had died on 21 August. His successor, Celestine IV, also died after only a little more than two weeks in office, and the papal chair was vacant for twenty months thereafter. Sanchia of Provence and her father refused to wait. She married Richard of Cornwall, brother of Henry III, while Raymond VII was soon embroiled in a military enterprise with fateful results.

## Conspiracy and Revolt in 1242

Quite unlike Trencavel's small and unsupported rebellion of 1240 the campaign of 1242 in Languedoc was part of a war waged by an international coalition against France, in which Hugh of Lusignan, count of La Marche, vented his dislike of Louis IX and Alphonse, the king's brother; Henry III of England resumed the old English-French feud; and Raymond VII sought to force a revision in his favour of the settlement of 1229. Raymond is sometimes described as the chief instigator of the affair. It is probably more accurate to depict him as a victim of an incautious search for allies and over-eager to take advantage of events he could not greatly influence.

The count of La Marche had married Isabella, widow of King John of England. Count Hugh himself was disgruntled when Louis IX, having knighted his brother Alphonse in June 1241, invested him with the counties of Poitou and Auvergne. Isabella, a haughty woman, never forgetful that she had been a queen, very much disliked the queen mother of France, Blanche of Castile. Dislike became furious hatred when Louis IX and Blanche treated Isabella coolly – contemptuously she thought – at Poitiers during the festivities of Alphonse's investiture. Her nagging carried Hugh to a decision to go to war. He enlisted the English seneschal and the barons of Gascony, as well as the citizens of Bordeaux and Bayonne, on his side. Henry III of England, when informed of Hugh's plans, impetuously decided to join him, although his barons refused to support the war.

The count of Toulouse also had early word of the disaffection of Hugh and Isabella. In October 1241 Raymond VII made a treaty of alliance with the count of La Marche[3] and then crossed the Pyrenees in search of further allies. Raymond Trencavel gladly joined him and Jaime I of Aragon may have promised some co-operation; at least he was informed of the plans. The conspirators hoped also to draw in Navarre and Castille. Rumour added Frederick II to the lift of plotters, but there is no evidence of his involvement.

Meanwhile the French court had learned of the conspiracy in Poitou and Gascony through a secret agent – Raymond VII was not mentioned in the report – and by January 1242 Louis IX was ready for war. From that point on the allies' plans met little but frustration and the coalition began to fall apart at the first setback. Even before Henry III landed at Saintonge with 300 knights and some Welsh mercenaries, Louis IX had begun methodically to reduce rebel castles in Poitou. In March Raymond VII fell so ill at Penne d'Agenais that his life was despaired of. Barely recovered, he summoned the southern nobility to him on 5 April. The counts of Armagnac, Comminges, and Rodez, the viscounts of Narbonne, Lautrec, and Lomagne, and many other southern lords agreed to fight; the young Roger of Foix (1241–1265), who had just succeeded to that county, gave a fiery declaration of support and the townsmen of Albi pledged their aid. The southerners, however, did not take the field until June. By that time Henry III had moved his army to Taillebourg, where he refused Louis IX's suggestion of negotiations, only to learn that Hugh of La Marche had already decided to try for peace. Raymond VII attempted to keep the coalition alive by a proposal of marriage with Hugh's daughter, Marguerite.

Support which was not truly welcome came to the count of Toulouse from another quarter. His plans, which, of course, were no secret in his county in the spring of 1242, aroused hope in the dwindling group of fiery devotees of the Cathars and led them to a brutal stroke against the hated inquisitors who had resumed their activities in mid-1241. On the night of 28 May 1242 an armed party from the heretical refuge at Montségur murdered William Arnold, Stephen of St Thibéry and their companions, who were quartered for the moment at Avignonet, about twenty-five miles southeast of Toulouse. The episode will be recounted in more detail in the following chapter. It caused exultation among partisans of the heretics and those who feared prosecution, but it cast a shadow over Raymond VII's campaign and undoubtedly cost him support among those who hated the French but had no wish to see heresy revived.[4]

In June and July Raymond led his army through southern

Languedoc, not far from the places where Trencavel had been welcomed, and again the inhabitants rallied to the rebels, although they had been badly weakened by events of 1240. The count avoided Carcassonne. At Narbonne, early in August, Viscount Aimery hailed him with the title of duke. Archbishop Peter Amiel and his clergy had already fled to Béziers, whence he issued a sentence of excommunication of all the rebels and their supporters. The Inquisitor, Ferrier, also excommunicated the count of Toulouse.

But even while Raymond VII was having his small successes, the French had defeated Henry III at Taillebourg on 20 July, forcing him back to Bordeaux. Hugh of La Marche surrendered on 20 August and, although Louis IX no longer led his army because of illness, a substantial detachment under Humbert of Beaujeu was already moving toward Languedoc. At the end of August Raymond tried to encourage his last remaining ally by a treaty with Henry III in which each agreed to make no separate peace, but the coalition was beyond repair. On 5 October, as the count was attacking French troops who had occupied Penne d'Agenais, Roger of Foix withdrew his allegiance and went over to Louis IX.

The situation of Count Raymond was hopeless. Bishop Raymond of Toulouse had not lost his good will of recent years, however, and acted as intermediary in suggesting negotiations to the king. Louis IX insisted on full capitulation and, on 20 October, Raymond sent to him and Queen Blanche his unconditional surrender. The clerk who later arranged the royal archives wrote in the margin of Raymond's letter: 'The humiliation of Raymond, former count of Toulouse, after the last war.' It was an accurate description.

King Louis, it was said, contemplated harsh measures against the rebellious count but was persuaded to a milder course by his mother. Blanche was Raymond's cousin, yet one may think her attitude was shaped less by that relationship than by a determination to see the inheritance of Toulouse come undiminished to her son Alphonse. Thus, the commission sent by the king to make preliminary arrangements required only the surrender of Bram and Saverdun as cautions. In January 1243 Raymond journeyed to the court at Lorris to conclude the peace. He threw himself and his lands on the king's mercy; agreed to require all barons, knights, and townsmen under his authority to swear fealty to Louis; surrendered three additional castles for five years; and reiterated the promises of 1229 and 1241 about destruction of recent fortifications. To Queen Blanche Raymond made a special commitment to purge his lands of heresy. He was then required to travel throughout his county, accompanied by the king's commissioners, to get from his subjects oaths of fealty to king and church and obedience to the treaty of 1229.

Aimery of Narbonne and Raymond's other southern allies made similar submissions. Count Roger of Foix rendered direct homage to the king, thus declaring his county independent of Toulouse. One result was intermittent war between the former allies over border territories. As for the other conspirators, Henry III, after complaining bitterly that he had been betrayed by the count of Toulouse, arranged a five-year truce with Louis IX in April 1243 and the count of La Marche was humbled by being forced to beg for mercy and by loss of castles. A rumour soon put about that his countess had attempted to poison the king and his mother is probably false, but illustrates contemporary opinion of the depth of her hatred.[5]

The failure of the revolt of 1242 ended any hope of a change in the territorial settlement of 1229 by force. Raymond VII could henceforth only continue to seek a marriage in the hope of a male heir. A more immediate need was to restore his standing with the church, without which there could neither be success for his marital plans nor for the effort to have his father buried in consecrated ground. Therefore, although he again complained to a council at Béziers in April 1243 about the Dominican inquisitors' antipathy toward him, he promised the prelates to support episcopal prosecutions of heretics, and he made no effort to oppose the pursuits which the friars had resumed in 1241.[6]

## The Reconciliation and Last Years of Raymond VII
Full reconciliation with the church awaited the election of a new pope. In the interim Raymond VII half-heartedly resumed his war in Provence but was easily persuaded to accept a truce. Then on 24 June 1243 the long interregnum in Rome ended with the election of Sinibald Fieschi of Genoa as Pope Innocent IV. The new pontiff was a man of native shrewdness tempered and refined by legal study and, because he was thought not to be implacably hostile to the imperial cause, hopes rose momentarily for an end to the long contest of pope and emperor. In pursuit of his own ends Raymond VII became an agent in the attempted reconciliation.

The count of Toulouse approached Rome by way of the court of Frederick II at Malfi. The emperor understood very well

L

political tactics adopted under pressure, such as Raymond's defection in 1241, and willingly restored the title of marquis of Provence which he had withdrawn at that time. Innocent IV was hardly more difficult to approach for Louis IX had generously seconded Raymond's reconciliation. Preliminary negotiations obtained the count's promises to obey the church and make satisfaction for damages he had done to it. He was then absolved from Friar Ferrier's excommunication, a fact which the prelates of Languedoc were instructed to proclaim. The pope also took Raymond under his protection, forbidding for five years any excommunication of him without pontifical permission.

One reason for Raymond's easy reception in Italy was that both Innocent IV and Frederick II recognized in him a useful go-between, for he was experienced in negotiations, not ardently committed to either side, and free from the personal rancours that had arisen between members of the curia and Frederick's ministers. In the early months of 1244 the count was one of the negotiators who worked out articles of peace which were given their first reading on Holy Thursday. But the papal–imperial controversy was not so easily to be ended. Frederick II backed away from final acceptance of the terms; Innocent IV fled Rome for the safety of Genoa; and although Raymond VII followed him there with the emperor's offer of further discussion, the breach was complete. The pope resolved to cross the Alps to hold a council which would muster the church at large for war with the emperor. Frederick defended himself in letters to the courts of Europe in which he declared that Count Raymond would testify to the sincerity of his efforts for peace.

From that involvement in great affairs Raymond VII returned to Languedoc with praise from both sides for his mediation. He and Viscount Aimery obtained absolution from their ex-communication by Archbishop Peter Amiel of Narbonne. Free from ecclesiastical censure for the first time in years, the count held a gala court at Toulouse at Christmas, 1244, when he created 200 new knights. Winter and spring were passed in administering local affairs, pressing the quarrel with Foix, skirmishing with the count of Armagnac, and acquiring a stronger position in the government of various towns, including Toulouse, where Raymond was moving toward a position of real influence over the consulate.

Raymond's hopes for marriage and an heir revived in 1245. At the council of Lyon, which convened in May, he encountered Count Raymond Berengar of Provence. The skirmishing of former years and failure of one matrimonial plan had left no great gulf between them and Raymond Berengar listened approvingly to the proposal for a match between the count of Toulouse and his last unmarried daughter, Beatrice, his favourite and heiress. It was necessary to bring the pope into the discussions in order to obtain two necessary dispensations: Raymond's unconsummated marriage contract of 1242 with Marguerite, daughter of the count of La Marche, had to be annulled, and a dispensation was needed to allow marriage within the prohibited degrees to the princess of Provence. Innocent IV seemed to agree to the plan, and at the end of the council a perfunctory investigation laid the basis for the annulment. The counts of Toulouse and Provence left Lyon in expectation of prompt action on that and the dispensation they had requested.

Again Raymond VII's hopes were to be dashed. Raymond Berengar died on his homeward journey in August. The count of Toulouse was urged by an adviser in Provence to press his suit for Beatrice at once, but was also warned by the guardians to whom her father's will entrusted her that, in view of past hostilities, it would be unwise for Raymond to appear in Provence at the head of an armed force. Moreover, the papal court was dilatory; the annulment of the marriage with Marguerite did not come until 25 September, permission to marry Beatrice not at all. At last the count sent an envoy to France to beg Queen Blanche's intervention with the pope for removal of that final barrier.

Raymond VII had totally misunderstood the mind of the queen. Blanche was determined to see Provence in Capetian hands, and the guardians of the heiress had already been in touch with her. In a week-long meeting at Cluny Blanche and Louis IX had discussed with Innocent IV the king's proposed crusade, the war with Frederick II, and, no doubt, the fate of the county of Provence. Thus it was that Raymond's messenger, who was to ask Blanche's aid for the count, met en route a French army moving toward Provence in escort of Charles of Anjou, the youngest of Blanche's sons, whose marriage to Beatrice had been quietly arranged and took place in the following January. We have no information on Raymond's reaction to the new frustration. His marital hopes were now a matter of gossip, which reported a journey to St James of Compostella and a secret meeting at that shrine with a Spanish princess. Nothing resulted.

Louis IX was now devoting himself to preparations for a crusade against the Saracens, in which he desired the support of all his major vassals. To leave the count of Toulouse behind would be folly; thus, early in 1247, the king urged him to take the cross. Powerful inducements were offered: Louis promised to restore the duchy of Narbonne and to contribute 20,000 pounds toward Raymond's expenses; Innocent IV pledged 2,000 marks to be paid on the count's arrival overseas and, in return for a new promise to eradicate heresy, allowed him to draw on church funds raised from southern sources for the crusade. Raymond could not but agree and undertook preparations, including commissioning a special vessel to be fitted out in Brittany. Inhabitants of Languedoc benefited by the activity. Louis IX ordered an inquest in all lands acquired by the crown since the death of his father to remedy past injustices, while Innocent IV allowed inquisitorial sentences of imprisonment or of wearing crosses to be commuted to the crusading vow and somewhat later the pope sent his penitentiary through the land with power to change sentences of imprisonment to fines for the benefit of the crusade and the church.

Even though now in the good graces of the church, in one matter Raymond VII was rebuffed. On taking the cross he had again requested of the pope permission for burial of his father's bones and Innocent IV had appointed a commission of investigation. Raymond himself and more than a hundred other witnesses testified before it. Perhaps the papal bureaucracy was not sufficiently rewarded to press the case with the pope; in any event the report was found lacking in necessary detail and Innocent IV adopted the bureaucratic manoeuvre of calling for a new inquiry. It does not appear that the case was again seriously considered. The body of Raymond VI continued to decay in its unburied coffin in the precincts of the Hospitallers at Toulouse.

Like that vain attempt to obtain his father's burial, other acts in the last year of Raymond VII's life awoke echoes of what had gone before. Louis IX, journeying down the Rhône in 1248, encountered unpleasantness at Avignon, where antagonisms surviving from the siege of 1226 provoked brawls between the citizens and the king's party. Raymond VII bade farewell to the king at Aigues-mortes in August, but the vessel on which the count was to follow did not reach Marseilles until the end of the safe sailing season and, as so often before, Raymond postponed his departure. Early in 1249, holding court at Agen, the count intervened on behalf of a vassal, the count of Armagnac, against the count of Lomagne. In that dispute, the count of Lomagne had the support of the English governor of Gascony, Simon of

Montfort, earl of Leicester, son of the leader of the Albigensian crusade. Apparently Raymond and Simon did not meet in person to revive the old enmity of their parents.

Toward heresy, Raymond VII's attitude had hardened. His *baillis* were now more active in seizing suspects, and in 1248 the count complained to Innocent IV of the ineffectiveness of the church's pursuits. He ordered his officials to require people to attend the inquisitors' sermons, and, when eighty persons accused as heretics or defenders of heretics were brought before him at Agen in 1249, the count had them burned without further ado.

In August 1249 Raymond was again at Aigues-mortes for farewells to his daughter and Alphonse of Poitiers, who were taking reinforcements to Louis IX in Egypt. The count's own plans are not revealed. Perhaps it was to make final arrangements for his absence that Raymond was on tour through the Rouergue not long afterward, when he fell ill of a fever serious enough to induce him to make a last confession and to draw up his will. He managed to get to Millau and there, as courtiers, consuls, and bishops gathered, on 27 September 1249, at the age of fifty-two, Raymond VII died.[7]

### The Succession of Alphonse of Poitiers

By the treaty of 1229 the possessions of Raymond VII were to pass to his daughter and her husband jointly, but in his will Raymond named Jeanne as sole heir. The distinction would be important if a question about the right to dispose of the county should arise in the future; therefore, Queen Blanche acted promptly to claim the county for her son on the basis of the treaty alone. Two knights and Alphonse's chaplain were at Toulouse by 1 December 1249 to receive oaths of fealty from the count of Comminges and other notables. The consuls of Toulouse, however, delayed until a delegation to the queen had been assured that ancient rights and liberties would be respected. Agen held out longer on the same pretext, and Najac declared its independence of the new count, for which it was assailed as a nest of heretics and endured severe hardships before submitting. The marquisate of Provence was the scene of even more trouble. Avignon and Arles declared themselves republics and only yielded to Alphonse and Charles of Anjou when they appeared in person in 1251.

Count Alphonse and his wife returned from the crusade in June 1250. He had been taken prisoner in Egypt with Louis

IX, was ransomed, and came back from Acre when the king went on to Syria. Alphonse paused to accept the pledges of loyalty of some towns along the Rhône and from various lords of Languedoc before going on to pursue without success the commissions given him by his brother to persuade Innocent IV to make peace with the emperor in order to send aid to Palestine and to urge Henry III of England to come to the assistance of the crusaders. Alphonse and Jeanne then came to Toulouse in May 1251, where they swore to observe the customs and privileges of the town in return for the citizens' oaths of fealty. The count employed a group of jurisconsults to find Raymond VII's will invalid on technical grounds as a preliminary to petty haggling by which he persuaded abbeys and churches to accept far smaller amounts than the bequests Raymond had made. A tour through upper Languedoc followed, before the count and countess returned to France, not to reappear in Languedoc for nearly two decades.

Only a sketch of the further political destiny of the county is possible here. Alphonse entrusted the oversight of his inheritance to four seneschals and in the 1260s he created a parliament; the new system only gradually affected local rule and customs. There were serious quarrels over the liberties of Toulouse in 1255 and other disputes over the government of Montpellier and the respective rights of the bishop and count in Albi. Inquests established the count's rights to specific properties, notably those confiscated from condemned heretics. In 1270 Louis IX again went on crusade, Alphonse and Jeanne following him, and on 25 August of that year the king died. His son was immediately crowned as Philip III. Since Alphonse and Jeanne died in Italy within days of each other in that same month, Philip III also took possession of their lands. That he ruled the county of Toulouse as successor to its former counts by the treaty of 1229 and that it was not formally merged with the realm until the next century did not disguise the fact that politically all of Languedoc was now part of Capetian France. Its full acceptance of that union had to wait until the national ordeal of the Hundred Years War.[8]

# References

1. See p. 156 below.
2. The report of the seneschal on the defence of Carcassonne is in *HGL*, VIII, 1043–5; A. Molinier describes the campaign, *ibid.*, VII, 448–61; see

also Poux, *La Cité de Carcassonne*, Vol. II, Ch. 3. The fortunes of the Trencavel family are traced in L. D'Alauzier, 'L'Héritage des Trencavels', *AM*, LXII (1950), 181–6; and for the fate of a rebellious town, see A. Sabarthès, 'L'Albigéisme à Limoux et le prétendu déplacement de cette ville', *BPH*, 1924, 193–222.
2. The relationship may be shown thus:

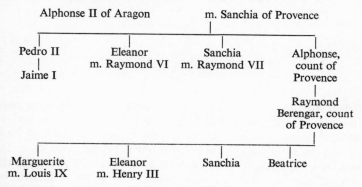

(Sanchia, daughter of Raymond Berengar, would soon marry Richard of Cornwall and her sister, Beatrice, was later wed to Charles of Anjou).
3. The allies were not strangers. In 1226, fearing that he would be denied a negotiated peace by Cardinal Romanus, Raymond VII had made a secret pact with Henry III and Hugh, but nothing came of that arrangement.
4. See pp. 169–71, below.
5. See C. Belmont, 'Le Campagne de Poitou, 1242–1243: Taillebourg et Saintes', *AM*, V (1893), 289–314; E. Berger, *Histoire de Blanche de Castille*, 345–53; E. Boutaric, *Saint Louis et Alfonse de Poitiers*, 43–61; Y. Dossat, 'Le Prétendu concile de Bourges', *BPH*, 1959, 461–71.
6. See pp. 169–70 below.
7. There is no satisfactory biography of Raymond VII, nor do biographies of his great contemporaries give him much attention; see, for example, E. Kantorowicz, *Frederick the Second, 1194–1250*, trans. by E. O. Lorimer (2nd ed.), 580ff.; M. W. Labarge, *Saint Louis*, 85ff. I have depended much on *HGL*, VI, 760–808, for these last years. The execution of heretics in 1249 is the subject of P. Merklin, 'Les Brûlés de Béoulaygues', *CEtC*, XXI, 2nd ser., No. 45 (1970), 20–33. On the attempt to have Raymond VI decently buried, see C. Molinier, *La Question de l'ensevelissement du comte de Toulouse Raimond VI en terre sainte (1222–1247)*.
8. For the history of Languedoc after 1249, see the works of Dognon, Michel, Molinier and Wolff, cited on pp. 63, n. 2, 150, n. 1; also J. Rogozinski, 'The Counsellors of the Seneschal of Beaucaire and Nîmes, 1250–1350', *Speculum*, XLIV (1969), 421–39. Transfer of the county of Toulouse to Philip III is the subject of Y. Dossat, *Saisimentum comitatus tholosani*.

# X The Inquisition Resumes

When Raymond VII shifted his allegiance from emperor to pope in 1241 his attitude toward the Inquisition had continued to be ambivalent. Publicly he urged the bishop of Agen to keep up the prosecution and he did the same before prelates at the council of Béziers in 1243. Each time, however, he protested the role of the Dominicans, who were, he insisted, animated by malice toward him and should be kept strictly subordinate to the bishops. But Gregory IX had consistently rejected reliance on the episcopate and Raymond's protests had no result.

Despite the count's declared opposition the friars seem to have taken his change of course as a signal to resume their activities. Peter of Seila was first in the field at Montauban and Moissac in May 1241, then in various nearby places in December and during Lent of the following year. In sessions of a few weeks at a time he delivered a total of 732 sentences. So many, issued so rapidly, indicate that these were penances imposed on those who came voluntarily to confess during periods of grace. The offences, extending back over several decades, often included fervent devotion to Cathars or Waldenses, but also there were only casual contacts, such as by a boatman who unwittingly transported heretics or a servant sent on an errand to them. Numerous persons, especially around Montauban, had gone to the Waldensians for medical advice. It was not unusual for a person to admit that he had heard Waldenses preach and venerated Cathars as well. There were references to disputations between members of the two sects. The penalties varied. Only one was to imprisonment. Men of fighting age were ordered to go to the Latin Empire of Constantinople; others were assigned one or more pilgrimages – as many as eight in certain cases – to St James of Compostella, Le Puy, St Gilles, or Canterbury. Well-to-do persons were occasionally required to support a priest or a pauper for periods varying from a year to life. Many of the penitents had to wear a cross on the breast for periods varying from a year to life and for others one on the back as well was stipulated.

The renewed activity of the inquisitors probably stimulated other pursuers. We know, for example, that the abbot of St Papoul captured two heretics in 1241, because witnesses before the Inquisition in 1245 described a plan to liberate the prisoners by bribery or force. It came to nothing.[1]

Late in 1241 William Arnold and his Franciscan colleague, Stephen of St Thibéry, were in the region of Lavaur and they continued their pursuits in the following year in the region southeast of Toulouse. Eventually they reached the walled village of Avignonet, shortly before 28 May 1242, their last day of life. They were quartered that evening in a room of the little ungarrisoned castle which served as the residence of the count's *bailli*.

Avignonet was not a safe place for inquisitors. From that region many faidits had fled across the Pyrenees or to Montségur to nurse their hopes of revenge. With Raymond VII's willingness for military action being openly rumoured and an inquisitorial party within reach, desperate men saw an opportunity for a blow at the hatred tribunal.

The fortress of Montségur, in the mountains southeast of Foix, had come into the possession of Raymond of Pereille earlier in the century, under the nominal overlordship of the Trencavels. After the crusade Raymond of Pereille installed his faidit son-in-law, Peter Roger of Mirepoix, as commander and came there himself after his condemnation for heresy in 1237. Over the years the castle and the huts clinging to the cliffs outside its walls had become a place of refuge for perfected Cathars who could not endure the life of the hunted. Guilabert of Castres and Tento, Cathar bishops of Toulouse and Agen, respectively, were often there, as was Bertrand Marty, Guilabert's successor after about 1240. Fugitives from prosecution and faidits who had ridden with Trencavel joined them. Believers came frequently to adore the Good Men and, toward the end of life, to die among them.[2]

One of the contacts between the garrison at Montségur and men outside who equally hated the French and the Inquisition was Raymond of Alfaro, son of a noted Navarrese leader of mercenaries and Williametta, illegitimate half-sister of Raymond VII. In 1242 he was the count's *bailli* in Avignonet. When he learned the itinerary of the inquisitors, Raymond of Alfaro sped the news to Montségur. Peter Roger of Mirepoix assembled a party of armed men, most of them exiles from the area of

Prouille, Limoux, and the Lauragais, who set out on the fifty-mile ride to Avignonet. During a stop for rest near Gaja they were met by others, including men armed with axes. Peter Roger remained there with a reserve; the group charged with the assassination went on. By nightfall of 28 May, the eve of Ascension Day, they had gathered outside the town, making contact with Raymond of Alfaro through a messenger who went in and out to report the actions of the inquisitorial party: that they were dining, that they had retired for the night. There were eleven of the intended victims in all: the inquisitors William Arnold and Stephen of St Thibéry with two other Dominicans and a Franciscan as companions; Raymond Scriptor, one-time collaborator with the crusaders, now archdeacon of Villelongue and an assistant to the inquisitors; his clerk; the inquisitorial notary; two servants; and the prior of Avignonet, who had the bad luck of having come to stay with the visitors.

The gates were opened to the raiders and they were guided into the castle, where Raymond of Alfaro met them with men and torches to light the way to the hall where the inquisitors lay. Axes made short work of the barred door. The two servants ran to an upper story as the murderers burst in; they were killed and tossed to the floor below. The friars had only time to begin to chant the *Te Deum* before swords and axes hacked them down. The blood-stained attackers, shouting boasts to each other of blows they had struck, shared out the booty: garments and bedding, a little money, some books, no doubt inquisitorial registers, which were later sold, a box of ginger, and other trifles, valuable only as grisly souvenirs. The inquisitors' horses, too, were taken as the killers retired through the village, speeded by Raymond of Alfaro's 'Good luck as you go'. Reunion with the party waiting at Gaja was marred only by Peter Roger's reproaches that no one had brought him William Arnold's shattered skull, from which he had hoped to fashion a drinking cup. On the return to Montségur, there was a pause for rest at a village where the riders were applauded by the people and a priest gave the leaders a meal.

The massacre at Avignonet, an act of unreasoned fury in a losing cause by men who refused to give up hope that they could still strike to win, would, perhaps, have been only one more bloody entry in the annals of brutality of those years if it had occurred at another time. But, because it coincided with Raymond VII's attack on the French in Languedoc, it drew opprobrium on his enterprise.

It was widely believed at the time and has often been asserted since that Raymond VII had encouraged the murders at Avignonet. Raymond of Alfaro, it was said, had told the conspirators that he was acting for the count; there was also a statement from the wife of one of the murderers that her husband had known Raymond to be involved. Such reports of support from high places are understandable when so desperate a plot is in the making. But the sentences of excommunication of the count, nearly a month after the event, by the archbishop of Narbonne and the inquisitor, Ferrier, do not accuse Raymond VII of the murders. Montségur was not under his jurisdiction. There was nothing for him to gain by the act and much to lose; he could not have forgotten what happened to his father after the murder of Peter of Castelnau nor the censure he himself had endured after a bloodless expulsion of the friars from Toulouse. And when some of the conspirators fell into his hands, he hanged them.

## Montségur Is Captured

Once the revolt of 1242 had collapsed, the murders at Avignonet gave the incentive for an assault on the place where the plot was hatched. Already in 1241 Raymond VII had promised Louis IX to reduce the fortress of Montségur and had made a half-hearted attempt to do so. A more formidable attack was launched in mid-summer of 1243 by Hugh of Arcis, the royal seneschal of Carcassonne, with troops provided by the archbishop of Narbonne and the bishop of Albi added to his own.

The castle of Montségur perched on a mass of rock rising more than a thousand feet from a valley surrounded by even higher peaks. It was reached by a steep climb up the southwest slope. The other sides dropped more sharply from the summit. So situated, it controlled little; its value was in its remoteness and defensibility. Quick storming of the walls was out of the question and the seneschal planned to starve out the besieged; even that proved impracticable without enough troops to encircle the base of the rock. Patrols could not prevent local guides from leading people in and out. Food was not a problem for the defenders, for in addition to stockpiles on hand, more was carried in during the siege. Somehow the water supply held out through the summer.

In October or November the attackers, supervised by the bishop of Albi, with enormous effort erected a rock-throwing machine close to the summit. Even though the siege was thus tightened and the castle's occupants were now constantly endangered by projectiles, messengers continued to come and go. A bishop of the Cathars of Lombardy sent greetings. Heretical sympathizers nearer at hand dispatched couriers to discuss matters with the chieftains in Montségur, sometimes encouraging the hopeful rumours that always arise or are deliberately put about in a desperate situation. Raymond VII, who had gone to Rome to ask for his own absolution, was, as we have seen, also occupied in the peace negotiations of Innocent IV and Frederick II. The defenders of the castle told each other that a message had come from him: could they but hold out until Easter, the count would come to their relief with troops furnished by the emperor. One or two fighting men did slip through the lines from time to time, and a skilled artilleryman was sent in to construct a catapult for counterfire on the attackers' machine. A famous mercenary captain contracted to bring twenty-five men at arms to bolster the defence; either he could not find the men for so risky a venture or they could not get through.

The attackers held their position near the crest through the winter months, suffering the weather and fighting off at the cliff's edge sorties against them and the catapult. Hugh of Arcis grimly maintained the pressure and refused to release the militia from Albi when they wanted to go home. His own men were professionals. Inside the castle morale sank so low that the Cathars decided to send out their 'treasure', funds accumulated over the years by contributions and bequests, perhaps also precious books and Bibles.

The end came in March. There had been a major setback for the defenders when local guides led an assault party to seize one of the outer defensive works in a daring night attack. Thereafter, although vicious fighting continued at the outworks, it was clear that unless the attackers suddenly lost the nerve and determination that had carried them through the winter, the castle must fall. Peter Roger of Mirepoix and Raymond of Pereille opened negotiations for surrender, delivered hostages for their good faith, and obtained terms which were no doubt tempered by the fatigue which must have beset the besiegers: the armed defenders were promised their lives and amnesty for past acts of violence but, like all the others, must appear before the Inquisition for questioning; heretics and their believers must abjure their faith or die.

The negotiations took time and during those last days about twenty persons within the castle decided to make their final gesture of loyalty to their faith and received the consolamentum. Apparently, the evacuation was by groups: wives of the defenders and women not committed to heresy, then heretics, and men-at-arms last, between 13 and 20 March. During that time two of the Good Men were hidden, were lowered by night from the cliffs, and escaped to preserve knowledge of the hiding place of the treasure that had already been smuggled out. The most dramatic scene came when two hundred persons who were unwilling to recant heresy were led, pushed, or carried down the mountain. Among the perfected heretics were Bertrand Marty, Cathar bishop of Toulouse, Raymond Aguilher, the elderly bishop of Razès, and two or three deacons. The legend is firmly established that on 16 March 1244, in an open meadow on the lower slopes, piles of brush were heaped within a palisade, the heretics were herded in, and torches were flung on the tinder. Local tradition is said to have long preserved tales of hearing the spirits of 'the holy ones' in the night wind. A legend, however, may be more romantic than accurate. The victors at Montségur were not crusaders, eager to 'kill them all', as at Béziers. Nor, in 1244, was it by any means the practice of inquisitors to hand over victims for burning without a hearing. Furthermore, Yves Dossat has found evidence that some, at least, of the heretics were taken to Bram and were burned there after some kind of inquisitorial process. Yet, in all probability the legend will not die and the *prat dels crematz* (field of those who were burned), now marked by a monument to the memory of the martyrs, will continue to be pointed out as the site of the holocaust.

Wherever the executions, the fall of Montségur was a terrible event for Catharism. The hierarchy, if not destroyed, had lost devoted leaders. A rallying place and refuge was gone; one other remained at Quéribus, but it was less frequented and it also surrendered in 1255. More deadly to the heretical church was the toll among its believers and defenders after the inquisitors Ferrier and Peter Durand had completed their interrogations of the survivors, who were persuaded to reveal every experience of heresy they could dredge from their memories. Who had been consoled? Who attended the ceremonies? Who took meals with the heretics? Who heard them preach? Who sheltered them, guided them, sent them food? The records were invaluable for years to come.[3]

*Inquisitorial Procedures*

At the time that all the information they could give was being drawn from the prisoners of Montségur the structure of the Inquisition was being fixed. There were now two centres. From Carcassonne Friar Ferrier, working successively with Pons

Gary and Peter Durand, had responsibility for most of the ecclesiastical province of Narbonne, while Friars Bernard of Caux and
John of St Pierre, who had succeeded Peter Seila in 1242, were
assigned to the dioceses of Cahors and Agen and part of the
diocese of Toulouse. The two headquarters apparently shared
jurisdiction in Albi and Rodez, and the territorial limits were
not always observed, especially while Ferrier and his colleagues
were following up leads obtained after the fall of Montségur.
In 1245 Bernard of Caux and John of St Pierre, then established
in Toulouse, began a general inquest of the state of religion in
the whole diocese. Adjacent areas, such as Foix, were also visited,
but in 1248 the pope forbade the Languedocian inquisitors to
summon subjects of the king of Aragon, where an independent
tribunal was being established. Montpellier was added to the
jurisdiction of the inquisitors of Carcassonne in 1246. There is
no information about activities of the tribunal at Avignon except
that vigorous resentment at it was expressed there in 1246.[4]

The judges were assisted by other persons, casually or regularly
employed. In the first category were fellow Dominicans who might
sit for a day as delegate (*vice gerens*) of one of the judges or be
designated to handle a particular case, perhaps in a place remote
from where the inquisitors were sitting. The presence of two
witnesses at interrogations were required; larger numbers of
persons attended the sessions when sentences were announced.
These assistants were probably called as circumstances and
locality permitted; William Pelhisson was the only Dominican
regularly and frequently associated with the Toulousan inquisitors
in 1245–1246. Notaries and scribes were the most important of the
regular employees, for they were involved in every step from
inauguration of an inquiry until its conclusion.

During these years procedures were worked up on the basis of
experience, while higher authority gave precision and elaboration
to their legal basis. Pope Innocent IV, himself a capable canonist,
by his directives and decisions took a leading part, keeping also
so watchful an eye on the inquisitors' activities that they complained openly of his interference. The bishops who had acted
on their own initiative in the first decade of peace were now
content with an advisory role. Church councils – Narbonne
(1243/1244), Béziers (1246), Valence (1248) – legislated on heresy
and the conduct of the inquisitorial office, providing definitions
of various levels of guilt, stipulating action in the cases of those
who confessed during the period of grace or as a result of later
investigation, establishing guide lines for penances, and exhorting

the inquisitors to work always in the spirit of mercy to obtain confessions and save souls. Problems of a special nature were referred to the bishops in council or to individual prelates, and the record of similar consultations in Italy was accepted in Languedoc. In 1245 or 1246 Peter of Collemieu, cardinal-bishop of Albano, was instructed by Innocent IV to set down certain rules for the work of the judges. About 1248–1249, the inquisitors drew up a little manual on the conduct of their office for the benefit of colleagues elsewhere, the first of many such guidebooks that would be produced during the next hundred years. Thus, a substantial body of laws, rules, precedents, and customary procedures accumulated in the archives.

Documents produced by the investigations were much more numerous, for every step in the processes which will be described in following pages was carefully recorded. Scribes wrote down confessions and responses to questions, not verbatim but in standardized phrases which incorporated the essential points. These depositions were then copied into registers, rearranged as necessary to bring together those which had some affinity, such as the parish from which they came or their bearing on a particular case. The sentences of the inquisitors were also enregistered according to the type of penance imposed. Such records, of course, aroused fear and hatred among those whose activities were described or who feared that their names appeared in the depositions. The seizure of books of the murdered inquisitors at Avignonet and the burning of records taken from messengers of the Inquisition who were ambushed at Caunes, near Narbonne, in 1247 taught the need of security. Thus, when documents were dispatched to other inquisitors or were needed by judges intending to visit a distant place, copies were made, while the originals remained under guard. Of all that material, what has survived is only a fraction, yet it allows a fairly clear picture of the tribunal at work. A summary will show how the judicial pursuit of heresy had developed on the existing legislative base and out of daily experience.

The requirement that all persons assist in the prosecution of heresy was now widely enforced. Priests issued the notices of a forthcoming visit of inquisitors to their parishes and were employed to deliver individual citations; notaries could be drafted to record confessions if the staff of the tribunal needed help; local personages sat as witnesses to the proceedings and authenticated the written record of confessions. The role of bishops in the investigations, however, and their responsibility for approving the sentences of the friars were not entirely agreed on. Most prelates were content with no more than token participation. Secular lords, their vicars, *baillis*, and consuls of the towns were required to carry out verdicts involving confiscation of property or destruction of houses, and it was their duty to arrange for the prompt execution of the condemned whom the inquisitors abandoned to them.

When the inquisitors proposed a session in a locality, they selected a place convenient for their purpose and instructed the parish clergy to announce their arrival. In 1247 the pope gave orders that the site be chosen with an eye to security from ill-wishers. The party would include the judges and their companion friars, notaries, necessary servants, and guards to protect against violence. Innocent IV reprimanded inquisitors in 1248 for travelling with an excessive retinue and ordered, their attendants limited to the absolutely indispensable. Ordinarily, only inhabitants of nearby parishes would be required to come to the place where the court was sitting, but in the great inquest of 1245–1246 people from the whole diocese had to appear in groups at Toulouse. There, the house which Peter Seila had given to Dominic in 1215 was the official home of the Inquisition but, since it was small, most of the interrogations and the sentencing took place in the cloister of St Sernin in the bourg.

At the start of an investigation in a particular place, the people of the district were called to a 'general preaching', *Baillis* of the count of Toulouse were ordered in 1248 to enforce attendance, even on work days. One of the friars in a sermon would add to his exhortations about the faith a statement of the authority under which he acted and would demand from all his hearers an oath to support the church, avoid heresy, and assist in apprehension of the guilty. Men and women from the ages of fourteen and twelve, respectively, were required to swear, and even younger persons, if they had knowledge of heresy, were not excused. If no time of grace had hitherto been granted, the inquisitor could announce that for a period of six to twelve days, or occasionally a little longer, persons who confessed about heresy of their own free will would be assured lenient treatment. It was in his power to grant immunity from the more severe penalties, or even from all, to anyone who had not previously been convicted, if that person revealed what he had done or what he knew about 'the fact and crime of heresy'. By 1246, however, a period of grace had probably already been extended to most inhabitants of the county of Toulouse, and it was not normally renewed when they were again subjected to investigation.

In the sweeping inquiry of 1245–1246 and in other general inquisitions each person was asked questions and the answers were recorded by notaries who, in view of the large number of persons to be interrogated, were probably themselves the questioners. The inquisitors supervised and, in the case of important testimony such as that from a convert or a person long searched for, would take personal charge. From the surviving records it appears that the usual questions included the following: Have you ever seen any heretics or Waldenses? Have you heard them preach? Attended any of their ceremonies? Adored heretics? Have you ever seen anyone receive the consolamentum? When and where? Who was present? Have you ever accepted the kiss of peace from heretics? Did you believe their teaching? Did you believe that they were good men, teaching a good faith? Have you ever given or sent them anything? What, to whom, when? Have you ever guided them or arranged for them to be escorted from place to place? Who sheltered them? What do heretics say about the creation of the visible world? Have you heard them speak of the sacraments, the nature of Christ, resurrection of bodies? Did you ever make an agreement to keep silent about these things? Have you ever appeared before another inquisitor?

The intent of the questioning was obviously less to elicit information about erroneous doctrine, on which the inquisitors felt themselves amply informed by experience or from treatises written for the purpose, than it was to ascertain who was in any way contaminated by association with heretics. Witnesses were found whose memories stretched back ten, twenty, forty years, to produce details of time and place of heretical assemblies and names of dozens of persons who had attended, on whom the investigators could turn their subsequent attention. No reticence was permitted; husbands must inform on wives, children on parents. Failure to speak freely could lead to a charge of defending heretics or being a heretic oneself. Any sign in word or deed by which a man or woman had shown evidence of belief in heresy or respect for heretics had to be revealed, and a plea of faulty memory was no excuse, indeed, could bring a summons to return after reflection. Each deponent was finally required to abjure heresy entirely and again take oath to oppose it. To permit the use of these depositions as legal evidence, they were authenticated by at least two witnesses, drawn from attendant local clergy or the companions of the inquisitors.

Even if the witness was hard-pressed by his interrogator there could not always be certainty that the answers were complete

**M**

or accurate. Many references are found to threats against persons summoned to testify: 'Take care to say nothing of your neigh-bours,' men were warned, and some deponents spoke of mis-treatment to prevent them from testifying or to punish them for having done so. Inhabitants of a place, hearing that the inquisitors were coming, would agree among themselves to reveal nothing incriminating; others conspired to give false testimony. The care with which the records were checked and correlated is demon-strated by the fact that we know of such acts because they were detected and the perpetrators were summoned to make new and better confessions.

The action against a person already under arrest because damaging evidence had been accumulated or against one who had failed to appear at the general preaching or who was discovered to have lied under oath began with a statement of charges presented to the accused when he came before the court. A written summation of them would be given him, if desired, and time was usually allowed for preparation of a reply, but no lawyer could take part for the defendant,[5] nor were the names of witnesses against him disclosed. The most one could do was to name persons believed to be personal enemies, with the inquisitors' promise that their hostility would be taken into account in weighing the evidence. The accused might be allowed to call in friends who would swear that the alleged enmities in fact existed. No other witnesses for the defence were called; on the other hand, testimony against the suspect was allowed whatever the source. The evidence of heretics, criminals, accomplices, and young children, forbidden in other courts, was admissible before the inquisitors. They would very often already have a dossier on suspects, including the record of previous appearances before the same or other inquisitors, in which it might be noted, for example, that an accused had been seen to adore Cathars or was known to have heard Waldenses preach; that he had been present at the consolamentum of a neighbour so many years before; that he had been seen to eat bread blessed by the Good Men or had shared in the Waldensian Eucharist; that he had the reputation of being a believer of heretics and had been heard to speak sneeringly of the Roman church. Two witnesses to guilty acts were normally thought necessary for conviction, yet there were cases in which insub-stantial suspicions became accusations and random encounters were taken as proof of heretical sympathies. The judges' duty was to obtain an admission of guilt,[6] for the church put confession and repentance by the suspect as its highest aims.

Only the most hardened and impenitent or, on the other hand, those who were utterly stubborn in insisting on their innocence refused eventually to make a confession of some kind and to ask for forgiveness. How were the confessions obtained? The use of torture in the inquisitorial process had not yet appeared. Scrutiny of the very few references to it in Languedoc before 1250 and, indeed, until nearly the end of the century, reveals that torture was the action only of secular officials who were dealing with heretics without reference to the Inquisition.[7] However, suspects could be held long in custody and summoned again and again until they yielded. In the early years, prolonged confinement for the purpose of obtaining a confession was probably not much used because of lack of prison space, yet it may be surmised that harsh conditions when it was imposed were potent inducements to full confession. Probably the great majority of the accused recognized that there was no escape from some kind of penalty and confessed to what they feared could be proved. The prestige and power of the tribunal and the dread of what its books contained would overawe the ordinary suspect.

If the accused offered no demur and agreed to accept whatever penance might be imposed, a case, apart from the sentence, could be concluded in one session. When delay occurred and a day was assigned for another appearance, surety had to be given in money or by the oaths of other persons to guarantee that the suspect would return. Those who were under graver charges or who were already in detention would be remanded to prison to await their next appearance. There, too, were sent those who had confessed to crimes which would bring on them the severer penances.

When one or more cases had been brought to a conclusion, the inquisitors prepared the sentences. Penance could be imposed only on one who was willing to accept it and whose agreement to do so was part of the record, but to refuse that assent would be evidence of contumacy. The law required consultation between inquisitors and bishops in whose dioceses they were operating, and from an early date the sentences contain such phrases as 'having consulted with bishops and men of good counsel', or 'having had the assistance of men skilled in law', and the like. We know that judges after about 1270 did present a summary of the interrogations to groups of lawyers and theologians and sometimes engaged in genuine discussion of the punishments they proposed. This could not have been done in any effective way in the years 1241–1249. The records show that conferences with prelates and advisers immediately preceded the delivery of the verdicts and afforded no real opportunity for review; they were no more than announcements of the decisions in which neither bishops nor legal experts had a real voice.

The proceedings to this point had supposedly been secret. The general sermon, however, in which the sentences were announced, was normally a public affair to which clergy and people were invited. Penitents and condemned were arrayed before the court in the sight of the spectators. Again, the repentant were required to abjure not only their own admitted errors but heresy of every kind. Then the verdicts were read. First came the condemnations, that is, the abandonment of the recalcitrant to the secular officers for execution, excommunication of the contumacious who had taken to flight, and orders for exhumation of the defunct. There followed announcement of the penances of those who had repented and confessed, to whom imprisonment, pilgrimages or other good works were enjoined. Although relatively simple in form at this period, the general sermon had all the essentials of the elaborate and terrifying ceremonial of *auto-da-fé* that would develop in later years.[8]

### The Penalties

The inquisitors devised no new punishments to add to those which had already been authorized before the tribunal existed; their contribution was rather to regularize the application of penalty to offence. Toward the unrepentant they neither wished nor were allowed to show mercy, but for those who had confessed they could use discretion in weighing the gravity of the offence and their estimate of the sincerity of repentance. The price of lenient treatment normally was to give proof of good faith by revealing all that the offender knew about perfidious acts of other persons.

Death at the stake, recognized in civil and canon law as the punishment for the obdurate heretic, was, in theory, never the sentence of the ecclesiastical judges. A perfected Cathar or a Waldensian preacher who refused to recant or a believer who persisted in his loyalty lost the protection of the church and was handed over to the secular power. The same fate was possible for a relapsed heretic who had abjured error but returned to it 'like a dog to his vomit'. Death was the penalty also for an accused person who maintained his innocence in the face of evidence which the judges believed convincing of his guilt. When such culprits were relaxed to civil officers, the inquisitors' plea that mercy be shown them was an empty formula, for an official who failed to carry out an execution became a defender of heretics.

Comital or royal officials were the usual executioners. The sites where the stakes were erected are not now precisely known; the one in Toulouse was probably the count's meadow, near the Château Narbonnais which had served for earlier burnings; in Carcassonne a spot outside the city on the banks of the Aude was used. There are no contemporary descriptions of executions, but they surely did not vary greatly from the ones described in histories of the Albigensian crusade or in documents of much later date. Probably the victim was bound to a stake atop a pile of faggots by chains about the torso and legs. A crude sketch of a figure in that position amid the flames was drawn by a clerk in the chancery of Alphonse of Poitiers on the back of an unused memorandum about 1254. There is no mention of the mercy of strangulation before the fire was kindled.

Far more common than death was imprisonment, which was considered to be an act of penance. The inquisitors before 1250 imposed prison sentences in many cases in which they could have decreed death. Fugitives who had been recaptured, the relapsed, perjurors, and persons who had been long and seriously suspect were usually sentenced to prison for life (*in perpetuum carcerem*), although at the judges' discretion the term could subsequently be reduced, especially if the prisoner showed repentance by remembering things that would aid in other prosecutions or, more rarely, if his family suffered unusual hardship. Even while they exercised discretionary powers and often granted mercy, the inquisitors were jealous of their prerogatives, as is revealed by complaints to Innocent IV in 1245 that suspects who deserved worse were being lightly penanced when they took their cases to the papal curia. Interference by the pope in commutations of punishments in 1248–1249 was also to lead to a serious crisis.

Prisons were a problem. The attempt of the council of Toulouse (1229) to put the responsibility for them on the king or on the lay lords who received property confiscated for heresy was not very effective. The prison for heretics in Toulouse in 1237 was that of the bishop, although the Château Narbonnais was used in certain circumstances. In 1245 or 1246, the inquisitors bought a house near St Sernin to be used as a prison. It was later given to the hospice of St Raymond, a foundation attached to St Sernin, for the use of poor scholars. The king's prison in Carcassonne was also used before 1240. The council of Narbonne (1233/

1234), declaring that stones and cement for construction were in short supply, referred the problem to the pope, but Innocent IV in reply sharply reminded them of their duty and in 1249 reproved bishops for failing to provide necessary facilities for prisoners. Although fines for heresy were formally opposed by a provincial chapter of the Dominican order and abandoned by the council of Narbonne, the council of Béziers in 1246 reinstated them in the hope of obtaining funds to construct prisons and feed poor prisoners. Louis IX ordered his seneschal in 1246 to continue to put the royal dungeons at Carcassonne and Béziers at the inquisitors' disposal and to furnish bread and water for prisoners whose goods had fallen to the crown. He was still urging action in prison building in 1258. Ultimately, after the county of Toulouse had entered the royal domain, the costs for all prisons for heretics in Languedoc were assumed by the crown.

The lot of the prisoners was unenviable. Early conciliar legislation made food their own responsibility, unless they were too poor, in which case the bishop was supposed to furnish bread and water. Pope Gregory IX in 1231 had ordered, and the council of Béziers repeated the prescription, that solitary confinement be the rule; it was an edict probably impossible to carry out for lack of cells. In later years, the judges would make a distinction between harsh and easy conditions (*murus strictus, murus largus*), that is, between confinement in chains as opposed to a little freedom of movement with visiting privileges, but this did not prevail in the early decades.

Sentences of death or imprisonment carried the additional penalty of confiscation of property by the civil power, as did relapse into heresy after abjuring it, even if no other penance than wearing crosses with double transverse arms was then imposed. Neither the king's officials nor Raymond VII nor those prelates who had been granted rights of confiscation in lands of which they were overlords hesitated to take advantage of this. Innumerable problems arose when confiscations did not respect the dower rights of an innocent wife, interfered with feudal obligations or with mortgages held by orthodox persons, or when they were made illegally by over-zealous officials. Suits for justice in such cases would occupy comital and royal courts for decades to come. Both count and king sold or gave away confiscated property. They also entertained pleas for restoration to former owners or their heirs. A notable example of this occurred in 1279, when King Philip III gave up his rights to what had been confiscated for heresy or other crimes in Toulouse between 1229 and 1270.

At least two hundred and seventy-eight inhabitants of Toulouse who had thus been punished appear in the document, including many we know to have been condemned between 1229 and 1250.

The inquisitors could also impose a variety of less severe penances, as we have already seen. One was pilgrimage to one or more holy places, during which the penitents might be required to wear crosses on their garments and had to obtain from clerics of places they visited letters attesting that they had completed the journey. The easiest such requirement would be to visit churches or chapels in the area where the guilty acts had been committed, there on Sundays and feast days to be scourged. Travel to distant shrines, especially if more than one pilgrimage was imposed, could amount to exile for months or years, leaving one's family to the mercy of circumstances. Taking the cross for crusade as penance for heresy came into question. It had been favoured in 1229, but many persons had avoided compliance; the council of Narbonne withdrew it from the list of approved penances; that of Béziers restored it; and when Raymond VII was preparing to accompany Louis IX on crusade, commutations of imprisonment to allow men to go with them were encouraged by the pope.

Less taxing physically was the very common penance of wearing crosses of cloth on the clothing for a term of years or for life. The dimensions were stipulated – two palms in height and breadth at first, later somewhat larger – and the cloth was provided when the sentence was issued, but replacing worn out crosses was the duty of the penitent. A commutation from imprisonment to wearing crosses usually required that they be cut with double transverse arms as a sign of more serious crime. This was also the form used for perjurors. To cease to wear these badges of guilt without permission was regarded as relapse into heresy. What may seem to have been a simple burden was, in fact, universally detested, for the crosses exposed the wearer to contempt and maltreatment and there were complaints that they prevented men from finding employment.

Banishment was rarely decreed. Destruction of houses which heretics had frequented was required by law, but often avoided; houses in Toulouse which Cardinal Romanus had ordered destroyed in 1229 were still standing in 1236; and probably some of them entirely escaped demolition. Attempts were also made to prevent the guilty from wearing ostentatious dress or adornments. If heretics died before beginning their penance, their heirs were required to make satisfaction for their misdeeds by fines.

Not everyone who came to the inquisitors' attention suffered the penalty that law required. There are numerous references to those who took to flight before or during the trial; a relatively small number are known to have broken out of confinement after being sentenced. Lombardy had become a place of refuge during the Albigensian crusade and continued to harbour exiles thereafter. An exceptional person with money and friends might avoid imprisonment for a long time without leaving his homeland, as did Alaman, a member of the wealthy Roaix family of Toulouse, who had refused to make the pilgrimage to the Holy Land ordered by Cardinal Romanus in 1229, was excommunicated as a recalcitrant in 1237, yet remained free for another decade. Many persons also removed their crosses or concealed them under other garments. We know, of course, only of the considerable number who were detected.[9]

The surviving records for the first two decades of the Inquisition are too sparse to permit an accurate statement of how far its net was cast or how great a catch it made. Such estimates as can be made are owed largely to the careful analysis of documents pertaining to the years 1245 to 1257 by Yves Dossat. In the diocese of Toulouse in 1245–1246, Dossat estimates that there were 105 sentences to imprisonment and 840 to lesser penances; the number of verdicts that led to death at that time cannot be known. Records for the years 1249 to 1257, however, show the proportion of death sentences to other penalties as follows:

| | |
|---|---|
| Death | 21 |
| Relapsed | 5 |
| Fugitives | 30 |
| Posthumously condemned | 11 |
| Prison | 239 |
| | |
| Total | 306 |

The number of persons given crosses or pilgrimages is not recorded. Thus, of 306 severe sentences in eight years, not more than twenty-six; or 8·5 per cent (if we include the relapsed, who may have got off more lightly) led to execution. An earlier examination of prosecutions in a limited area around Montauban led to comparable estimates: of 800 persons cited there only six were sent to the stake and about twenty sentenced to prison for life.

On the basis of these and other calculations by Professor Dossat the following rough estimate of penalties for heresy in the middle years of the thirteenth century in southern France may be made: out of every hundred persons who received some punishment one was sent to death and ten or eleven to prison. In the case of the latter we must take account of shortening or commutation of sentences. And about one person in every four who came to the inquisitors' serious attention escaped by flight.[10]

Data derived from acts of inquisitors, however, give less than the full story, for they do not include the results of independent secular actions. In 1249 Raymond VII by his own authority had eighty persons burned. If we take into account the holocaust at Montségur we may calculate that in the decade after 1240 the secular power, on its own responsibility, killed more persons for heresy than were released to them by the Inquisition for execution.[11] Nor did lay actions cease to be harsh. In the 1250s officers of Count Alphonse of Toulouse burned a number of heretics whom the inquisitors had sentenced only to prison.

The Inquisition, then, was fully established and efficiently operating throughout the years after 1243. The tribunals rightly aroused dread, for the judges were zealous and their memories, aided by documents, were long. To have been interrogated and dismissed or to have completed one of the lighter penances gave no immunity from further summons if fresh evidence was discovered. The ideal, repeatedly expressed by popes and councils, was to avoid punishing the innocent, and inquisitors declared that they convicted no one except on sure evidence. The conclusion cannot be avoided, however, that stern and strong-minded men sometimes felt that necessity overrode principle, and that expedients adopted in the aftermath of war and amidst imminent dangers of conspiracy became established procedure. On the other hand, implacable as they seem to modern eyes, the inquisitors did act in a scrupulously legal manner, as they saw legality in those early years, did use discretion in fitting penance to the offence, and were not without conscience. There are no documents, other than the dry phrases of the manual of procedure of 1248/ 1249, to reveal their reflections on their duties, and it is, perhaps, unwarranted to carry back to the middle of the thirteenth century evidence from seventy years later, yet the words of Bernard Gui, written not long before 1323, illustrate the problem which an inquisitor had to resolve in his own mind:

For it is exceedingly difficult to catch heretics when they themselves do not avow error but conceal it, or when sure and sufficient evidence against them is not at hand. Under such circumstances, serious problems beset the investigator from every side. For on the one hand, his conscience torments him if an individual be punished who has neither confessed nor been proven guilty; on the other, it causes even more anguish to the mind of the inquisitor, familiar through much experience with the falsity, cunning, and malice of such persons, if by their wily astuteness they escape punishment to the detriment of the faith, since thereby they are strengthened, multiplied, and rendered more crafty.[12]

After 1243 there was little to restrain the inquisitor's pursuits. Raymond VII had ceased to protest their activities, the citizens of Toulouse no longer dared to do so, and, for the time being, the bishops had only a nominal role in operations of the tribunal. The zeal of the friars was tempered by their respect for legality, but their pride in office was also great. There are hints that it drew criticism even from their friends. As mentioned earlier, Innocent IV criticized the inquisitors for travelling with too numerous a retinue. Superiors in the order could not interfere with the work of the inquisitors, who, although they were named to the office by provincial priors, drew their powers directly from the pope. There could be, however, attempts to regulate their conduct as friars. In 1242 and 1245 provincial chapters at Montpellier and Avignon instructed inquisitors to attend chapter meetings as regularly as possible. They were forbidden to ride horses except in emergencies or in places known to be dangerous. They were to avoid personal participation in captures, imprisonment, or executions. They should avoid imposing fines or acting in any way that might make it seem that the order profited from their work. On the other hand, their colleagues were warned to give little credence to malicious stories that were circulated about them. One may fairly conclude that the inquisitors were subject to the temptations of power. Eventually their pride and dedication conflicted with the determination of Innocent IV to maintain papal authority to produce a tense situation.

## Crisis and Continuity in the Inquisition
It was probably at the inquisitors' instigation that a group of southern bishops and abbots in 1245 urged the pope to be less charitable to persons who, in fear of prosecution or even after conviction, came to the papal court and received more lenient treatment than they deserved. A similar issue resulted in a direct clash of wills in 1246, when more than 150 inhabitants of Limoux were allowed by the pope to put off the crosses to which they had been sentenced in favour of lighter penances. In vexation

the inquisitors annulled their verdicts entirely and dismissed the petitioners scot free. Innocent IV presently yielded and withdrew his instructions, but the friars did nothing in response and it was left to the archbishop of Narbonne in 1249 to inform the inhabitants of Limoux that they must resume the crosses they had thrown away.

That intransigence did not deter the pope from exercising his authority in other cases. In 1248 he charged an old acquaintance, William II, bishop of Agen with general oversight of inquisitorial procedures. What followed must have been galling to the judges, for the bishop was encouraged to commute sentences of imprisonment to participation in the crusade on which Louis IX was embarked. In January 1249 the archbishop of Narbonne was instructed to remove the crosses to which six persons in Foix had been sentenced. The papal penitentiary also dealt with the case of a knight of Narbonne without reference to the inquisitors and ordered the release of seven prisoners at Toulouse.

Such infringement on their authority in the matter of sentences, coupled, no doubt, with the shock of the murder of their assistants and the theft of registers at Caunes in 1247, seem to have discouraged the inquisitors at Carcassonne, William Raymond and Peter Durand. In 1248 they withdrew from their office. Bernard of Caux and John of St Pierre transferred from Toulouse to Carcassonne for a time, but they too apparently found papal and episcopal supervision difficult to endure and in 1249 they also retired. Bernard of Caux busied himself with the establishment of a Dominican house at Agen until his death in 1252.

Prosecutions did not cease. The bishop of Carcassonne assumed responsibility for trials in his diocese early in 1250, utilizing existing records and attempting to reconstitute the registers stolen at Caunes. Officials of the bishops of Toulouse, Rodez, and Cahors, and the archbishop of Narbonne also moved into the seats of the inquisitors in their dioceses. The episcopal inquisition for which Raymond VII had pleaded long before became a reality in the year after his death.

The bishops soon tired of their unpopular and onerous duties. The new count of Toulouse had no wish to see prosecutions wane or confiscations decline. And Innocent IV cannot be accused of desiring to see heresy revive for want of diligence against it.

The pope, therefore, soon requested the friars in Languedoc to resume their function; when there was no response, he appealed to the Dominican prior at Paris to appoint new judges. That, too, went unanswered. In 1254 the pope proposed to the Franciscans that they take up the task of extirpating heresy in the county of Toulouse. Before a decision had been reached, he died.

The accession of Alexander IV (1254–1261) ended the stalemate on the inquisitors' terms. Judges for Toulouse were appointed by the prior of the Dominican convent of Paris early in 1255; their powers were gradually extended to Quercy, Albi, and the Rouergue, and after 1258 they were joined by friars assigned to other places in the kingdom of France. The Dominicans returned triumphant, for they now had authority to work without significant interference from superiors in their order or bishops or even from papal legates. When, in 1256, Alexander IV granted them power to absolve each other from canonical irregularities occurring in the performance of duty, their independence was almost complete. Henceforth, inquisitors constituted something of a caste within their order, although the consultations and manuals of procedure that were written emphasized regularity of procedure and careful definitions, showing the desire of legists to make inquisitorial actions conform to established legal principles.[13]

### The Waning of Heresy in Languedoc

Great inroads had been made on the numbers of the Good Men before 1249. A well-informed Italian inquisitor, Rainier Sacconi, estimated that in 1250 there were fewer than 200 perfected Cathars left in the churches of Toulouse, Albi, Carcassonne, and 'the almost totally destroyed church of Agen'. Many heretics and believers had fled to Lombardy, where for some years a church of 'French' (*francigene*) Cathars existed. Messengers maintained contact between the exiles and the dwindling number of believers in Languedoc, who mourned to each other that the sweetness had gone out of the land with the passing of the Good Men. Waldenses, too, were far less active, although they maintained themselves in Burgundy and in the Alpine foothills beyond the Rhône.

Although relentless pressures drove heretics and adherents to furtive and secret existence, the inquisitors would not admit that the danger from heresy had passed. Spies infiltrated groups of exiles in Lombardy and the Pyrenees, occasionally luring one of them to a place where he could be arrested. Prosecutors raked over the records of earlier inquests and called in persons who had been interrogated years before, or opened posthumous investigations. A case was heard in 1263 against Count Raymond of Foix, dead since 1241; Arnold, viscount of Castelbon, was condemned as a heretic four decades after his death. The inquisitors found evidence for their fears that heretical disaffection was still rife in the protests against their conduct that went to the king of France from Carcassonne between 1280 and 1285, and again after 1291, and in a more serious crisis involving Albi and Carcassonne after 1299, which was acerbated by the resolute attacks on the Inquisition by Bernard Délicieux, a Franciscan. The inquisitors dealt with these 'heretical plots' vigorously; with the help of the bishop the prosecution was especially ruthless in the case of Albi. Undeniably, among the challengers of the Inquisition were members of families with a tradition of attachment to heresy; there were even a few professed Cathars, but it is also evident that alarm over the unrestrained power of the tribunal and its interference with political and economic interests was as much at the root of the plots and protests as was attachment to the old faith.

Documents from the first quarter of the fourteenth century preserve the names of fewer than a score of Good Men in Languedoc. None were bishops; an organized Cathar church had disappeared. There was a brief localized revival of Catharism in the county of Foix, fostered primarily by the labours of Peter Autier, who returned from Italian exile in 1295 to strive with the help of his brother and nephew to keep the dying faith alive. Nine-tenths of those to whom they preached were peasants or artisans. Side by side with dwindling, sometimes perverted, expressions of Cathar or Waldensian dogma were now appearing criticisms of orthodox doctrines on rationalist or materialistic grounds.

The inquisitors pursued the participants in that feeble revival with all vigour, yet their searches were much less fruitful than in former times. Peter Autier was burned in 1310; between 1300 and 1330 some 650 persons were accused of heresy and apprehended, while 300 or 400 more were incriminated but not brought to trial. For comparison we may note that in 1241–1242 Peter Seila alone had given penance to more than 700 persons and more than 5,000 had been questioned in the big inquests of 1245–1246.

After the middle of the fourteenth century the heresies of Waldenses and Cathars were little more than memories in Languedoc. Now and then doctrines which were bizarre reminiscences would be espoused by individuals and small groups. The waning of the great sects did not mean the end of heresy. Indeed, as long as the conviction that unity of faith was vital to the health of society, profound criticism and dissent had no logical end but heresy. Moreover, fundamental religious impulses, especially those toward moral regeneration through voluntary poverty, could not disappear quickly from a society in which spiritual values had paramount place. They showed their vitality in the fourteenth century in sects such as the Apostolics in Italy, the Brethren of the Free Spirit in northern Europe, and the dissident faction in the Franciscan order who were called the Spirituals. But the focal points of dissent, apart from some lay followers of the Spiritual Franciscans, were no longer in Languedoc. Mystics, prophets, visionaries, and the heretical sects of the very late Middle Ages awakened little response in southern France.

Why did the big thirteenth century heretical sects disappear? An element of internal fragility may be suggested for Catharism which, after about 1224 ceased to develop an intellectual content that could rival the appeal of Catholic theology as preached by the mendicants. There is, indeed, evidence that Catharism absorbed folk beliefs and superstitions which, however attractive to countrymen, failed of reception among the literate element or intellectuals. Internal doctrinal conflict, such as was evident in Italy, might have sharpened wits, but it was lacking.

Two other factors deserve greater credit for the victory of orthodoxy over the Cathars and the lesser but real success in curbing the Waldenses. One was the steady pressure from the Inquisition which had the central role in prosecutions, with two interruptions, after 1234. Yet it must be noted that to the same end worked the policies of the Capetians, while the division of the large diocese of Toulouse into an archbishopric with seven suffragans made ecclesiastical discipline easier. Equally important with prosecution must be judged the erosion of a social base. The disastrous consequences of revolt in 1240 and 1242 on the nobility, especially in rural areas, deprived the Cathars of important protectors. Transfer of comital authority to Alphonse of Poitiers weakened the ability and will of important urban groups to risk the penalties for supporting heresy. Descendants of both groups put their efforts into salvaging what property was left.

Yet defeat of the heresies was not an unqualified triumph for the church, for in part the victory was bought at the cost of centralizing authority, loss of flexibility, unwillingness to absorb innovative movements but willingness to resort to force against dissent. Even as the heresies of the high Middle Ages waned, the popes were challenged anew by monarchs, schism scandalized the faithful, nascent nationalism disrupted administration. Internal energy for religious reform fell off, and clearly the formal services of the church became no more satisfying as a medium of genuine religious expression. On the one hand, mysticism or a lay piety that was fundamentally orthodox, on the other hand indifference were the result. In northern Europe the paths that would lead to the great religious revolt of the sixteenth century were already being marked out.[15] Yet until the upsurge of Protestantism, Languedoc was to know no religious unrest to compare with the swirling movements of dissent of the twelfth and thirteenth centuries.

# References

1. On Peter Seila's work, see Albe, 'L Hérésie albigeoise et l'Inquisition en Quercy', *RHEgF*, V (1910), 280–91. The plot to rescue the two heretics is described in Toulouse, Bibliothèque municipale MS 609, fols. 31v–40v, *passim*.
2. Montségur has become a source of legend and a shrine for present-day groups who cherish its memory as a symbol of southern independence – for which it scarcely qualifies – but more as a sacred place of the Cathars. Annual commemorative services are held by 'neo-Cathars' who revere the Good Men as exponents of a pure Christianity animated by the spirit of the Gospel of John and as exponents of spirituality in the Manichaean and Gnostic tradition. Novelists and dramatists have written of the esoteric qualities of the Cathars, for whom, it is said, Montségur was a temple as well as a refuge, and have mourned the loss the world suffered from its passing. By a romantic alchemy, the treasure which was smuggled from Montségur in 1244 has become the Holy Grail. Between these modern partisans of the Cathars and historians whose emotions are not thus engaged or who fail to find documentary evidence for such interpretations a little war of words occasionally breaks out.
3. A recent sketch of the massacre at Avignonet is Y. Dossat, 'Le Massacre d'Avignonet', *CFan*, VI, 343–59. Montségur, as indicated in the preceding note, inspires various sentiments. A close student of the records and the site is Fernand Niel, whose *Montségur, temple et fortresse des Cathares d'Occitanie* is the most recent of several works he has devoted to the subject. Niel's thesis that the stronghold was also a temple deliberately designed for religious rites connected with some kind of veneration of the sun has drawn sharp criticism, as in J. Ferlus, *Autour de Montségur: de l'histoire ou des histoires*, and in articles in *Archeologia*, XIX (1967), esp. 19, 22–3. See also A. Moulis, *Montségur et le drame cathare*. It is Niel's thesis also that Raymond VII encouraged the defenders to hold out while he negotiated on their behalf with the pope. But the count had been actively pursuing and punishing heretics since 1243 (Dossat, *Les Crises de l'Inquisition toulousaine*, 212–13, 274–5). Why should he wish to help those at Montségur? My own examination of the career of one alleged go-between, Raymond of Niort (see 'The Family of Niort', *Names*, XVIII [1970], 291–2), and of the interrogations of survivors in Collection Doat, Vols. XXII and XXIV, convince me that the evidence does not support Niel's suggestion. The study by Dossat referred to in the

text is 'Le Bûcher de Montségur et les bûchers de l'Inquisition', *CFan*, VI, 361–78.

4. To glance briefly at the contemporary Inquisition in other areas: Robert the Bulgar continued his extravagant and fiery career in northern France – he had 180 persons burned in one holocaust in May 1239 – until at least 1241, but was finally halted and deposed. Thereafter, there were Dominican inquisitors in the kingdom of France, under the oversight of the prior of the order at Paris. Their operations were less noteworthy, or are less well-documented, than those of their southern colleagues. The Inquisition in Dominican hands did not exist in German lands at the middle of the century, although a variety of heresies were prosecuted by bishops. In Aragon King Jaime I encouraged the episcopal pursuit of heretics, and an Inquisition staffed by friars took shape after 1237, modelled on the tribunals of Languedoc, but never acting on a comparable scale. Crown and bishops co-operated against heresy in Castile, without the assistance of the friars. In northern Italy, where Cathars, Waldenses, and other sects were established, papal-imperial rivalries and the turbulence of city politics were considerable obstacles to consistent prosecution. Dominicans, of whom Roland of Cremona was one, combined preaching and inquisition in the decade after 1230; by the 1240s tribunals had been set up in various Lombard towns, although their permanence was not assured for another decade. Even then unsettled political conditions made their task difficult, and the victory of orthodoxy over Italian Cathars was by no means sure until the end of the century, while new but less numerous sects arose to draw the attention of the judges.

5. The rule originally enunciated by Innocent III in 1199, was that no advocate or notary could assist a known heretic. In strict law, counsel could be had by one whose guilt was not yet proved, but it would be a brave advocate who would risk the charge of defending heresy, and in the records of the thirteenth century no instance is found of counsel for the defence before the Inquisition. The council of Valence in 1248, entirely forbade the participation of lawyers, lest their argumentativeness retard the proceedings (Mansi, *Concilia*, XXIII, 773). W. Ullman, 'The Defence of the Accused in the Medieval Inquisition', *Irish Ecclesiastical Record*, 5th ser., LXXIII (1950), 481–9, makes the best case for the inquisitors' protecting rights of the accused, but on the basis of canonists' commentary, not the actual practice.

6. In manuals written for their colleagues by inquisitors of the later thirteenth century, there were sometimes warnings of the wiliness and evasiveness of the accused. Modern historians, on the other hand, have found the tactics of the questioners repugnant. Lea, for example, in his *History of the Inquisition*, (I, 410–16), writes of the ruthlessness of the inquisitors, the sophistication of their interrogations, and their willingness to use any method to make a witness say what they wished to hear. His work is based on the sources, but those of a period rather later than ours, when the Inquisition had become much more experienced. The questioning may have been equally resourceful and insistent before 1250, but, apart from the allegations made against Ferrier (see p. 151, n.10 above), we do not have evidence of that in the documents. We do know, moreover, of a considerable number of persons who managed on first appearance to escape with light penance, although their offences, it was later discovered, were serious and they concealed the truth when first questioned.

7. Innocent IV authorized use of torture by secular officers in Italy in 1252 to obtain confessions, but forbade inquisitors to have any part therein. Four

years later, Alexander IV, by allowing inquisitors to absolve each other for 'irregularities', made it possible for them to send prisoners to the question or even be present during torture.

8. The preceding paragraphs draw heavily on Dossat, *Les Crises de l'Inquisition toulousaine*, 152–72, 206–46. Space forbids citing older studies, for which the reader is referred to the Bibliography (Ch. 8). The advice of Peter of Collomieu on procedure is printed in Dossat, *op. cit.*, 348–9; similar 'consultations' are found in F. Valls Tabernier, 'El diplomatari de Sant Ramon de Penyafort', *Annuari de la Biblioteca Balmes*, V (1929), 254–61; and in Mansi, *Concilia*, XXIII, 356–66, 715–24. The manual of procedure of 1248–1249 is translated in Appendix VI below. On all these and inquisitorial manuals of later date see A. Dondaine, 'Le Manuel de l'inquisiteur (1230–1330)', *AFP*, XVII (1947), 85–194. I have also consulted documents of the period before 1250: in manuscript the Collection Doat of the Bibliothèque nationale, Vols. XXI–XXIV (interrogations and sentences); and MS 609 of the Bibliothèque municipale of Toulouse (interrogations); in print, C. Douais, *Documents pour servir à l'histoire de l'Inquisition*, II, 1–114; and P. Cayla, 'Fragment d'un registre inédit de l'Inquisition', *Mémoires de la Société des arts et sciences de Carcassonne*, 3rd ser., VI (1941–1943), 382–9.

9. On the respective responsibilities of church and state for the death penalty, consult the studies of the Inquisition listed in the Bibliography (Ch. 8), especially those of DeCauzons and Tanon. The sketch of a heretic at the stake is in *Layettes du trésor des chartes*, III, 215. On prisons at Carcassonne and Toulouse, see Poux, *La Cité de Carcassonne*, II, 156–60, which corrects in some details Molinier, *L'Inquisition dans le Midi de France*, 435–8; Dossat, *Les Crises de l'Inquisition toulousaine*, 161, 167, 194–5, 262; and the same author's 'Une Figure d'un inquisiteur' in *CFan*, VI, 259, 267–8, which follows and corrects C. E. Smith, *The University of Toulouse*, 67–8. On escapes see Wakefield, 'Friar Ferrier', *CHR*, LVIII, 220, n. 2. The rules on solitary confinement are in Auvray, *Les Registres de Grégoire IX*, Vol. I, No. 562, and Mansi, *Concilia*, XXIII, 720. On confiscation and disposition of property, see P. Timbal, 'La Confiscation dans le droit français', *Revue de droit français et étranger*, 4th ser., XXII (1943), 44–79; XXIII (1944), 35–60; Dossat, *Les Crises de l'Inquisition toulousaine*, 297–320; and the numerous cases in A. Molinier, *Correspondance administratif d'Alphonse de Poitiers*; also, n. 107 to Appendix III, below. The case of Alaman of Roaix is treated in Appendix IV.

10. These figures may be compared with the more precise data from the sentences of Bernard Gui, inquisitor at Carcassonne from 1308 to 1323:

| | |
|---|---|
| Death | 42 (3 others to be executed if captured) |
| Fugitives | 40 |
| Posthumously condemned | 69 |
| Prison | 307 (17 more would have been imprisoned if alive) |
| Crosses | 143 |
| Pilgrimages | 9 |

In the total of 930 sentences in this register there are also 271 reductions of penances from imprisonment to wearing crosses, or release from crosses. There are also a number of miscellaneous penalties: pillory, degradation of clerics, exile, and destruction of houses: see Douais, *Documents*, I, 205, for the full tabulation.

N

11. But this statement should be balanced against the more than two hundred persons Robert the Bulgar sent to the stake in northern France between 1233 and 1239.

12. The quotation from Bernard Gui is found in his *Practica inquisitionis*, translated in Wakefield and Evans, *Heresies*, 377. As indicated in the text, Dossat, *Les Crises de l'Inquisition toulousaine*, 246–68, is the fundamental study of penalties as actually applied. The figures for the Montauban area are given in C. Daux, *L'Inquisition albigeois dans le Montalbanais*, 9. On Raymond's execution of heretics in 1249, see p. 165, above; on unauthorized burnings under Alphonse of Poitiers, Douais, *Documents*, I, 157. Expenses of the inquisitors are not discussed here because of lack of documents dated before 1250. Some accounts for the years 1255–1256 are analyzed in E. Cabié, 'Comptes des inquisiteurs des diocèses de Toulouse, d'Albi, et de Cahors', *Revue . . . du Tarn*, XXII (1905), 215–29; and in Dossat; *Les Crises de l'Inquisition toulousaine*, 90–101. In 1269 Alphonse de Poitiers suggested that the inquisitors of Toulouse might reduce the heavy expenses of which they complained by transferring their seat to Lavaur: Molinier, *Correspondence administratif d'Alphonse de Poitiers*, I, 610.

13. On attempts to regulate the inquisitors' conduct, see C. Douais, *Acta capitulorum provincialium ordinis fratrum praedicatorum*, 22–3, 27. Development and resolution of the crisis of 1249–1256 is traced in Dossat, *Les Crises de l'Inquisition toulousaine*, 175–88; and in the same author's 'Une Figure d'inquisiteur: Bernard de Caux', *CFan*, VI, 262–8. On legal aspects of the Inquisition in the later thirteenth century, see P. Ourliac, 'La Société languedocienne au XIIIe siècle et le droit romain', *CFan*, VI, 209–13.

14. The waning of heresy in Languedoc is discussed in Guiraud, *Histoire de l'Inquisition*, Vol. II, Chs 9–13, where more vigour is ascribed to the sects than I believe they still had. On migration to Italy, see E. Dupré-Theseider, 'Le Catharisme languedocien et l'Italie', *CFan*, III, 299–313. Plots and prosecutions of the later thirteenth century are also discussed in J. L. Biget, 'Un Procès d'Inquisition à Albi en 1300', *CFan*, VI, 273–341. The revival under Peter Autier is the subject of articles by J. M. Vidal: 'Les derniers ministres de l'albigéisme en Languedoc'; and 'Doctrine et morale des derniers ministres albigeois', *RQH*, LXXIX (1906), 57–107; LXXXV (1909), 357–409; LXXXVI (1909), 5–48, respectively. J. Duvernoy has edited *Le Registre de l'Inquisition de Jacques Fournier, évêque de Pamiers*, which was compiled at that time. An inquisitor's view of heresies in the early fourteenth century is translated from Bernard Gui's *Practica* in Wakefield and Evans, *Heresies*, 375–445. One sect not mentioned by Bernard Gui is studied in R. Lerner, *The Heresy of the Free Spirit in the Later Middle Ages*. On all movements after 1250 one may consult G. Leff, *Heresy in the Later Middle Ages*.

15. A causative link, as opposed to mere similarity of characteristics, between the medieval sects and major movements of the sixteenth century reformation has not been established. See comments on the question in Nelli, *Spiritualité de l'hérésie*, 207–24; C. P. Clasen, 'Medieval Heresies in the Reformation', *Church History*, XXXII (1963), 392–414; and D. Walther, 'Were the Albigenses and Waldenses Forerunners of the Reformation?', *Andrews Theological Seminary Studies*, VI (1968), 178–202.

# Appendix 1

# A Northern View of Heretics and the Crusade

The attitude of northern Europeans toward the Albigensian crusade and the stories that were told of the heretics are illustrated by the following excerpt from the work of a contemporary Cistercian monk in Germany. Caesarius of Heisterbach (*ca.* 1180–1240) wrote a *Dialogue on Miracles* for the instruction of novices in his monastery not far from Bonn, filling his book with tales of all sorts to point up the edifying conclusions he wished to impart. The date of writing of this passage can be placed after 1220 and before 1228, probably in 1220–1223, by the references to Conrad, cardinal-bishop of Porto, who was appointed as papal legate late in 1219, and to Honorius III, who died in 1227.

The translation is from Caesarius of Heisterbach, *Dialogus miraculorum*, V, xxi, ed. by Joseph Strange (2 vols, Cologne, 1851), I, 300–3. There is also an English translation of the whole work by Henry von Essen Scott and C. C. Swinton Bland, *The Dialogue on Miracles* (2 vols, London, 1929).

*Monk*: In the days of Pope Innocent [III], the predecessor of Honorius [III] who now holds the papacy, while the quarrel was still going on between the kings of the Romans, Philip and Otto,[1] by the devil's ill-will the heresy of the Albigenses began to sprout or, to speak more accurately, to mature. Such was its potency that all the grain of faith of that people seemed to change into the weed of error. Abbots of our order, together with some bishops, were sent to weed out the tares with the hoe of Catholic preaching, but man's enemy, who had sown the weeds resisted, and they accomplished little there.

*Novice*: What was the error of these persons?

*Monk*: Some of their heresiarchs selected tenets from the teaching of Manes, others chose from among the errors which Origen is said to have written in the *Peri archon*,[2] and they also added a great many which they contrived in their own hearts. With Manes, they believed in two principles, a good God and an evil one, the latter the devil, who, they say, created all bodies, just as the good God created all souls.

*Novice*: Moses proves that God created bodies and souls by saying, 'And God formed man,' that is, the body, 'of the slime of the earth and breathed into his face the breath of life,'[3] which is the soul.

*Monk*: If they would accept Moses and the prophets, they would not be heretics. They deny the resurrection of bodies; they scoff at anything that may be done by the living for the benefit of the dead; they say that it is of no use to go to church or to pray in church. In so doing, they are worse than Jews or pagans, who believe in these things. They have cast aside baptism; they blaspheme the sacrament of the body and blood of Christ.

*Novice*: How can they endure so much persecution by the faithful if they do not anticipate recompense in future life?

*Monk*: They say that they look to a glory of the spirit. A certain monk among the aforesaid abbots noticed a knight on horseback talking with his plowman and guessing that he was a heretic, as he was, went up to him to ask, 'Tell me, good sir, whose is this field?' When the other replied, 'It is mine'; he went on 'What do you do with the yield?' The man answered: 'I and my family live from it; also I give some to the poor.' Then the monk, 'What good do you hope for from this charity?' And the knight answered with these words, 'That my spirit may pass on in glory after death.' The monk, 'Pass on where?' The knight said: 'That depends on its merit. If it lives rightly and is deserving in the eyes of God, when it leaves my body it will enter the body of some future prince or king or that of some other great man, where it may take delight. If, however, it lives wickedly, it will enter the body of someone wretched and poor, in which it will be oppressed.' The stupid man and other Albigenses believed that the soul, according to its merit, will pass through various bodies, even those of serpents and animals.

*Novice*: What a filthy heresy!

*Monk*: The error of the Albigenses waxed so strongly that in a short space of time it had infected as many as a thousand cities, and, if it had not been reduced by the swords of the faithful, I am sure that it would have corrupted all Europe. In the year of our Lord 1210,[4] the crusade against the Albigenses was preached throughout Germany and France, and in the following year there assembled against them from Germany Leopold, duke of Austria; Englebert, then provost and later archbishop of Köln; with his brother, Adolph, count of Altenberg; William, count of Jülich;

and many others of various rank and status. The same occurred in France, Normandy, and Poitou. The preacher and leader of all these was Abbot Arnold of Cîteaux, later archbishop of Narbonne.

When they reached the great city of Béziers, in which more than a hundred thousand people were said to live, they besieged it. Before their eyes, the heretics befouled a copy of the Holy Gospel, threw it from the wall toward the Christians, and shot arrows after it as they shouted, 'Here is your Law, you wretches!' But Christ, the sower of the Gospel, did not leave unavenged the insult offered Him. For certain sergeants, aflame with zeal for the faith, like lions and in imitation of the ones of whom we read in Machabees,[5] set up ladders and bravely scaled the walls and, while the heretics were heaven-struck by terror, they opened the gates to the remainder and took the city. From the confessions of some of these people, they were aware that Catholics were intermingled with the heretics, so they asked the abbot: 'Lord, what shall we do? We cannot distinguish the good from the wicked.' The abbot, as well as others, was afraid that the heretics would pretend to be Catholics only in fear of death and after the Christians' departure would return to their perfidy. He is reported to have cried: 'Kill them! The Lord knows those who are his own.'[6] So untold numbers were slain in that city.

In the same way, by divine power, they won another great city which is located near Toulouse and called 'Beautiful Valley' from its location.[7] When the people therein were questioned and all others had declared their wish to return to the faith, 450 remained who were hardened in their obstinacy by the devil. Of them, 400 were consumed by fire, the others hanged from a scaffold. The same was done in other cities and strongholds, the wretches of their own accord presenting themselves for death. Now, the Toulousans, under coercion, promised every reparation, but deceitfully, as was revealed later. For, after the prince and chief of all the heretics, the treacherous count of St Gilles,[8] gave up all his possessions at the Lateran Council, to wit, his fiefs, allods, cities, and castles, the greater part of which had by right of war been occupied by the Catholic man, Simon of Montfort, he himself proceeded to Toulouse, from which, to this day, he does not cease to harass and attack the faithful.

Thus, in this very year, Conrad, cardinal-bishop of Porto, a legate sent against the Albigenses,[9] wrote to the chapter at Cîteaux that one of the more important citizens of Toulouse did something in hatred of Christ and to the shame of the faith so dreadful that it ought to trouble even those enemies of Christ. He befouled the altar of the cathedral and took the altar cloth to cleanse himself. Others piled madness on madness, for they led a prostitute to the holy altar and used her there in front of the crucifix. Afterward, they tore down the holy image itself and broke off its arms, behaving worse than Herod's soldiers, who spared the dead Christ and would not break His legs.

*Novice*: Who is not astonished at the great patience of God?

*Monk*: He is long suffering and 'a patient rewarder'.[10] He, who so terribly punished in neck and throat the people of Damietta after their victory, because they dragged a crucifix through the streets by a rope tied about its neck,[11] will not, I am sure, overlook these blasphemies.

Before the army of the Lord came against them, as I related above, the Albigenses besought El-Moulmenin, king of Morocco, to aid them. He came into Spain from Africa with an army of such incredible size that he might hope to win all Europe for himself. He even warned Pope Innocent that he would stable his horses in the portico of St Peter's and mount his standard above it. This was fulfilled in part, although differently from what he had planned. For, since God humbles all pride, at that time, which was the year of Grace 1212, on 16 July, 40,000 of the warriors of his army were slain. He himself went to Seville and died of grief. His chief standard, captured in the battle, was sent to Innocent and erected on the aforesaid cathedral to the glory of Christ.[12] We have finished with the Albigenses.

*Novice*: If there had been learned men among them, perhaps they would not have erred so much.

*Monk*: When learned men begin to err, by the devil's inspiration they act more foolishly and do worse than the ignorant.

# References

1. That is, the civil war in Germany after the death of Henry VI in 1197, between Otto of Brunswick and Philip of Swabia.
2. The *Peri archon* [first principles] of Origen (*ca.* 185–254) was a work of theological speculation now preserved in Latin under the title *De principiis*. It was held to contain various errors, among them, the assertion of the pre-existence of souls and metempsychosis.
3. Gen. 2:7.
4. Caesarius confuses the date, no doubt because 1210 was when Arnold Aimery and Bishop Fulk were sent north to recruit reinforcements in a time of need for Simon of Montfort, and the crusade was first preached intensively in Germany.

5. II Macc. 11:11: 'And rushing violently upon the enemy like lions ...'

6. Cf. II Tim. 11:19. This is probably the best-known anecdote of the crusade. It has often been called apocryphal (cf. Tamizey de Larroque, 'Une Épisode de la croisade des albigeois', *RQH*, I [1866], 168–91), but there is an echo of it in the *Annales sancti Albini Andegavensis* (L. Halphen [ed.], in *Recueil des annales angevines et vendômoises*, 24), which states that when the crusaders captured Carcassonne and other places, they slaughtered many Catholics as well as heretics, because they could not tell them apart (*quos non potuerunt discernere*).

7. *Pulchramvallam*. It seems likely, because of the fate of the defeated which Caesarius describes, that the reference is to the fortress of Lavaur (see Appendix 2).

8. Raymond VI, whose ancestors had been counts of Saint Gilles.

9. Conrad was appointed legate late in 1219 and reached Languedoc in 1220. He left in 1223. It was he who was responsible for a widely circulated report that a certain Bartholomew, a native of Carcassonne and a heretic at that time active in Agen and the region around Toulouse, was an emissary of a heretical pope in the Balkans; see Thouzellier, *Un Traité cathare inédit*, 30–2, for discussion of Conrad's letter.

10. Ecclus. 5:4.

11. Caesarius is referring to a plague in Damietta which he described elsewhere (VIII. xxvii [II, 102–3]).

12. Caesarius' version of this historical episode is thoroughly garbled. The Almohads under Emperor Abd al-Mu'min had established a Berber confederation in Morocco by 1147, with its centre at Marrakesh. Under his successors, they invaded Spain, conquering the Almoravids and expanding territory under Moslem control. It was Mohammed III (Mohammed al-Nasir, 1199–1213) who was defeated at Las Navas de Tolosa in 1212. His standard was, indeed, displayed by the victors, but over the cathedral in Toledo. There was no connection between the war of Christians against Moslems in Spain and the Albigensian crusade except the participation in both of Pedro II of Aragon and Abbot Arnold Aimery, who led knights from Languedoc to join the Christian army at Las Navas de Tolosa.

# Appendix 2

## The Capture of Lavaur

A successful siege, with ruthless action following the victory, occurred in 1211 when Simon of Montfort attacked the fortified place of Lavaur. With the capture of Minerve and Termes in 1210 his fortunes had risen from their low point of the preceding winter. In January 1211 Pedro II of Aragon had accepted his homage for former Trencavel lands, while Count Raymond VI's interviews with Simon and the legates had led to excommunication of the count by a council at Montpellier on 6 February.[1] Having decided that it was time to carry the war against Toulouse Montfort needed to protect his rear by reducing some still obstinate strongholds. Cabaret was yielded to him without a fight. Lavaur, however, standing on the west bank of the Agout River, where the steep drop of the banks added to the strength of the defences, not only had a reputation as a refuge of heretics – it had been besieged in 1181 in the crusade led by Cardinal Henry[2] – but as a formidable and well-garrisoned fortress. For the attack in April–May, 1211, Simon of Montfort had at hand a recent influx of crusaders from France and Germany and could count on more to come. The story of the siege is told by the contemporary historians of the crusade, William of Tudela in his *Chanson de la croisade albigeoise*;[3] William of Puylaurens in his *Cronica*;[4] and the crusading monk, Peter of Les Vaux de Cernay, from whose *Hystoria albigensis* (Pascal Guébin and Ernest Lyon [eds.] [3 vols., Paris, 1926–1939], §§215–27 [I, 214–28], the following translation is made.[5]

215. *The siege of the castle called Lavaur*. Now that castle was very famous and very large, standing above the Agout River at a distance of five leagues from Toulouse. That traitor, Aimery, who was lord of Montréal,[6] was in the castle with many other knights, to the number of eighty, enemies of the cross who had occupied and fortified the castle against us. The lady of the castle, a widow named Geralda, was the worst of heretics and Aimery's sister.[7]

216. When our people came up to the castle they besieged it on only one side for our army was not enough to lay siege to it all around.[8] And so, after the passage of a few days while machines were being built, we began to attack the castle in the usual way, the enemy to defend it as well as they could. Indeed, there was in the castle a countless multitude of men, equipped with the best of arms; in fact, the defenders were nearly as numerous as the attackers. We should not fail to note that when we approached the castle the enemy sallied therefrom and captured one of our knights and, taking him inside, killed him at once. Moreover, although our people attacked at one point, they were split into two forces and stationed in such a way that if an emergency arose, one detachment could come to the other's help only at some risk.[9] But not long afterwards many noble men arrived from France, namely, the bishop of Lisieux, the bishop of Bayeux,[10] and also the count of Auxerre,[11] with a number of other pilgrims.[12] So they besieged the castle on another side and, furthermore, when a wooden bridge was built across the Agout River, our people crossed the stream to besiege the castle all around.

217. Now the count of Toulouse persecuted the church of God and the count [Simon of Montfort] as much as he could, but not openly, for provisions still reached our army from Toulouse. In the course of these events the count of Toulouse came to the army. The count of Auxerre and Robert of Courtenay, who were his blood relatives,[13] undertook to advise the count to come to his senses and to obey the commands of the church, but, since they had no success, the count of Toulouse parted from the count of Montfort in wrath. The men of Toulouse who were at the siege of Lavaur also quit the army.[14] In addition, the count of Toulouse forbade the citizens of Toulouse to carry further provisions to Lavaur. Here we must tell the story of a heinous and most wicked deed of the counts of Toulouse and Foix, an unheard of treachery.

218. *The count of Foix slays pilgrims.* While the conference on peace with the count of Toulouse and about the reformation of Holy Church was going on near Lavaur,[15] as we have described, a large number of pilgrims[16] came from Carcassonne toward the army. Those ministers of evil, practitioners of treachery, to wit, the count of Foix[17] and Roger Bernard, his son, and Gerald of Pépieux,[18] and many of the count of Toulouse's men, stationed themselves in ambush with a very large force of mercenaries in the castle called Montgey, near Puylaurens;[19] when the pilgrims

reached it, they fell on them and, since they were unarmed and unsuspecting of treachery, killed great numbers of them;[20] and, carrying off all the money of the slain to Toulouse, divided it among themselves. O the harsh betrayal! O the madness of the wicked! O the blessed troop of the slain! O precious in the sight of the Lord the death of his saints! . . .[21]

220. *The hypocrisy of the count of Toulouse.* We believe that we ought not to fail to note that the count of Toulouse, the enemy and the cruellest persecutor of Christ, solely out of hatred for the Christian religion secretly sent one of his seneschals and several knights to the castle of Lavaur[22] – there wherein lay the source and origin of every heresy – to defend it against us, although it did not belong to the count of Toulouse, but for many years had fought the Toulousans. Our count discovered the men there after the castle was taken and held them in prison in chains for a long time. What an unusual kind of treachery! He [Count Raymond] set his knights inside the castle to defend it; outside, as if he were lending us aid, he allowed provisions to be brought from Toulouse, for at the start of the siege of Lavaur, as we said earlier, provisions were carried to the army from Toulouse, but in modest amounts. Yet, although provisions came from Toulouse the count of Toulouse strictly prohibited the transport of machines.[23] Also, at the urging of their venerable bishop, Fulk, the citizens of Toulouse, to the number of about 5,000, came to our aid in this siege.[24] Even the bishop himself, going into exile for the Catholic faith, came there. Moreover, I do not think it superfluous to recount the manner of his leaving Toulouse. . . .[25]

224. While these events were occurring, our people constructed a machine commonly known as a 'cat'[26] and when it was built dragged it up to the castle moat.[27] Thereafter, with very great effort, they brought wood and branches, of which they made bundles to cast in and fill the ditch. But the enemy, being very crafty, dug a tunnel reaching almost out to our machine and, coming out through that passage by night, picked up and carried back into the castle the wood and branches which we had thrown in the ditch. Furthermore, some of them, moving up to the machine, tried secretly and deceitfully to seduce into desertion those who, under cover of the machine, ceaselessly worked with picks[28] to fill in the ditch. Besides this, one night the enemy, emerging from the castle through the tunnel, came up the ditch and hurled darts, fire, flax, fat, and other combustibles in an attempt to

burn the machine. But two German counts of the army were on guard at the machine that night; a clamour was at once raised for the army, it was called to arms, and the machine was saved. These German counts and the Teuton soldiers with them, realizing that they could not get at the enemy who were in the ditch, with great courage jumped into the ditch amidst many hazards and bravely attacked the enemy, threw them back to the castle, killing some of them and wounding many in the process.

225. Meanwhile our men began to be much disturbed and to despair of capture of the castle by any means, particularly since whatever we could throw into the ditch by day the enemy hauled out and carried into the castle by night. But, even while our people were worrying over this, some of them put their heads together with good effect to find an effective counteraction to the enemy's strategems, in that they had green wood and branches thrown at the entrance of the tunnel which the enemy used for sallying out. Thereafter they put small dry sticks, fire, fat, flax, and other inflammable material over the exit of the tunnel and then threw wood and green stalks and a great deal of vegetation on top. The smoke pouring from the fire at once so choked the tunnel that the enemy was no longer able to come through it because of the smoke, which, since it could not rise through the wood and green stalks heaped on top, filled the whole tunnel, as we have said. As they realized this, our men easily filled up the ditch in the usual way and, when it was filled, our knights and armed sergeants dragged the machine up to the wall with great exertion and set the sappers at the wall. Those in the castle threw fire, wood, fat, stones, and great sharply-pointed stakes down on the machine without a pause, but, because our people defended the machine bravely and miraculously, they were unable to set fire to it or to drive the sappers away from the wall.

226. While our men laboured to the utmost in the attack the bishops who were there, together with the venerable abbot of La Cour-Dieu of the Cistercian order[29] – who by the legates' command was acting in their stead with the army at the time – and all the clergy gathered in a group and with the utmost devotion sang, 'Veni, Creator Spiritus'.[30] At the sight and sound, the enemy, as God ordained, was thunderstruck and almost completely lost their ability to fight back; for, as they later confessed, the singers terrified them more than the warriors, those who chanted more than those who mounted the attack, those who prayed more

than the assailants. And when the wall was broken through our people pushed in and the enemy surrendered because they could resist no longer. God willing it and His mercy being with us the castle of Lavaur was captured on the feast day of the Invention of the Holy Cross.[31]

227. Aimery, he of whom we have already spoken, who was the lord of Montréal, and other knights to the number of eighty were immediately taken outside the castle. The noble count [Simon of Montfort] declared that all should be hanged from a gibbet, but when Aimery, who was more important than the others, was hanged, the gallows collapsed because through haste it had not been solidly planted in the ground. Realizing that there would be a considerable delay the count ordered the others killed. This the pilgrims undertook with the greatest eagerness and at once put them to death on the spot.[32] The lady of the castle, who was Aimery's sister and the worst of heretics, was thrown into a pit, and the count had her buried under stones.[33] Our pilgrims also burned innumerable heretics with great rejoicing.[34]

# References

1. See pp. 104–5 above.
2. See pp. 85–6 above.
3. In the following notes the edition of Martin-Chabot is cited by *laisses* [stanzas] and lines, with volume and page in parentheses. This episode appears in *laisses* 68–72 (I, 162–74).
4. Chs 16–18, 132–3 in the edition by Bessyier.
5. The citation is to numbered paragraphs with volume and page in parentheses. I am much indebted to the documentation provided by the editors for notes to this translation.
6. Aimery's mother was Blanche, the great lady of Laurac and a perfected Cathar, grandmother also of the fierce Niort brothers. Aimery had abandoned Montréal and made his peace with Simon of Montfort at the onset of the crusade in 1209, but soon thereafter he subverted the ecclesiastic to whose custody Simon entrusted Montréal and reoccupied the castle. (The traitorous cleric was dragged to death at the heels of a horse when Montfort later captured him.) Aimery then offered Montréal to Pedro II of Aragon, but the proposal fell through because of the king's demand for other castles as well. In 1210, therefore, Aimery again surrendered the stronghold to Simon of Montfort on the promise of compensation by grant of lands elsewhere. However, he re-entered the war against the crusaders not long afterward. His repeated defections account for his fate after capture.
7. Geralda was a widow whose husband's name is unknown.
8. The siege began about 1 April 1211. The first investment was on the western side.

9. The two camps were separated by a deep ravine.

10. They were Jordan of Lisieux (1201–1218) and Robert of Bayeux (1206–1231).

11. Peter II of Courtenay (1184–1218).

12. *Peregrini*, the usual word for those who took the cross.

13. Peter and Robert of Courtenay were grandchildren of Louis VI of France through his son, Peter. Raymond VI was grandson of Louis VI through his daughter, Constance.

14. But others took their places, as will be seen below. See also p. 105 above.

15. That was the conference at Montpellier, February 1211, mentioned in the introduction to this translation.

16. A northern chronicler, Alberic of Trois-Fontaines, set their number at 1,500, of whom, he says, about 1,000 were killed: *Monumenta Germaniae historica, Scriptores*, XXIII, 892. See also n. 20, below.

17. Raymond Roger of Foix (1188–1223). Peter of Les Vaux de Cernay elsewhere (§§197–209 [I, 199–208]) gives a long diatribe against him.

18. After briefly allying with Simon of Montfort, Gerald had turned against the crusaders and took a notable part in some campaigns. It was not he but a relative of the same name, who was arrested and imprisoned for heresy about 1238, but escaped from prison and was with Raymond Trencavel in the revolt of 1240. In French mopping-up operations in November of that year, Gerald of Pépieux was captured and hanged: Wakefield, 'Friar Ferrier', *CHR*, LVIII (1972), 227.

19. It is about six miles south-east of Puylaurens.

20. William of Puylaurens (*Cronica*, Ch. 17, p. 132) merely says that the crusaders were not on the alert. William of Tudela's account of the ambuscade is somewhat different (*Chanson*, 69–70 [I, 168–72]). There were, he says, some 5,000 German and Frisian crusaders, marching in armed column. Surprised, they fought hard in the wooded area along the road, but were cut down. Peasants and mercenaries finished off the wounded with stones and staves. One squire who escaped the slaughter carried news of the fight to Lavaur, from which a party rode in pursuit of the count of Foix and his troops, but in vain. Peter of Les Vaux de Cernay, in a later passage (§232 [I, 231]), relates a marvellous sign: As the army marched away from Lavaur after its capture, they beheld a hovering column of fire and on investigation found every body of the slain lying with arms outstretched in the form of a cross.

21. Omitted here is the tale of the slaughter of a cleric by Roger Bernard, son of the count of Foix.

22. According to a later report, the seneschal was Raymond of Ricaud who was related to the seigneurs of Lavaur.

23. That is, the stone-throwing artillery needed for a siege. William of Tudela (*Chanson*, 69, lines 9–12 [I, 162]) remarks that the purchase and transport of food to the army came at high cost and that the Toulousans banned the shipment of arms, lances, and shields to the besiegers.

24. Raymond VI tried to prevent these troops, recruited by Bishop Fulk among the White Confraternity in Toulouse, from leaving the town, in a dramatic gesture barring the gate with his own person, but they circumvented him: see William of Puylaurens, *Cronica* (Bessqier ed.), Ch. 17, p. 133.

25. Paragraphs omitted here describe Fulk's quarrel with Count Raymond and his expulsion from the city (see p. 105, above). Also omitted is the incident of destruction of a cross erected by the besiegers.

26. A tower armoured with hides to protect troops against missiles from the walls. See also the use of a cat at Toulouse, pp. 120–1, above.

27. William of Tudela (*Chanson*, 67, line 5 [I, 162]), speaks also of catapults battering the walls.

28. *Uncinis ferreis*: poles with a hook or barb, used as grapples.

29. The abbot's name was Hugh. Other ecclesiastics present were those named in n. 10, above; also Bishop Fulk of Toulouse; Dominic; Peter of Nemours, bishop of Paris (1208–1218); and his brother, William, archdeacon of Paris and expert in siege machinery.

30. 'Come, Spirit Creator,' a hymn much used on ceremonial occasions. During the crusade, it became a battle-chant for the clergy at the beginning of an assault.

31. 3 May. Great booty was found, according to William of Tudela (*Chanson*, 71, lines 16–19; 72, lines 1–6 [I, 174]) – horses, steel armour, grain and wine, rich cloth and clothing – but Simon of Montfort had to hand much of this over to Richard of Salvanhic of Cahors, a banker who had financed him during the preceding year and continued to loan him money until at least 1212.

32. William of Tudela (*Chanson*, 71, lines 8–10 [I, 172]) writes that Aimery and a few knights were hanged, about eighty other prisoners put to the sword.

33. Robert of Auxerre (*Chronicon*, in *Monumenta Germaniae historica, Scriptores*, XXIII, 892) repeated the nasty rumour that Geralda was pregnant from incest with her brother. But William of Tudela, who was no friend of heretics, wrote of her death: 'That was a misery and a sin, for you may truly know that no man in the world ever departed from that lady without having had something to stay his hunger' (*Chanson*, 68, lines, 22–3 [I, 166]). Also, after describing the death of Geralda, 'crying out, weeping, and screaming' as she was thrown into the pit and stoned, he relates that a 'courteous' French noble released all the other female captives (*ibid.*, 71, lines 11–15 [I, 172]).

34. William of Tudela (*Chanson*, 68, line 19 [I, 165]) says 200 were burned in a field outside the walls. William of Puylaurens (*Cronica*, Ch. 17, 133) gives the number as 300, saying that many heretics had gathered at Lavaur 'in the hope that many would fall wounded there, whom they could take into their sect and so get possession of their money'. None of the sources informs us how the heretics were singled out from other inhabitants.

# Appendix 3

## The Chronicle of William Pelhisson

The memoir here translated was written by William Pelhisson of the convent of Friars Preachers at Toulouse. It is the most important source we have for the story of the turbulent first years of the Inquisition in Languedoc:

William Pelhisson was a native Toulousan but nothing is known of his life before he joined the Dominican order, probably soon after 1230. He speaks of himself and other friars in Toulouse in 1234 as young, yet at that time he was mature enough to act as an inquisitor and in the following year to risk martyrdom in the service of the tribunal.[1] Beyond that, his words are modestly unrevealing of himself. Other sources disclose that he continued to be associated with the Inquisition in 1245 and 1246,[2] but such activities thereafter were, perhaps, limited by his duties as custodian of records of property (*operarius*) for the convent, of whose acquisitions in and around Toulouse he prepared a complete record in 1263. He died on 8 January 1268.[3]

William Pelhisson's narrative is not a polished literary work but the events recounted supply its vigour and a touch of drama. The author takes up his story about the year 1230, with a backward glance at the history of the friars in Toulouse and passing mention of the situation in 1229. The scene thereafter is chiefly Toulouse, yet he writes also of investigations conducted by the friars in Albi, Moissac, and Cahors. The last episodes described are those of 1237–1238. Pelhisson, however, did not write until after 1244, for he refers to the fall of Montségur, and an even later date is possible, because he characterizes Raymond VII (d. 1249) as 'the last Raymond'. Also, from his rather uncertain chronology, it appears that enough time had passed to blur some of the events of 1235–1237 in his mind.

The original of the chronicle is no longer known. Bernard Gui, the Dominican inquisitor and historian of the early fourteenth century, made a copy, appending an anonymous narrative of the events in Albi in 1234 to which Pelhisson only briefly refers.[4] In the seventeenth century an unknown hand made a transcript of the chronicle and its addition, faulty by omission of words and by other mistakes, but it was this version that was first edited, by Charles Molinier in 1880.[5]

A year later Célestin Douais printed the text of the fourteenth-century copy made by Bernard Gui, in his *Les Sources de l'histoire de l'Inquisition dans le Midi de la France au XIIIe et XIVe siècles* (Paris, 1881), 81–118. The translation is made from Douais' text, amended in a few places by reference to the edition of Molinier.

There is a French translation of the chronicle by Jean Duvernoy, *Chronique de Guillaume Pelhisson* (Toulouse, 1958).

### The Chronicle of William Pelhisson of the Order of Friars Preachers[6]

Friar William Pelhisson of Toulouse, a religious, one of the first friars, wrote on paper with his own hand that which follows, which has been transcribed here, word for word, as a remembrance for posterity.[7]

To the glory and praise of Almighty God and the Most Blessed Virgin Mary, mother of Christ, and of the Blessed Dominic, our father, and of all the heavenly court, I wish to preserve the memory of what the Lord brought to pass in Toulouse and in the region around Toulouse through the friars of the Order of Preachers and other faithful persons in those parts, by the merits and prayers of the Blessed Dominic, who by his will inaugurated and ordained that order against heretics and their believers, through ordainment of the Holy Spirit in his time, by permission of the Lord Pope Honorius,[8] and with the assistance of Lord Fulk, bishop of Toulouse of happy memory.[9] Let no detractor or rival or envious person think that this is said or done to the exaltation of members of our order or other persons, because we seek not glory of our own – since it is nothing – but I write so that successors in our order and whatsoever other faithful persons who examine these matters may know how many and what sufferings came to their predecessors for the faith and name of Christ, that they may praise the Lord and herefrom may faithfully take courage against heretics and all other unbelievers, and so that they may stand ready to do – or rather to endure – as much or more, if need be or the occasion arise. For, after the numerous, the countless trials borne patiently, devoutly, and with good results by the Blessed Dominic and the friars who were with him in that land, true sons of such a father shall not be wanting; nay, sons have arisen in the place of the fathers. Nor shall they be 'children of withdrawing'[10] and degenerates, like 'the sons of Ephraim, who bend and shoot with the bow',[11] as the Psalmist says of some; but seeing that the affair is good, they will set their shoulders wholly to bearing the yoke of the Lord and the burdens of the church and of the orthodox faith.

Passing over, however, the deeds which the Blessed Dominic and his sons performed, I shall give a faithful account of some which were done after the peace made at Paris[12] in Holy Week in the year of our Lord 1229 between the lord king of France and the church on one hand and the noble Count Raymond and his counsellors on the other.[13] For, just at the moment when the church thought to have peace in that land, heretics and their believers girded themselves more and more for numerous ventures and stratagems against her and against Catholics, with the result that the heretics did more harm by far in Toulouse and that region than they had even during the war. The friars of the Order of Preachers and Catholics grieved at the sight.

At that time, too, a considerable number of masters of Paris and scholars had been sent to Toulouse to establish a university[14] there and to teach the faith and all the liberal arts. This was ineffective in uprooting heresy; rather, heretical individuals, regarding them with hostility and hearing unfamiliar things, mocked at them in manifold ways.

The Friars Preachers were at that time occupying the church of St Romain in Toulouse, which Lord Fulk, bishop of good memory, father and friend of the order, gave to them. But, since the church was small and the site was very constricted and impossible of extension, the friars transferred themselves within the same city[15] to the place which was called the Garrigues's garden, in the year of our Lord 1230, on the Sunday before the birthday of our Lord Jesus Christ. Lord Pons of Capdenier, a burgher of Toulouse, bought and gave to the friars that garden on the edge of the city and another on the edge of the bourg.[16]

The conventual prior at that time was Friar John of Johannia[17] and the provincial prior was Friar Raymond of Le Fauga, who became bishop of Toulouse not long afterward.[18] He accepted the gift of the site, where the friars built houses, very poor, small, and humble because of the poverty of the place and the lack of money. Our friars also for a long time, in the name of Christ and for planting the faith, led a very mean and poor life in respect of food as well as clothing.

At the release of Friar John, the aforementioned prior, Friar Peter of Alais[19] was made prior to succeed him. Lecturing in theology there at that time was Master Roland, who came from Paris where he had become master in theology at the cathedral.[20] One day one of our friars, while preaching, declared in his sermon

o

that heretics lived in the town and that they held assemblies and disseminated their heresies there. The people of the town became very disturbed and agitated at hearing this. Hence, the consuls of the town summoned the prior to the town hall and ordered him to tell the friars not to dare to preach such things in the future and said that they would take it very ill if it were said that there were heretics there, since no one among them, so they insisted, was any such thing. These and other remarks to the same effect they uttered as threats. When Master Roland heard the story from the prior, he replied with the words, 'Surely it behooves us now to preach more and more against heretics and their believers.' This he did and others manfully and powerfully did the same.

In those days, A. Peter, a donat of St Sernin, died in the bourg and at death was made a canon with the surplice and was buried in the cloister.[21] He had before that been hereticated on his death bed, without the knowledge of the canons. As soon as he heard this Master Roland went to the spot with friars and clerics and had the body dug up, dragged to the fire, and burned.

At that time there died in the bourg a certain heretic, Galvan by name, a leading figure[22] among the Waldenses. The fact did not escape Master Roland, who announced it publicly in a sermon and, when the friars, clergy, and some of the people had assembled, they went boldly to the house where the aforesaid heretic died and razed it to the ground, making a refuse-pit of it. They dug up that Galvan and took him from the cemetery of Villeneuve where he had been buried, then in a great procession dragged his body through the town and burned it in the common field outside the town.[23] This was done in praise of our Lord Jesus Christ and the Blessed Dominic and to the honour of the Roman and Catholic church, our mother, in the year of the Lord 1231.

At that time, after the death of Lord Fulk, bishop of Toulouse, on Christmas Day in the same year of the Lord 1231, Friar Raymond of Le Fauga of Miramont, the provincial prior, was elected bishop of Toulouse and was installed in the see on the Sunday of Lent when *Laetare Jerusalem* is sung.[24] Friar Romeu[25] was made provincial prior in the province of Provence.

In those days, Brother Peter of Alais was released from the office of prior and Master Roland left Toulouse to go to his homeland; in his place, Master John of Saint Gilles,[26] a good and holy man, gracious in appearance and life, lectured in theology at Toulouse. He had been master in theology at the cathedral in Paris. Also, Friar Pons of St Gilles[27] was chosen as prior at Toulouse. He bore himself courageously and vigorously in the business of the faith against heretics, together with Friar Peter Seila,[28] who was a Toulousan, and Friar William Arnold,[29] a jurist, who was from Montpellier. Them the lord pope appointed as inquisitors against heretics in the dioceses of Toulouse and in Cahors as well. The lord legate, archbishop of Vienne,[30] also made Arnold Catalan,[31] who was then of the convent at Toulouse, an inquisitor against heretics in the diocese of Albi, where manfully and fearlessly he preached and sought to conduct the inquisition as best he could. However, the believers of heretics would say virtually nothing at that time, rather, they united in denials; yet he did sentence two living heretics, Peter of Pug Perdutz, that is of Podiumperditum, and Peter Bomacip, or Bonusmancipius, and both were burned, but at different times. He condemned certain other deceased persons and had them dragged away and burned. Disturbed by this, the people of Albi sought to throw him into the River Tarn, but at the insistence of some among them released him, beaten, his clothing torn to shreds, his face bloody; yet even while being dragged along he cried out, 'Blessed be the Lord Jesus Christ!'[32] [This happened] in the year of the Lord 1234, in the week of Pentecost.[33] Many misfortunes overtook those people later in the time of Friar Ferrier,[34] the inquisitor, who seized and imprisoned a number of them and also had some burned, the just judgement of God thus being carried out.

In addition to those already named, there were in the convent of Toulouse at that time Friar Maurice, an excellent preacher against heretics;[35] Friar Dominic of Baretge; Friar John of St Michel; Friar Geoffrey, an Englishman and great cleric; Friar Nicholas; Friar Stephen *Methensis*; Friar Stephen of Salignac of Limoges; Friar B. of Périgueux; Friar Luke *Amadyensis*; Friar Bertrand *de Pineto*; Friar William of St Amans; Friar John of Alias, the subprior; Friar B. of Saint Frégulf; Friar P. of St Laurent; Friar Odo; Friar P. *de Sorers*; Friar William Pelhisson the Toulousan; and many others, young, virtuous, studious, and religious. Also, a little later were present Friar P. of Marseillan, the subprior, a prudent and religious man; Friar B. of Martres; Friar Raymond of Foix; Friar Guy Navarre of Limoges; Friar Giran; and Friar Raymond of Vilar, the last two senior in the order; and Friar Roderick. There were at that time more than forty friars in the convent.

Moreover, in that land in those days Catholics were harassed and in several localities those who searched out heretics were killed, although Lord Raymond, the count, had promised in the treaty of peace that over a period of five years, for every heretic, male or female, he would give two silver marks to the one who seized them and after five years one mark.[36] This happened many times. But the chief men of the region, together with the greater nobles and the burghers and others, protected and hid the heretics. They beat, wounded, and killed those who pursued them,[37] for the prince's entourage was notably corrupted in the faith. And consequently many wicked things were done in the land to the church and to faithful persons.

It happened then that a certain citizen of Toulouse, named Bernard Peitavin, who was reputed to be a Catholic, had a quarrel with another man, one suspected of heresy, Bernard of Soler by name, and in the exchange of words called him a heretic. Hence, the latter laid a complaint of unjust accusation before the consuls, and the first-named was haled before the Council and castigated with words and threats by the many believers of heretics who at that time held the consulate and the town in their power. Finally he was sentenced to several years' exile, to pay monetary damages to Bernard [of Soler] for the affront and to the consuls of the town on behalf of the community, and to declare on oath in the town hall that the other man was honest and Catholic and that he himself had lied in the affair just described. On hearing that, the man was very much aggrieved about the money and especially, he declared, about perjury – for he would make the statement against his conscience – and about the disgrace inflicted on him and other Catholics and on the church. He sought a stay from the Council. This being granted, he came to the friars to ask advice and help. The friars told him that since it was a case involving the faith he should appeal to the lord bishop and then they would stoutly and strongly defend him. Taking their sound advice, he did so. Both men without delay appeared before Lord Bishop Raymond, and the heretical sympathizer brought with him to court a number of burghers and important people, all of whom took his part and raised violent and clamorous outcry against the other man. The latter [Bernard Peitavin] brought with him trustworthy witnesses against the other, together with Friar Peter Seila and Friar William Arnold, who so stoutly defended him that the other miserable fellow gave up and fled to Lombardy. His partisans stayed behind in confusion. Blessed be the Lord and blessed be Dominic, His servant, who thus defends his own.

At that time the inquisitors made their inquisition in Toulouse and summoned many people of the town before them. Among them was a man from the bourg, John Textor by name. He, like the other man [Bernard of Soler], had many of the important heretical sympathizers of the town to defend him. Now this wicked John spoke out before everyone: 'Gentlemen, listen to me! I am not a heretic, for I have a wife and I sleep with her. I have sons, I eat meat, and I lie and swear, and I am a faithful Christian. So don't let them say these things about me, for I truly believe in God. They can accuse you as well as me. Look out for yourselves, for these wicked men want to ruin the town and honest men and take the town away from its lord.' Then the case was pressed against him in such fashion that the friars heard witnesses against the aforesaid John, with the result that being publicly haled into the cloister of the friars, in the presence of the vicar and many other persons, he was condemned. But when the vicar, who was Durand of St Ybars,[38] sought to drag him away to the stake, those who defended the man raised an outcry against his doing any such thing, and everyone was muttering against the friars and the vicar. So the aforesaid John was taken by the vicar to the bishop's palace and put in the prison there, since he was still declaring that he was a good Christian and a Catholic.

The town was now very much stirred up against the friars; there were even more threats and speeches against them than usual, and many heretical persons incited the people to stone the friars and destroy their houses because, the cry was, they were unjustly accusing decent married men of heresy. And so they made many plots against the friars.

There were at that time many who had taken the cross to go overseas because of their acts against the faith, and there were some others singled out for other penances by Lord Romanus, legate of the apostolic see, because William of Solier,[39] a convert from heresy, had denounced them. They and many other persons were in constant opposition to the church and to Catholics. The Lord God, who in time of troubles always knows how to give help, aided the friars wonderfully; they threw themselves entirely on Him, praying and entreating Him to save His faith and church from the wicked and to preserve them without disruption in this situation.[40]

Then it happened at that time that William of Le Mas,[41] bailiff of Lord Raymond, count of Toulouse, for the district of Lavaur, brought some heretics whom he had seized to hand over to the lord bishop of Toulouse. They were thrown into the prison where John Textor lay. That John was pretending to be sick and was asking incessantly, albeit falsely, for the body of Christ. When he saw the heretics at his side, however, and recognized them for what they were, he gave himself to them and they hereticated him. Also, when the heretics were taken out for trial, John said that he wished to go with them and to follow their way in all things. Then Lord Bishop Raymond summoned before him in his court the friars, the consuls, the vicar, and many other upright men, and a large number of heretical sympathizers. He had John brought from prison with the heretics and, in the presence of all, the heretics were examined and sentenced, the said John with them, because he had confessed before everyone that his faith was in every respect that of the aforesaid heretics and he wished to follow their way. And although repeatedly urged by the bishop and the friars to recant, he was unwilling to return to our faith. All who had previously defended him were now covered with confusion, and they damned and cursed him, at least as far as words go, and he was burned at the same time as the others.[42] In all things, blessed be God, who delivered the friars who were in grave danger, and magnified His faith in the face of His enemies. Hence, Catholics rejoiced greatly, and heretical sympathizers were confused and refuted.[43]

At that time the friars inquisitors Peter Seila and William Arnold made inquisition against the heretics in Cahors, where they condemned some deceased persons, whom they caused to be dragged through the town and burned. They also condemned the deceased Humbert of Castelnau, but his son stole the body secretly from the cemetery and it was not found.[44] And Raymond of Broelles, an important believer of heretics, fled; when he reached Rome, he was drowned in the Tiber.

The same friars made inquisition also in Moissac and sentenced the living John of Lagarde, who, fleeing to Montségur, became a perfected heretic and later was burned there with 210 other heretics.[45] They also cited Falquet of Moissac, who in fear became a monk in the abbey of Belleperche, but they proceeded against him nevertheless. At the news he fled to Lombardy. John Christofols, an advocate of Moissac, likewise fled to Lombardy when summoned.[46] Then the inquisitors condemned these men as contumacious heretics, and great fear was aroused among the heretics and their believers in that land.

At that time, while those inquisitors were in the diocese of Cahors, Friar Arnold Catalan with Friar William Pelhisson was making inquisition against heretics in Albi, where twelve persons of that city took the cross to go overseas. Friar Arnold and Master William of Lombers,[47] his colleague, condemned Peter

of Podiumperditum and Peter Bomacip, both living. They were
burned, to the terror of many heretics and the exaltation of the
faith of Jesus Christ.

Meanwhile, Friar Pons of St Gilles, the prior of Toulouse, had
caused Arnold Sans,[48] an artisan of Croix-Baragnon,[49] to be
summoned several times and had heard many sworn witnesses
against him, who testified about the many things he had done
contrary to the faith. The man denied everything, saying nothing
in his own defence except that the charges were not true. When
they heard this, the prior and the friars, after taking counsel
with discreet men who were present, condemned him in the
presence of the vicar and many other faithful persons as a heretic,
because he was a great believer of the heretics. This accomplished,
Durand, the vicar, took him to the stake because he refused
to confess his heresy, although Arnold cried out as he was led
through the streets: 'Look, all of you, at the injustice they do
to me and the town, because I am a good Christian and believe
in the Roman faith!' and shouted out many such plaints, demanding his release. Hence, many of the people were very stirred up
against the friars and the vicar, but the vicar burned him nonetheless. Many of the people were both terrified and apprehensive;
knowing themselves to be guilty, they were grievously afraid for
themselves, and the whole town complained.

In the year of the Lord 1234, the canonization of the Blessed
Dominic, our father, was proclaimed at Toulouse and Lord Friar
Raymond of Miramont, bishop of Toulouse, first said solemn
Mass in the house of the Friars Preachers of Toulouse and,
when the holy office had been devoutly and solemnly completed,
the bishop, his attendants, and the friars washed their hands in
preparation for dining in the refectory. At that moment, by
ministration of divine providence, through the merits of the
Blessed Dominic, whose feast day[50] they were celebrating, a
person from the town came up to the prior as they were entering
the rectory and informed him that some heretics had gone in to
hereticate a sick woman quite nearby, in the street called l'Olmet
sec.[51] The prior then told this to the bishop. At once, before they
ate, they went there, that is, to the house of Peitavin Boursier,
who for a long time had been something of a general courier
for the heretics in Toulouse. Peitavin's mother-in-law was
suffering from a high fever, or at least was afflicted with a serious
illness. One person then called out to the invalid, 'Look, my lady,
the lord bishop is coming to see you'; but because the bishop
and the others entered quickly he could not warn her further.

The bishop, moreover, seating himself beside the invalid, began to talk to her at length about contempt for the world and for earthly things and, perhaps because she understood what had been said to mean that it was the bishop of heretics who visited her, for she had already been hereticated, she freely responded to the bishop in all things. The lord bishop, with great care, drew from her what she believed on many points and almost all of it was just what the heretics believe. Then the bishop went on to say to her: 'For the rest, you must not lie nor have much concern for this miserable life,' and words of that sort; 'Hence, I say that you are to be steadfast in your belief, nor in fear of death ought you to confess anything other than what you believe and hold firmly in your heart.' On hearing this, she said, 'My lord, what I say I believe, and I shall not change my commitment out of concern for the miserable remnant of my life.' Then said the bishop: 'Therefore, you are a heretic! For what you have confessed is the faith of the heretics, and you may know assuredly that the heresies are manifest and condemned. Renounce them all! Accept what the Roman and catholic church believes. For I am your bishop of Toulouse, and I preach the Roman Catholic faith, which I want and urge you to believe.' He made these and many like remarks to her in everyone's presence, but he accomplished nothing as far as she was concerned; rather, she persevered all the more in heretical obstinacy. Forthwith, the bishop, who at once summoned the vicar and many other persons, by the virtue of Jesus Christ condemned her as a heretic. Moreover, the vicar had her carried on the bed in which she lay to the count's meadow and burned at once. Seized at the time were Peitavin, her son-in-law, who was a messenger and agent of the heretics in Toulouse, and Bernard Aldric of Drémil, who was his associate. They subsequently confessed at length about heresy and courageously exposed many prominent persons. And after the bishop and the friars and their companions had seen the business completed, they returned to the refectory and, giving thanks to God and the Blessed Dominic, ate with rejoicing what had been prepared for them.[52] God performed these works on the first feast day of the Blessed Dominic, to the glory and praise of His name and of His servant, the Blessed Dominic, to the exaltation of the faith and to the discomfiture of the heretics and their believers.

In the year of the Lord 1235, on Good Friday,[53] many persons came to confess in the matter of heresy, and the friars were kept so busy that there were not enough of them to hear the confessions. Hence, some Friars Minor and parish priests of the town who were present at the hearings were called on. At that time the prior, acting in co-operation with the vicar of Toulouse, seized certain persons of the town who refused to come of their own free will, among whom was a wine-seller,[54] named Arnold Dominic. He, when he realized that the vicar threatened his death unless he fully exposed heretics, was terror-stricken and promised to betray eleven heretics whom he knew. He was given hope that he would be released. Then he led Peter of Mala Fayda, the abbot of St Sernin, and the lord vicar and some armed men to the stronghold called Les Cassès, where they captured seven heretics. The others got away with the help of peasants of the locality. The aforesaid Arnold Dominic made his confession and was released, but afterward he was murdered one night in his bed, at Aigrefeuille, in the region of Lanta.

The abbot just mentioned, together with the vicar, seized Peter William Delort in his house in the bourg of St Sernin. He was a noted believer of heretics. When they tried to take him away with them Raymond Roger, his elder both in age and wickedness, and Peter Esquivat, together with some other people of the bourg, snatched him from their custody. He took flight thereafter and was, I believe, condemned as a heretic.[55]

At the news of this event, all the inquisitors came to Toulouse and called many to confess, giving them a time of grace. If, within this period, they made a good and full confession without deceit, the inquisitors offered solid hope that they would not be imprisoned, be exiled, or lose property, because Lord Count Raymond had agreed with the friars that any penitent who confessed the truth would lose nothing. Subsequently, those who honestly confessed found this to be true.

At that time the bodies of certain deceased persons who had been hereticated, namely Bertrand Peyrier[56] and some others, were dragged through the town and burned. The whole town was excited and aroused against the friars because of the Inquisition and appealed to the count. He came to the inquisitors to ask them, out of consideration for him, to call a halt for a time, adducing his trifling reasons.[57] This they refused to do. Then the count complained to the legate about them, alleging also that Friar Peter Seila, who had been a member of the court of his father and was a citizen of Toulouse, was now his enemy. He laid a request before the legate that for the future Friar Peter should not act as inquisitor in the diocese of Toulouse, but only in Cahors. Then Friar Peter, when he was transferred from this region, made inquisition in the diocese of Cahors with Friar Pons Delmont and Friar William Pelhisson as his colleagues, where, travelling about to many strongholds and towns, they heard confessions about heresy and preserved the memory of them in books.

At the same time Friar William Arnold, the inquisitor, went to Carcassonne with a certain archdeacon associated with him for this purpose. He cited the nobleman, Bernard Oth of Niort, lord of Laurac, together with his brothers, William of Niort and Gerald, and their mother.[58] Bernard Oth and William responded to the summons, but would confess to nothing about heresy and, having received permission to leave, withdrew. But the next day the seneschal[59] of the king of France seized them and they were held in the city of Carcassonne and repeatedly interrogated. Bernard Oth would not confess, although many acts against the faith and many heresies were proved against him. And so, after conference and discussion, the inquisitors condemned him as a heretic. They held William of Niort prisoner because he had confessed, albeit not voluntarily, and did the same to Bernard. When the seneschal made preparations to burn the latter, the French of the region, with the exception of the marshall of Mirepoix,[60] dissuaded him, fearing that war would result; indeed, Gerald of Niort, his brother, put the castles of Laurac and Niort and such other territory as he could in a state of defence. When he and his mother were cited for this by the inquisitors, they refused to appear and were therefore condemned by them. Many others, both clergy and laity, were condemned at that time.

On his return to Toulouse, Friar William Arnold, the inquisitor referred to above, cited twelve believers of heretics of Toulouse, namely, Sicard of Gameville or of Toulouse, a knight;[61] Arnold Gui the elder;[62] Raymond of Mirepoix;[63] Vital Melic[64] of Cassamilh; Maurand the elder;[65] Bernard Seguier;[66] Raymond Centolhs;[67] Raymond Roger the elder;[68] and certain other persons. They refused to appear or to answer concerning their faith; rather, they uttered threats and dire warnings to make him desist from his activities. But when they realized that he did not intend to dismiss them, but proposed to proceed against them, after joint consultation, acting at the wish and with the assent of the count of Toulouse, they ordered him to leave the town or to halt the Inquisition. But he was advised by the friars not to pause, but to proceed against them vigorously. Thereupon, the consuls of Toulouse and their accomplices took direct action and expelled the friar inquisitor from the convent and town, manhandling him as they did so. The entire convent accompanied him in procession to the head of the Daurade Bridge over the Garonne. There the consuls announced that they would allow him to stay in the town with the other friars if he would give up the Inquisition; otherwise, on behalf of the count and themselves, they enjoined him strictly to leave the count's lands without delay. Therefore, he took Friar Giran as companion and went to Carcassonne. From there, he wrote instructions to the parish priests of Toulouse and to the prior of St Stephen's to issue a second citation on his behalf to those same persons who had once been summoned. This they did diligently, although the townsmen voiced many threats and menacing words. The consuls at that time were Griffus of Roiax, Arnold Barrau, Curvus of Turres, Bernard of Miramont, Arnold of St Ybars, Pons of Seilh, Bernard Seguier, Raymond Borel, and Raymond Roger, and their associates were Maurand of Belpech and Aldric Maurand.[69] When they learned of Friar William's action, they sent after nightfall for the prior of St Etienne and for William Vaquier and the other priests who had issued the citation and held them at the town hall for part of the night; then they expelled them from the town, with the declaration and threat that if anyone issued summons for them in this affair in the future, he would be killed at once. Hence, none of the clergy or religious dared to cite them again.

At the same time the consuls made proclamation by herald throughout the town on behalf of the count and themselves that, on penalty of corporal punishment and fine, no one was to give, sell, or lend anything whatever or to give assistance in any form to the Friars Preachers. They also applied this edict to the bishop of Toulouse and to the canons of St Etienne. It came about then that the bishop had to leave the town, because he could not obtain the necessities of life within it; no one dared to bake him bread or do other such things.[70] We friars did have the essentials in sufficient supply from friends and Catholics who, despite the danger, handed us bread, cheese, and eggs over the garden walls and by every other possible means. When the consuls of the town learned of this, they set their guards at our gates and also on the garden, watching the house day and night to prevent any necessities being brought in. They even cut us off completely from the water of the Garonne. This was a more serious blow to us, because we were unable to cook our vegetables in water. Then Catholics grieved, matrons lamented, the faithful sighed, murmured and groaned, but at night many threw good large loaves and cakes and cheese to us over the walls into the garden, taking care lest the guards see them. Thus, by God's grace, we were well enough off for about three weeks, spent in rejoicing and exulting in the Lord and devoutly singing the office in the church.

At that point Friar William Arnold, the inquisitor, wrote from Carcassonne to Friar Pons of St Gilles, our prior, instructing him that, since others dared not cite the heretical persons, he was to depute two of our friars to summon peremptorily on his behalf those heretical persons to appear at Carcassonne to answer to him concerning their faith; two other friars should be added to them as witnesses of the summons. The prior ordered the bell tolled and, when the friars had gathered, said with joyful countenance: 'Now brethren, rejoice and be exceeding glad, for I am now to send four of you by martyrdom to the court of the Highest King. Such is the command I have from Friar William, inquisitor and defender of the faith, and there is every reason to believe that whoever cites them peremptorily this time will be slain on the spot. So say the consuls, and others who have been summoned have made this threat. Therefore, let me hear from you whether you are prepared to die for the faith of our Lord Jesus Christ. I want those who are so prepared to prostrate themselves as for pardon.' At this, all, acting as one, prostrated themselves in the chapter.[71] Rejoicing, he bade them rise and said in response, 'Blessed be the Lord that I find you ready.' And he talked to us at length, concluding, 'Because of the fact that all wish to go, I must decide whom to send, for all are not needed.' He then chose Friar Raymond of Foix and Friar John of St Michael in the Limousin to deliver the summons; he selected Friar Guy Navarre of Limoges[72] and Friar William Pelhisson as their associates and witnesses.

When they had made full confession and had received general absolution for all their sins from the prior, as sons of obedience they observed that duty bravely and joyfully; diligently and fearlessly they executed it, so much so, indeed, that they were not content to seek out those persons in the streets and at their houses, but even sought them in their inner bedchambers. When they were in the house of Maurand the elder in search of them, his sons, Maurand and Raymond Maurand the One-eyed,[73] came running and hustled the friars out of doors, heaping abusive words on them, dragging them by the hair and thrusting them out of the house, shouting as they struck them, and trying to slash them with knives, but some persons present thwarted them by holding them back, among whom was the burgher, Peter of Coussa, who restrained them from the deed, for he was a Catholic.[74]

Once the serving of the summons had been completed, the consuls conferred with heretical persons with a view to expelling all the friars from the town on the grounds that they had not given up their activities nor did they seem to fear death. They said, 'It would be much better for us if we expelled them from the town than if they were killed.' On this plan they agreed. Then some of our friends reported it to the prior. When he conferred with friars of the house and with Friar Lawrence,[75] who had arrived that very day from Paris to lecture in Toulouse, for Master John of St Gilles and his associates had already left the house, they agreed with his proposal to remove all the books, chalices, and ecclesiastical robes from the house and to entrust them all to their friends for the time being. This they did.

On the following day, Tuesday after the feast of All Saints, the nones of November,[76] in the year of the Lord 1235, after the conventual mass had been celebrated, the prior exhorted the friars to bear themselves with propriety and patience in all; no one was to go out unless thrice compelled. Realizing that the consuls were somewhat slow in coming because they were gathering their confederates and everyone else they could, he remarked that it would be well to eat, whatever happened. The hours were said and when the friars, numbering about forty, were at table the consuls arrived with a great crowd, their sergeants crying out for the doors to be opened at once or they would be broken down. The doorkeeper went to report it to the prior, who thereupon went out to them and besought the consuls to allow the convent to dine, since they were at table. This they were quite unwilling to do; on the contrary, their hangers-on pushed into the house forthwith. Then the prior rang the bell, the friars all rose from the table and in procession entered the chapel, singing *Miserere mei Deus* as is the custom, gave thanks to God, and remained there. On behalf of the count and themselves the consuls sternly ordered the prior and his whole convent to depart from the town at once; if not, they would expel them by force. The prior told them that under no circumstances would he do so and advanced some sound justifications of himself and the friars, which the others entirely refused to accept. In the meantime their hangers-on went to the refectory and ate and drank what they found there. Then the prior took the cross and the coffer containing relics that was at the foot of the cross and seated himself in the cloister, the cross in his hands, and the whole convent sat down there in front of the consuls and their confederates. Again and again the prior and convent were warned to depart at once. The friars refused to do so. Then Bernard Seguier, Raymond Roger, Bernard of Miramont, and some other men took the prior by the arms and dragged him roughly out of the cloister. The other hangers-on and sergeants of the consuls dragged all the friars in the same way out of the cloister. As the friars were at the door of the convent, Friar Lawrence, who had come to teach, and Friar Arnold Catalan threw themselves on the ground. Raymond Roger and others seized them by head and feet and carried them through the gate by force.

And thus they expelled all the friars, dragging and driving them outside the town; however, they did not strike them more than has already been described. At the moment that they undertook to eject him, the prior, and with him the convent, began to chant loudly the symbol of faith as it is sung in the Mass, then *Te Deum laudamus*, and, when they were in front of the church of St Mary of La Daurade, the *Salve regina*. However, the consuls left certain sick friars, seven in number, in the house, together with the very aged Peter Dalbius, who for a long time had been priest in the church of La Daurade and also in La Dalbade, but a few days later they expelled them also from the town, allowing only Friar Dalbius to stay in the church of La Dalbade with a lay brother.

Now the friars who were expelled from the town went to the farm of St Etienne which is called Braqueville, on the other side of the Garonne. The people of the town did not dare to aid the friars in exile nor to give or send anything because of the edict of the consuls, who even sent out agents to guard against any kind of assistance to them. The next day the prior distributed his friars among the convents of the province. He himself stayed for some days near Toulouse and at Portet-Saint-Simon received into the order Master William of St Gaudens, who had been master in logic and had taken a degree in physics at Montpellier. He was a man of great sanctity and admirable austerity; later he was lecturer in theology in several convents. Also, while the friars were grieving[77] over the expulsion from Toulouse, Friar Raymond Thomas of Toulouse, a religious and good man, entered the order and proved himself prompt and assiduous in obedience. He wished to be in the order with the friars during their tribulations.

At this time, Friar Pons of St Gilles went to Rome[78] with Friar Raymond of Foix and reported to Lord Pope Gregory and to the cardinals what had been done against the faith in that land and how the friars had conducted themselves in the affair. Hence, the lord pope commanded the count of Toulouse, the last Raymond, to return the friars to Toulouse, to allow inquisition against heretics to be conducted in his lands, and to aid the friars therein. To discuss this matter, the legate, the archbishop of Vienne, together with the inquisitors, called the count to Carcassonne. After this parley the count did recall the bishop and inquisitors and received Friar Pons again in Toulouse, in the year following the expulsion, on the octave of the feast of the Blessed Augustine,[79] our father, in the year of the Lord 1236. Then the friars returned from the convents where they were to the convent of Toulouse.

At the same time Friar John of Notoyra, minister of the Friars Minor in that province, was assigned by the lord legate as associate to Friar William Arnold, inquisitor, for the conduct of the Inquisition. Because Friar John was kept too busy with his other duties, he deputized Friar Stephen of St Thibéry,[80] a modest man and highly experienced in the courts, in his stead. Then, with one mind and heart, both took up the inquisition with equal credit and merit and manfully they continued until the day of their martyrdom with their associates.

On 10 November, in the year of the Lord 1235, Friar William Arnold, inquisitor, sitting at the time in Carcassonne, pronounced sentence of excommunication as fautors of heretics against the consuls named above.[81]

At this time Friar Peter Seila, who was from Toulouse, a religious man and advanced in years, was made prior of Toulouse. When the friars had been in the convent of Toulouse for some time [after their return], the prior went to Montauban [and then to] the diocese of Cahors with Friar William Arnold, his colleague, to make inquisition against heretics there. While they were engaged there in the year of the Lord 1236, on the morning of 2 April, there came to our house at Toulouse Raymond Gros of Toulouse who had been a perfected heretic in these parts for twenty-two years or thereabouts.[82] Converted from heresy of his own free will, not as yet summoned or cited, he surrendered himself devoutly and humbly to the will of the friars in every way. Friar William Bonsolas,[83] the subprior, acting as prior, received him freely into the house as a voluntary convert from heresy. By order of Friar William Arnold and Friar Stephen, inquisitors, the subprior heard his confession of heresy, together with Friar John, minister of the Minors in Gascony; Peter, prior of the church of La Daurade; Master Arnold Pelhisson, precentor of

St Stephen's;[84] Master Nicholas of Pointis, priest of the church of La Daurade;[85] and certain other friars, and for several days they recorded it, to the confusion of many. Numerous persons then confessed the truth, and the Inquisition was thereby enlightened. The friars rejoiced greatly at the sight and knowledge of this; believers of heretics, who knew their own iniquities, were terror-stricken beyond measure. In truth, so well and fully did Raymond Gros confess the doings of heretics and their believers, in so orderly a fashion, with such accuracy, that no one should think it could happen without divine providence.

Moreover, the prior and Friar William Arnold, the inquisitor, came to summon many persons to confession. Many came of their own volition, fearing arrest. The Lord then bestowed such favour upon the business of the faith that although the aforesaid Raymond was the one and only witness in many instances, no one challenged his word or contradicted him; on the contrary, a great many said, 'Masters, you may know that it is all just as Master Raymond says it is'; and they even asked him to tell them what else should be said in their confessions, because he knew the whole truth.

At that time, many heretications of prominent men and others, now deceased, which had taken place in Toulouse and in other places outside the town, were revealed by Raymond Gros and the inquisition of heretics was entirely directed by him, as God disposed and ordered, to such an extent that prominent burghers, noble lords, and other persons were condemned by sentences, exhumed, and ignominiously were cast out of the cemeteries of the town by the friars in the presence of the vicar and the people. Their bones and stinking bodies were dragged through the town; their names were proclaimed through the streets by the herald, crying, 'Who behaves thus shall perish thus,' and finally they were burned in the count's meadow, to the honour of God and the Blessed Virgin, His mother, and the Blessed Dominic, His servant, who just as he happily laid the foundation of that order in Toulouse against the heretics, so on the first of his feast days there celebrated and on following days, as has been described, most happily brought about this work of the Lord.

At that time deceased persons who had been hereticated at death were condemned: Embry the elder; Peter Embry; Oliva, their mother; Alesta, wife of Embry; Raymond Isarn and his two sisters, Dyas, wife of Lord Arnold Barrau, and Raymonda, wife of Bertrand of Roaix; and some others from the bourg.[86] Their bones were dragged through the town and burned. From the city likewise were condemned the defunct Bertrand Peyrier;[87] John Salade;[88] Peter Jacmars; Magna, wife of Jordan of Villeneuve, and Raymonda, his daughter, the wife of Arnold of Villeneuve; a daughter of the aforesaid Jordan, wife of Bertrand of Saint Loup, knight;[89] Stephen of Spain;[90] Bernard Raymond Teuler and his wife; Fays and Blanqua of Gameville;[91] and some others from the city.

Some living persons were also condemned as heretics. Certain of them fled and became perfected heretics; some eventually returned. Among them were Bernard Embry; Raymond Centolhs;[92] Peter William Delort; Raymond Roger;[93] Arnold Roger, who was later a bishop of the heretics; Alaman of Roaix;[94] Sicard of Toulouse, knight; Stephen Masse; Peter of Roaix; Pons of Gameville;[95] William Mercadier and his sister, Cortesia; Arnold William Peyrier; his wife, Ondrada;[96] her mother and maternal grandmother;[97] the father of Arnold William Peyrier; Peitavin Lawrence;[98] Bartholomew Boers,[99] Maurand the elder, who became a perfected heretic, as did Arnold of Villeneuve, son of Jordan;[100] Peter of Beauville;[101] William Peter Duran; Michael of Pinu; and Mistress Cadolhe Brenguera,[102] daughter of Bernard Raymond, the money-changer. Many of these persons were afterwards burned at Montségur.

In like manner the friars also condemned many of those who were from outside the town, to wit, from Laurac, William of l'Ile and Bernard of St Martin, knights, and Balaguier. These men had been in at the death of the friars. The first two were burned at Montségur, the third was dragged and hanged.[103]

They also condemned Raymond of Pereille, lord of Montségur; his wife, Corba; Arnold Roger, brother of that Raymond, and Peter Roger of Mirepoix, lords of Mirepoix already mentioned;[104] Isarn of Tays of Pamiers; and Peyronet of Montmaur. Also they condemned Raymond Unald, lord of Lanta.[105] William Bernard Unald, father of the Jordan who became a perfected heretic, was burned at Toulouse. Him the abbot of St Sernin, namely, Peter of Mala Fayda, seized at Le Bousquet, together with the heretic Arnold Giffre. The latter was likewise burned at Albi because the lord legate was there and he had been taken before him.[106] Many other persons were condemned by these friars inquisitors and others who were their successors; their names were not written in the Book of Life, but their bodies were burned here and their souls are tortured in hell.[107]

This is the end of what Friar William Pelhisson, who was an eyewitness and participant in these events, wrote with his own

P

hand. He died eventually at Toulouse on the feast of Epiphany in the year of the Lord 1268.[108]

## The First Inquisition at Albi

What follows, the events which took place in those days, one who was both witness and participant wrote of in this way:[109]

We shall write a faithful account of what we saw and heard. Now, it happened in the year of the Lord 1234, on Thursday after the feast of Pentecost, that Arnold Catalan, a member of the Order of Preachers from the convent at Toulouse, having been sent at that time by the provincial prior of his order, pursuant to the instructions of the lord pope, to make inquisition of heretics in the diocese of Albi, proceeded thus in consequence of the duty laid upon him. At the third hour of the day, prior to the convening of a synod which was ready to assemble, he summoned the *bailli* of the court of the lord bishop of Albi[110] and ordered him to have exhumed a certain female heretic, named Boyssene, the wife of the heretic Brostaion, in execution of the sentence he had delivered against them in full court on the day before the feast of the Ascension of the Lord, in the presence of the *bailli* and many others. But, since the *bailli* and his assistants were afraid to go to the cemetery to carry out the order, Friar Arnold himself summoned some priests and a number of other persons and went to the church of St Estève, in the cemetery of which that heretic was buried and, taking a mattock, made the first strokes to turn up the earth. Then he bade the bishop's servants continue and returned to the church to attend the synod. And lo! the aforesaid servants came back at once to say that they had shamefully been driven from the cemetery by order of Pons Bernard.[111] Then the friar went there with some priests and numerous other persons, among them Master Bernard, chaplain to the lord bishop. When they reached the spot, lo! the sons of Belial, raging vessels of iniquity, heaped threats and insults upon them in the way they had learned from their father the devil.

Here, moreover, are inserted their names, which, no doubt, have been struck from the Book of Life: William of Le Puy, son of Pons Bernard; Raymond Donadieu and his brother, Hugo; Curvale; William Montinant; Michael Brostaion; Azemar Brose, son of Raymond Hugo; Maurin Amat; Maurin Guinho; Pons Caus senior, from Castelviel; Isarn Jacob; Bernard Fumet; Bonys; Isarn Bya and his brother, William Bors; William Roger;

William Ganach; William Fenasse; Arnold Fenasse; Aimery Guinho of Bonneterre; Azemar Froment of Cestayrols; Peter of Najac; Blausat; Peter Bot; John of Foissens; John of Ports; the son-in-law of Veselle.[112]

When these persons we have named and many others came up to them, first William of Le Puy laid violent hands on him [Arnold Catalan] and said, 'Get out of the city, you villain.' Those who followed him, seeing his act, also laid hands roughly on the persons of the friar and dragged him about, some striking him with their fists on the chest, some slapping his face; some dragged him by the hood, others tore his cloak, as was to be seen for many days thereafter. O woe! If you had seen how they beat him, some from the front, others at his back. Some of them, indeed, tried to drag him into the shops to cut his throat. He, seeing what his fate was to be, lifted his hands to heaven and exclaimed in a loud voice: 'Blessed be our Lord Jesus Christ,' and 'I give thanks to Thee, Lord Jesus Christ'; to those who were beating him and dragging him to his death, he said: 'May the Lord have mercy on you.' A great throng of people was clamorously following them, shouting: 'Away, rid the earth of this fellow! He has no right to live.' Thus, shouting, thus beating and dragging him, they crossed the first street and reached the second, which ran down to the River Tarn and, when they had gone a little further, some people overtook them, who snatched him from their hands. As he found himself free and they had ceased the beating, he returned to the cemetery and, crossing it, reached the church of St Cecilia.

Isarn, priest of Denat, who had seen him dragged toward death, had followed to watch the end. Him they seized and, as with the aforesaid friar, showered abuse and insults on him and tore his clothing. O what mockery by the infidels! As they [Arnold and Isarn] were going through the streets returning to the church of St Cecilia, people cried out, 'Death to the traitors!' Others cried, 'Why don't they cut off the traitor's head and stuff it in a sack and throw it in the Tarn?' More than two or three hundred who had assembled there shouted agreement with this sentiment and it was said, although it cannot be declared for a fact, that the whole city resounded with the same cries.

Thus, when he reached the cathedral, in the presence of the bishop, the people, and the clergy, Friar Arnold at once excommunicated the town. Then some of them, moved to repentance, promised to make amends for themselves and for the people and swore in the hands of the bishop that in this affair they would stand wholly in his recognizance. They besought Friar Arnold to forgive them for the harm done. He replied that he very willingly forgave the injury to his person, as far as he could or should, but the harm done to the universal church and the lord pope he could not and did not forgive, but, at the instance of the lord bishop and all who were present, he withdrew the sentence he had pronounced.

Witnesses to this affair were Bernard, chaplain to the lord bishop of Albi; Peter Guiraud, priest and notary of the city of Albi; Robert, priest of Fréjairolles; Déodat, chaplain and schoolmaster[113] of Castres; Peter Salomon, priest of Boissezon; William, priest of Montpinier; Raymond, priest of St Affrique; Peter of Fraisse, rector of the church of Sénégats; Master Peter of Vilhers; Henry, a French cleric; William Coderc; Bernard Roguier; Peter Pelfort; and Isarn, priest of Denat, who was his comrade in tribulation.

Here ends the book.

# References

1. See pp. 211, 214, 220, below. He was probably at least twenty-five years old in 1234; that was the minimum age Dominic had set for friars to preach outside the convent: G. R. Galbraith, *The Constitution of the Dominican Order, 1216 to 1360*, 43.

2. His name occurs repeatedly in connection with the investigations of Bernard of Caux and John of St Pierre in 1245–1246, as recorded in MS 609 of the Bibliothèque municipale of Toulouse; cf. Dossat, *Les Crises de l'Inquisition toulousaine*, 221, 241.

3. Bernard Gui, *De fundatione et prioribus conventuum provinciarum tolosanae et provinciae ordinis praedicatorum*, P. A. Amargier (ed.), 32–42 (hereafter cited as Gui, *De fundatione*).

4. That anonymous piece was also copied into the Doat Collection, XXXI, ff. 29v–32; and printed in E. Martène and U. Durand, *Thesaurus novus anecdotarum*, I, 985–7. A few phrases are common to William Pelhisson's chronicle and the anonymous work, and Pelhisson's presence in Albi during the events narrated might be thought to indicate his authorship but Bernard Gui gives no sign of suspecting it. Moreover, the list of names of townsmen and clergy of Albi and vicinity points toward an author quite familiar with the place; perhaps Isarn, priest of Denat, one of the victims of mob violence (p. 228, below) was a source of information or even the author.

5. *De fratre Guillelmo Pelisso veterimo inquisitionis historica.*

6. There is no title in the MS of Avignon edited by Douais. That of Carcassonne, edited by Molinier, has the title as given here, with the additional misleading words: 'concerning the Albigenses'. Differences in the two editions will be noted hereafter only when they affect the sense of the passage. The edition of Douais will be referred to as D; that of Molinier as M.

7. This sentence was, no doubt, prefixed by Bernard Gui when he copied Pelhisson's narrative.

8. Honorius III (1216–1227).

9. Fulk of Marseilles, bishop of Toulouse (1205–1232). There is a biography of him by S. Stronski, *Le Troubadour Foulquet de Marseille*.

10. Heb. 10:39: 'We are not children of withdrawing unto perdition.' This and the following passage are the only quotations of scripture in the chronicle, and it may be that Bernard Gui interpolated them.

11. Ps. 77 [A.V. 78]:9.

12. The words, 'Passing . . . performed', and the subsequent 'after the peace made at Paris', are not in M.

13. See pp. 127–8, above.

14. D: *studium generale*; M: *studium theologiae*. A proclamation inviting scholars to the university and painting an idyllic picture of their opportunities is translated in L. Thorndike, *University Records and Life in the Middle Ages*, 32–5.

15. Pelhisson normally uses *villa* [town] to refer to Toulouse or other urban communities; occasionally, to be specific about the bourg of St Sernin, he writes *burgum, suburbium*. *Civitas*, used here, rarely appears.

16. Pons of Capdenier was 'the Croesus of late twelfth and thirteenth century Toulouse' (Mundy, *Liberty and Political Power*, 62; cf. 68, 79). A more circumstantial account of the transaction appears in William Pelhisson's list of properties, copied in Gui, *De fundatione*, 32–3. The garden was purchased from Bernard Raymond Fuster. It lay along the Saracen wall, dividing city and bourg. An adjacent site of a demolished tower was also donated to the friars, and a garden with house and dovecoat on the side of the bourg was purchased, the brothers Garrigues giving up their rights over the latter. Another purchase of about that time is listed, *ibid.*, 39. Cf. D, 85, n. 2; M, 7, n. 3.

17. John of Johannia of Gargas was an early friar in Toulouse (Vicaire, *Saint Dominic*, 506, n. 123). He was prior *ca.* 1230–1232, and died about 1264: Gui, *De fundatione*, 47.

18. Raymond, called also 'of Miramont', was an early follower of Dominic and had been prior at Montpellier, then provincial prior (B. Gui, *De fundatione*, 247). As bishop (1232–1270), he was active against heretics, although this did not prevent friendly relations with Raymond VII after 1240. His later years were troubled by charges of luxurious living, simony, and fratricide, brought by Archbishop Maurin of Narbonne, but he was exculpated by the pope (*HGL*, VI, 877–9; VIII, 1528–41). Raymond was also one of several prominent ecclesiastics of the time who consulted a well-known fortune-teller (Douais, *Documents*, I, 78, n. 4).

19. He was prior in 1232–1233: B. Gui, *De fundatione*, 49.

20. Roland entered the order at Bologna in 1219, studied at Paris, and was the first religious to teach theology there: Stephen of Salagnac and Bernard Gui, *De quatuor in quibus deus praedicatorum ordinem insignivit*, Thomas Käppeli (ed.), 32 (hereafter cited as Salagnac–Gui, *De quatuor*); also M, 8, n. 4.

21. Differences in the MSS make identification somewhat uncertain, but the text is probably accurate. By contrast, M reads (10): 'John Peter Donat, a cleric of St Sernin, was hereticated at death with the surplice and there he who had been hereticated at death was buried in the cloister.' This is obviously corrupt. Quétif and Echard, *Scriptores ordinis praedicatorum*, I, 126, give

the passage as 'John Peter Donat, a canon of St Sernin, died in the bourg and was buried in the cloister with the surplice; he earlier had become a heretic without the canons' knowledge.' Thus, the individual may have been A. (or John) Peter, a donat (a donat was a layman who gave property to a religious house, receiving in return support for his old age and burial among the religious), or he might have been A. (or John) Peter Donatus, a family name not unknown in Toulouse. Identification of him as a donat named Arnold Peter is supported by the appearance of that name in a document of 1279 listing persons who had been convicted of heresy: see n. 107 below.

22. *Archimandrita* [abbot, archbishop]. No office with that title existed among the Waldenses. This is the only member of the sect mentioned by William Pelhisson. The relatively small number of Waldenses in the region of Toulouse may be accounted for by the example and influence of Durand of Huesca (see p. 46, above), according to Y. Dossat, 'Les Vaudois méridionaux d'après les documents de l'Inquisition', in *CFan*, II, 225.

23. John of Galand, an Englishman who taught at Toulouse at about this time, in his poem, *De triumphis ecclesiae* (Thomas Wright [ed.] 101), praises Roland for his preaching and for consigning to the flames the vanities of Galvan (*sed haereticum contudit ille nefas | Gaudi qui vana Galvani tradidit igni*).

24. 2 March 1232.

25 Romeu de Llivia had been prior at Lyon; he was provincial of Toulouse, 1233–1236, prior of Bordeaux, 1258–1260, and died in 1261 (C. Douais, *Les Frères prêcheurs en Gascogne*, 479–81, citing R. P. Cormier, *Le Bien-heureux Romée de Livia*). Stephen of Bourbon heard from him a story of Dominic's preaching at Fanjeaux, when a cat of horrible appearance and nauseous odour sprang among the congregation, disclosing thus the one whom heretics worshipped (A. Lecoy de la Marche, *Anecdotes historiques, légendes et apologues tirées du recueil inédit d'Etienne de Bourbon*, 34–5).

26. He was an Englishman, a former physician, who had studied and taught theology at Paris: M, p. 12, n. 2; Quétif and Echard, *Scriptores ordinis praedicatorum*, I, 100–2.

27. Pons was prior in 1234–1235 and again in 1258. In the interval he had been prior at Montpellier, 1250–1256: B. Gui, *De fundatione*, 51, 247; Molinier, *L'Inquisition*, 44, n. 1.

28. The name in Latin, *Cellani* in our text, *Sillanus Seilanus* in others, may also be transliterated as Sella or Silla; I follow the usage of Vicaire, *Saint Dominic*. Peter Seila was of a prominent family in Toulouse and had been one of Dominic's first companions. In 1219, he helped to found a convent at Limoges and one at Cahors in 1226, whence he returned to Toulouse in 1232, and was prior, 1235–1237. He died in 1257: B. Gui, *De fundatione*, 50, 57–9.

29. He became prior in Toulouse in 1237 and was assassinated at Avignonet in 1242: see pp. 169–70 above; Molinier, *L'Inquisition*, 44, n. 3; Salagnac–Gui, *De quatuor*, 16, 23–4; Gui, *De fundatione*, 30.

30. John of Bernin, archbishop of Vienne, papal legate in Languedoc, 1233–1238. Dossat, *Les Crises de l'Inquisition toulousaine*, 121–2, shows that the appointments of the inquisitors were made in January or February 1234.

31. All that is known of Arnold Catalan comes from William Pelhisson.

32. The incident described here is referred to again a little later (p. 214) and described in more detail in the anonymous piece annexed to the chronicle of William Pelhisson (pp. 226–8, below).

33. This sentence, incomplete in D, does not appear in M.

34. Ferrier acted as inquisitor in Narbonne (see p. 144 above) and in various other regions including Albi until about 1244, after which he was prior of Prouille, Carcassonne, and Béziers, successively. The date of his death is unknown: Wakefield, 'Friar Ferrier', *CHR*, LVIII (1972), 222–3, 233–4.

35. The list of names which follows is not in M, being replaced by the copyist's comment that about forty names appeared in the document before him.

36. The terms of the treaty, in fact, called for a bounty of two marks for the first two years, one mark thereafter, with no time limit.

37. For some of these disturbances, see Wakefield, 'The Family of Niort', *Names*, XVIII (1970), 107–10.

38. Durand of St Ybars had been Raymond VI's vicar for Toulouse about 1214, was again in that office in the 1220s, and was consul in 1231–1232. Raymond VII was heavily in debt to him when the crusade ended and as a result allowed Durand to collect certain comital revenues. Durand's conduct in this and subsequent cases perhaps shows that he hoped to acquire confiscated heretical property: Mundy, *Liberty and Political Power*, 112–14, 160, and notes on pp. 321, 326–7.

39. *De Consolario*. The name is *De Solerio* in William of Pylaurens' account (*Cronica*, Beyssier [ed.], 155). The reference is to events following the council held at Toulouse in 1229 (p. 134, above).

40. The passage from 'The Lord God' to 'situation' is not in M.

41. M: *de Manso*; D: *Denense*. The place is Le Mas-Saintes-Puelles. The raiding party bound for Avignonet in 1242 (see pp. 169–70, above) would pause there but William was not, as implied in M, p. 19, n. 1, a participant in the assassination. He may, in fact, have been the one member of this family, seigneurs of the place, who voluntarily gave up adherence to the heretics before the Inquisition began: MS 609 of the municipal library of Toulouse fol. llr; cf. Roquebert, *L'Épopée cathare*, 118.

42. A Juliana, widow of John Textor, perhaps the individual named here, was sentenced to perpetual imprisonment in 1247 as an adherent of heretics and a perjurer: Douais, *Documents*, II, 63.

43. The passage, 'In all things' to 'refuted' is not in M.

44. Albe ('L'Hérésie albigeoise et l'Inquisition en Quercy', *RHEgF*, I [1910], 276–7), suggests that the charges against Humbert of Castelnau might have included usury, since his son was later described as a money changer.

45. This sentence was interpreted by Guiraud (*Histoire de l'Inquisition*, II, 44) to mean that there was such a holocaust in Moissac in 1234. The reference, however, is clearly to the events at Montségur in 1244.

46. These were not the only fugitives: see Albe, 'L'Herésie albigeoise', *RHEgF*, I (1910), 277, n. 3.

47. This is the only mention in surviving documents of an inquisitor of this name; perhaps Pelhisson was referring to himself.

48. D: *Sancii;* M: *Sancerii;* see also, n. 107, below

49. A district so named from a cross situated at the intersection of today's Rue des Arts, Rue Tolosane, and Rue Croix Baragnon. The Baragnon, or Barahnon, were a prominent Toulousan family.

50. 5 August. Dominic had died on 6 August 1221; his feast day was announced by Gregory IX as 5 August in the original canonization, but was transferred to 4 August by Pius V: Vicaire, *Saint Dominic*, 387, 529, n. 46.

51. Today Rue Romiguières.

52. In Salagnac–Gui, *De quatuor*, 16–18, this incident is briefly described, with the added comments that after the meal Pons of St Gilles went out to confront an angry mob that had gathered,defying their shouts and exhorting all Catholics to aid the Inquisition; and that within a week a number of persons came to confess their offences.

53. Note the lapse of time, August 1234 to April 1235, and see the comment of Salagnac–Gui about confessions in the preceding note. Would the friars have remained so long inactive? Dossat (*Les Crises de l'Inquisition toulousaine*, 128) suggests that the events which William Pelhisson here puts after Good Friday 1235 might well have occurred in the preceding winter, especially those in which the vicar participated. Durand of St Ybars was not in office after 22 April 1235.

54. M: *fervicosus*, but Douais read *servicosus* in the same MS, and from the one he edited gives *cervinerius*. Duvernoy (*Chronique de Guillaume Pelhisson*, 30), renders it 'chaudronnier' [coppersmith].

55. On Peter William Delort, see p. 217, also n. 107 below; on Raymond Roger, pp. 218, 222, 225, and n. 107. A later sentence of Peter Esquivat survives. The inquisitors announcing it on 17 May 1246, noted that he had acknowledged his guilt before William Arnold and had agreed to accept a penalty, prison or exile, but thereafter had continued to consort with heretics: Douais, *Documents*, II, 17.

56. Cf. p. 225, below.

57. Already the count had protested to the pope, for a letter of Gregory IX of 18 November 1234 summarizes his complaints: L. Auvray (ed.), *Les Registres de Grégoire IX*, I, No. 2218.

58. The archdeacon was Guy, major archdeacon of Carcassonne, who had opened the case in collaboration with the bishop and the provost of Toulouse: see Wakefield, 'The Family of Niort', *Names*, XVIII (1970), 110; also Dossat 'La Répression de l'hérésie', *CFan*, VI, 241–7.

59. John of Friscamps.

60. Guy II (1219–1247), whose father had been one of Simon of Montfort's staunch companions.

61. This may well refer to two individuals, for both Sicard of Toulouse and Sicard of Gameville are listed in a later document (see n. 107) and Sicard of Toulouse is named again below (see p. 225). The latter was excommunicated for heresy before 24 July 1237 (Doat, XXI, fols. 146–8v; Dossat, *Les Crises de l'Inquisition toulousaine*, 344–6).

62. Arnold Gui had been given the penance of a trip to the Holy Land by Cardinal Romanus in 1229 and was at last making preparations to go in March 1237 (Mundy, *Liberty and Political Power*, 290, n. 18). Rica, his mother, was sentenced as a deceased heretic, 1237 (Doat, XXI, fols. 182–3). On both, see n. 107.

63. See also n. 107.

64. M: *Melicum*; D: *medicus*.

65. The Maurand family had long been implicated in heresy (see p. 84, above). On this individual, see pp. 220, 225, below and n. 107. Names of several others of the family appear in later pages.

66. D: *Sigarii*; M: *Siguareii*, in other documents *Signarii* (cf. Mundy, *Liberty and Political Power*, 184, 188). As consul, he was excommunicated for refusing to take action against convicted heretics on 24 July 1237 (Doat, XXI, fols. 146–8; Dossat, *Les Crises de l'Inquisition toulousaine*, pp. 344–6). He was sentenced to prison as a heretic on 22 February 1238 (Doat, XXI,

fols. 149–53). Some of his property went to the bishop of Toulouse in 1279: Toulouse, archives municipales, AA 4 (18).

67. See also p. 218, 225, below, and n. 107.

68. See pp. 217, 225.

69. All of these men except Pons of Seilh, Raymond Borel, and Raymond Roger were also consuls in 1237, when they were excommunicated for allowing various persons to avoid arrest after they had been condemned for heresy (Doat, XXI, fols. 146–8v; Dossat, *Les Crises de l'Inquisition toulousaine*, 344–6). We have seen that Bernard Seguier and Raymond Roger had already been cited for heresy. Although William Pelhisson does not mention the fact, Arnold Barrau, Raymond Borel, and Aldric Maurand were also prosecuted at some later time, for their property was confiscated: see n. 107.

70. William of Puylaurens (*Cronica*, Bessyier [ed.], 139), passes over the events here mentioned with these words: 'Now of the acts committed against the bishop and the canons of his church and his domestics, I deem it preferable to keep silent out of respect for the city, of which the body was basically sound, although at this moment and in this instance it was corrupted by a little ferment.'

71. It was a normal custom, when a friar was entrusted with some special office, for him to cast himself humbly on the ground (Galbraith, *Constitution of the Dominican Order*, 43).

72. Raymond is said to have earlier been prior of Cahors; he was to be prior in Toulouse from 1242 to 1258 (Gui, *De fundatione*, 50–1, 77; M, 35, n. 1). Nothing more is known of John of St Michael. Gui of Navarre was later inquisitor at Carcassonne and then prior of Agen (Gui, *De fundatione*, 112).

73. The two sons later came voluntarily to confess to inquisitors: Maurand on 21 March 1238, Raymond Maurand on 25 April 1238; both were given pilgrimages as penance. Raymond was also fined: Doat, XXI, fols. 177v, 178.

74. The Coussa were a patrician and orthodox family. Peter's father, Bernard Peter, frequently a consul, had acted for Simon of Montfort in governing Toulouse: A. Molinier, 'La Commune de Toulouse et Phillipe III', *Bibliothèque de l'École des chartes*, XLIII [1882], 38; but see also Mundy, *Liberty and Political Power*, 299, n. 53, for Bernard Peter's support of the revolt against Simon.

75. Lawrence had been an early companion of Dominic and had helped to establish the friars in Paris: Salagnac–Gui, *De quatuor*, 155.

76. It was either 5 November or 6 November. The text reads: *In sequenti vero die, feria tertia* [Tuesday] *post festum omnium sanctorum nonis novembris*. The nones, however, 5 November, fell on Monday. Gui (*De fundatione*, 50) noticed the ambiguity of the dating. D (105, n. 3) inexplicably gives the date as 3 November.

77. M: *Quando ... dolebant Fratres expelli*; D: *quando ... debebant Fratres expelli*.

78. Actually to Perugia, according to Dossat, *Les Crises de l'Inquisition toulousaine*, 133, n. 192.

79. Already mentioned (p. 148, above), has been Dossat's suggestion that William Pelhisson, by a slip of memory or of the pen, substituted the feast of St Augustine (28 August) for the earlier feast of the translation of St Augustine (28 February). He makes the following points: there was time and opportunity between November 1235 and 28 February 1236, for the count and legate to have negotiated the return; according to Pelhisson the friars

were in Toulouse by 2 April (see p. 223 below); inquisitors from Toulouse were at work in Quercy at the end of April; and the pope did not contest Raymond VII's statement that the friars returned after 'not many days'. The counter-argument offered by Duvernoy (*Chronique de Guillaume Pelhisson*, 3) is that Pelhisson ought to be trusted to have given the correct date and that when he wrote '1236' the year was actually 1237, for he was using the style of dating which began the year with Easter, which fell on 19 April 1237. Dossat has since abandoned his conclusion about the style of dating which led him to declare for 1236.

80. He is the first Franciscan friar known to have acted as inquisitor.

81. The sentence is printed from Doat, XXI, fols. 160–1 in Dossat, *Les Crises de l'Inquisition toulousaine*, 343–4.

82. There are numerous references to Raymond Gros, heretic, in the sources. It is possible that they involve more than one man of that name (cf. Duvernoy, *Chronique de Guillaume Pelhisson*, 40, n. 1). On a Raymond Gros who became a friar, see Appendix V, n. 31. Vicaire ('Saint Dominique et les inquisiteurs', *AM*, LXXIX [1967], 173–94), has shown that no credence should be given to the legend that St Dominic had saved Raymond Gros from death in 1216 or 1217 in foreknowledge of the services he would later perform for the faith.

83. In 1246, William Bonsolas, together with William Pelhisson, acted as assistant to inquisitors in receiving depositions (M, p. 43, n. 2), and he was later prior of Cahors until about 1265 (Gui, *De fundatione*, 151).

84. Arnold was to act as inquisitor in Toulouse during the absence of the Dominicans after 1250: Douais, *Documents*, I, 131, 136.

85. On Nicholas, see also Appendix 5, p. 245.

86. All the persons named in this sentence were of consular families. The sentences of Alesta and Dyas in September 1237 are preserved (Doat, XXI, fols. 179–80, 183–5). On Arnold Barrau, see n. 69. Bertrand of Roaix was sentenced to prison in February 1237 (Doat, XXI, fols. 149–53) and was still there in 1247 (see Appendix 5, p. 247) but was later pardoned (Douais, *Documents*, I, 218, n. 4. Dossat (*Les Crises de l'Inquisition toulousaine*, 355, n. 1) believes two persons of the same name should be discerned, but his explanation is not clear. Bertrand's son fled to Lombardy and was there between 1250 and 1256 (M, 46, n. 2). On all these persons see also n. 107.

87. Cf. p. 217, above.

88. His sentence is preserved (Doat, XXI, fols. 179–80). See also n. 107.

89. The sentence of Raymonda is preserved (Doat, XXI, fols. 17c–80). Jordan of Villeneuve and his son Arnold were also sentenced for heresy at some time; the wife of Bertrand of St Loup was named Mabriana: see n. 107.

90. His wife, Anglesia, was sentenced on 22 February 1238: Doat, XXI, fol. 149–53. See also n. 107.

91. On Fays and Blanqua, see n. 107.

92. On Bernard Embry and Raymond Centolhs, see n. 107. The latter was sentenced before 24 July 1237 (Doat, XXI, fols. 146v–8). A Raymond Centol of Toulouse was later reported to have died at Montségur (*ibid.*, XXIII, fol. 230v); a man of the same name testified about heretical teaching on 21 February 1244: *ibid.*, XXII, fol. 32r–v.

93. On both men see also n. 107. Raymond Roger has been mentioned several times previously. Even after he had been condemned as a heretic, before 24 July 1237, he and Alaman of Roaix were accused of molesting Christians in Toulouse without interference from the consuls: *Ibid.*, XXI, fols. 146v–8; Dossat, *Les Crises de l'Inquisition toulousaine*, 344–6.

94. On this notorious believer of heretics see Appendix 4.

95. Sicard was sentenced before 24 July 1237 (Doat, XXI, fols. 146v–8). Stephen Masse was sentenced on 22 February 1238 (*ibid.*, fols. 149–53). Peter of Roaix and Pons of Gameville were declared to be relapsed heretics on 18 March 1246 (Douais, *Documents*, II, 1–2). Peter's property was confiscated by Count Raymond VII (Dossat, *Les Crises de l'Inquisition toulousaine*, 350–1). His wife, Raymonda, was condemned as a deceased heretic on 5 September 1237 (Doat, XXI, fols. 179–80v). On all these persons see also n. 107.

96. William Mercadier and Arnold William Peyrier were seen in Lombardy between 1250 and 1256 (M., 48, n. 3; Mundy, *Liberty and Political Power*, 289, n. 18). Ondrada was sentenced before 24 July 1237 (Doat, XXI, fols. 149–53), Arnold William on 22 February 1238, at which time a Beatrix, called wife of Arnold William Peyrier, was also sentenced (*ibid., fols.* 149–53). See also n. 107.

97. The sentence of Ondrada's mother, Esclarmonde, as a deceased heretic, 5 September 1237, is in *ibid.*, fols. 179–80v.

98. He also fled to Lombardy: M, p. 48, n. 5.

99. D: *Boers*; M: *Brens*.

100. On the property of all the persons named to this point in this paragraph except Bartholomew Boers, see n. 107.

101. He also fled to Lombardy: M, 48, n. 3; Mundy, *Liberty and Political Power*, 289, n. 18; see also n. 107.

102. D, by inserting a comma after Cadolhe, makes this name refer to two persons.

103. All three of these men, fervent believers, acted as armed guards and bully-boys for heretics (see, for example, Doat, XXIII, fols. 94–5v, 148v; XXIV, 200). They joined Trencavel's revolt and were in the murder party at Avignonet (*HGL*, VIII, 1154–6). Their sentences as heretics *in absentia* were issued in October 1241: Doat, XXI, fols. 158–9v.

104. On them see p. 169, above.

105. Raymond Unald, who had fought the Albigensian crusaders (*Chanson*, III, 92, n. 2), had also done good service to one of his retainers (*armiger*) when the latter was condemned to death by the consuls of Toulouse for an undisclosed offence about 1231. Raymond and Alaman of Roaix escorted heretics to the gallows before the execution, where the man was given the consolamentum (Doat, XXII, fol. 86v; XXIV, fols. 85v–6; Bibliothèque municipale de Toulouse, MS 609, fol. 201v). He was condemned as a deceased heretic on 20 September 1237 (Doat, XXI, fol. 183–5). Some of his property went to the bishop of Toulouse in 1279: Toulouse, archives municipales, AA.4 (18).

106. Probably in April or May 1237, when the legate is known to have been in Albi: Dossat, *Les Crises de l'Inquisition toulousaine*, 138.

107. Comment on disposition of the property of many of the persons named in preceding pages has been deferred to this point. Document AA.34.3 of the municipal archives of Toulouse (described in E. Roschach, *Inventaire des archives communales de Toulouse anterieures à 1790*, I, 445–6) is a letter patent of Philip III, dated August 1279. It discloses that a controversy had arisen between the king's procurator and certain citizens of Toulouse over property to which title was in question because of convictions for heresy, murder, theft, counterfeiting, or other crimes. After investigation, the king by this letter: (1) abandoned all rights to such property, provided the acts had occurred before 1270; (2) forbade further disturbance of the petitioners; (3) ratified

all transactions with them by his predecessors in the county; (4) spared from destruction houses which were under such sentence and permitted others to be built where houses had been destroyed; (5) allowed sons and nephews of condemned persons full rights of inheritance. The letter gives 258 names and refers to at least nineteen other persons as sisters, wives, or brothers of named individuals. Many have been encountered in these pages. In alphabetical order of first name they are: Alaman of Roaix and his wife (probably Lombarda, since Joanne is named separately); Aldric Maurand, alias Pedas; Arnold Barrau; Arnold Gui the elder; Arnold Peter of St Sernin; Arnold Roger; Arnold Sans; Arnold of Villeneuve; Arnold William Peyrier; Bernard Embry; Bertrand of Roaix and his wife, Petrona; Bernard Seguier; Blanqua of Gameville; Cortesia, sister of William Mercadier; Dyas, wife of Arnold Barrau; Fays of Gameville; John Salade; Joanne, wife of Alaman of Roaix; Jordan of Villeneuve; Mabriana, wife of Bertrand of St Loup; Magna, wife of Jordan of Villeneuve; Maurand the elder; Ondrada, wife of Arnold William Peyrier; (the name Peitavin Laurence does not appear, but Laurentia Peitavin does); Peter of Beauville; Peter Embry; Peter of Roaix; Peter Esquivat; Peter William Delort; Pons of Gameville; Pons of Seilh; Raymond Borel; Raymond Centolhs; Raymond Isarn (this name appears twice); Raymond of Mirepoix and his wife; Raymond Roger the elder; Raymonda, wife of Arnold of Villeneuve; Riqua, wife of Arnold Gui; Sicard of Gameville; Sicard of Toulouse; Stephen Masse and his wife, Angelesia; Stephen of Spain and his wife; William Mercadier. We have no way of knowing how much advantage to them or their heirs there was in the king's action; presumably much of the confiscated property had already been given away or sold (cf. nn. 66, 105). My thanks are due to Professor John Mundy, who called this document to my attention and who intends to publish it.

108. This paragraph was, no doubt, supplied by Bernard Gui.

109. This sentence is attributable to Bernard Gui. I have supplied the title.

110. Durand, bishop of Albi (1228–1254).

111. Pons Bernard, then designated as knight, at a date unknown was sentenced to life imprisonment, but died before beginning his penance. Because he had given information about other heretics toward the end of his life, the penalty was remitted in 1264 and his son, William of Puy, was freed of further liability, in return for a payment of one hundred pounds, money of Tours: Molinier, *L'Inquisition*, 324–4.

112. There are numerous discrepancies in the transcription of names in D and M. It seems unnecessary to note all of them here. Some identifications which are possible show that heretical sympathies, or the suspicion that they existed, continued. Azemar Brose was consul of Albi in 1252 and a later generation of his family was charged with heresy. A Raymond Hugo (*Huc*) was charged with heresy in 1299–1300; so was a Berengar Fumet. The numerous and prominent Fenasse (or Fenassa) family had several members similarly suspected then, as did the related house of Foissens: see G. W. Davis, *The Inquisition at Albi, 1299–1300*, 270–2, 276–8, 287–8, 293; Biget, 'Un Procès d'Inquisition à Albi', *CFan*, VI, 273–341, especially p. 289.

113. M: *capellanus et capiscol*; D: *capellanus de Cabiscol*.

# Appendix 4

# Two Sentences by Inquisitors

The two sentences translated here were issued by Bernard of Caux and John of St Pierre in 1246 and 1248 respectively.[1] The first, sending six persons to prison, is typical of most verdicts of the period in its recital of guilty acts, statement of procedure, and the order for imprisonment, but has an unusual element in the respite allowed to one man on his father's behalf.

The subject of the second sentence was a citizen of Toulouse, prominent by reason of family and his own reputation as a believer of heretics. Alaman of Roaix belonged to one of the wealthiest families of Toulouse.[2] He had been one of the persons ordered to make a pilgrimage to the Holy Land by Cardinal Romanus after the council of Toulouse in 1229. He did not go and continued to be very active on behalf of heretics. His first and second wives, Lombarda and Joanne, were devoted believers, as were his two sons and two daughters.[3] In May 1237 Alaman was one of several persons excommunicated and sentenced *in absentia* by William Arnold and Stephen of St Thibéry. Part of their verdict is as follows:

Therefore, since we, the aforesaid inquisitors, have manifestly discovered through diligent inquest that the said Alaman of Roaix many times in many places, within and outside of Toulouse, before the peace [of 1229] and after,[4] had received heretics in his house and had often given them meals and often heard their preaching and often and frequently adored them; and before Christmas and at Christmas and for a long time afterward he sheltered them in his house, making a special hiding place for them; and, moreover, he lent his counsel and assistance in the performance of heretications by heretics; he carried the letters of heretics for the purpose of collecting sums bequeathed by will to heretics and in their names received money; and he approved of the faith of the heretics; and we found many other things against him which rendered him suspect of heresy. . . . The aforesaid Alaman of Roaix being absent and refusing to appear, we condemn him as a heretic. . . .[5]

The consuls and vicar of Toulouse, however, had refused to arrest Alaman and others condemned in 1237 and were, on that account, themselves excommunicated.[6] Alaman remained at liberty, taking refuge with fellow believers in the mountains and visiting Montségur before its capture.[7] His fortunes worsened, however, for in 1243–1244 he was existing on the generosity, real or shown under duress, of acquaintances.[8] We do not know whether Alaman surrendered or was captured in January 1248 but within three days of his recantation he was sentenced. No doubt his notoriety and the prominence of his family account for the presence of the bishop and the count of Toulouse at the condemnation and for the place where it was delivered; it is one of two in this collection of sentences which were handed down in the town hall of Toulouse.

The translation is from Célestin Douais, *Documents pour servir à l'histoire de l'Inquisition dans le Languedoc* (2 vols, Paris, 1890), II, 8–10, 69–72.

I

In the name of our Lord Jesus Christ, amen.
In the year of our Lord, 6 May 1246.

We, friars of the Order of Preachers, Bernard of Caux and John of St Pierre, deputed as inquisitors of heretical depravity in the city and diocese of Toulouse by apostolic authority:

Since it is made evident to us through the confessions of Pons Bladier, Peter of Albigeois, and Raymond Sabbatier,[9] made in the course of trial, that they knowingly saw heretics many times, adored them many times, heard their preaching and believed them to be good men, concealed the truth contrary to their oath, and are relapsed into heresy once abjured;

Also, since it is made evident to us that Pons Dominic saw heretics many times in many places, believed them to be good men, heard their preaching, adored them, received them in his house many times, made them gifts from his possessions, was present at a heretication, ate with heretics, and, after he had made his confession to other inquisitors and abjured heresy, received heretics in his house within a few years and thereafter;

Since Raymond Maurin and Arnalda, his wife, many times and in many places knowingly saw many heretics, believed them to be good men, heard their preaching, adored them, received them in their house and ate with them; and the same Raymond guided them and received the Peace[10] from heretics, and denied the truth contrary to his oath; and the said Arnalda was present at an *apparellamentum*[11] of the heretics and sheltered a female heretic, who died in her house, and was present at the burial;

We first absolve from the chains of excommunication by which they were bound by reason of the aforesaid crimes these citizens of Toulouse who, accepting sounder counsel, now, as they assert, wish to return to the unity of the church, provided that they shall have returned to ecclesiastical unity in good faith and shall have fulfilled the commands laid upon them. As they now, in response to lawful citation, appear before us on the day peremptorily assigned to them for receiving penance for the crime of heresy, it is our will, because they have rashly transgressed against God and holy church in the ways aforesaid, that they be thrust into perpetual prison to do condign penance, and we command them to remain there in perpetuity. And we enjoin them to complete this penance in virtue of the oath they have taken. If, indeed, they refuse to accomplish the aforesaid penance, we bind them by the chains of excommunication. However, we grant permission to Raymond Sabbatier to remain with his father, who is an invalid and who, it is reported, is a Catholic and a poor man, as long as his father shall live; and meanwhile he shall wear a black mantle and on each garment a cross with two transverse branches, and he shall provide for his father as best he can.

Done at Toulouse, in the cloister of St Sernin, in the presence of W. Bernard, abbot of Idrac; Arnold Auriol, prior of St Sernin; Pons of Albione [and] Peter of Drudas, canons of St Sernin; Peter, prior of Caslus in the diocese of Cahors; W., chaplain of Le Mas-Saintes-Puelles; Arnold of Brassac, chaplain of Labécède; R. Berengar and Bernard of Escalquens of the chapter; R. P. Aribert, P. of Montbiza, and Bernard of Gaus, scribes for the Inquisition.

## II

In the year as given above [1248], 19 January.

Alaman of Roaix, who was condemned for heresy because he saw and adored heretics, both men and women, many times in many places, harboured and sheltered them many times, ate with them and ate of the bread blessed by them many times, was present at many *apparelhamenta* and at the heretications of many persons, often guided and associated with heretics, often gave to and received from them funds, accepted the Peace from them often, and heard the heretics preaching errors about visible things – that God did not make them, that there is no salvation in baptism and matrimony, that the bodies of the dead will not arise, and that there are two gods, one benign and one malign – and he believed the aforesaid errors just as the heretics uttered them and for thirty years he believed the heretics to be good men; and he abandoned that belief on Thursday after the feast of the Blessed Hillary just past;[12] also, he admitted that all the things were true which were alleged against him in the matter of heretical depravity by the late Friar Stephen of the Order of Friars Minor and the late Friar William Arnold of the Order of Preachers, inquisitors of heretical depravity, with the exception of certain acts in violation of the peace,[13] for it was there alleged that they had been done after the peace; also, he lay under sentence of excommunication for heresy for ten years and more;

Having received the counsel of good men, we command him by virtue of his sworn oath today to enter the prison of St Etienne,[14] there to remain in perpetuity to do penance for the acts aforesaid. We order him also to provide for Pons, who was once the companion of Raymond Scriptor,[15] fifty *solidi* of Toulouse a year as long as Pons shall live; also that he make reparation to the Hospitalers of St John for the plunder he took from them and to all other persons whatsoever on whom he inflicted damage and injury.[16]

Done at Toulouse, in the town hall, in the presence of the lord bishop of Toulouse; the lord count of Toulouse; the provost of St Etienne; W. Isarn; R., prior of the Friars Preachers; Friar R. of Paonac; John of St Gaudens; and P. Aribert.

# References

1. They are among the sentences of 192 persons in 52 general sermons between 1244 and 1248, recorded on 12 leaves of a parchment register, which may originally have run to 172 or more folios. The fragment was saved in the late eighteenth century, when a scholar discovered the parchment being used to bind schoolbooks. It is now MS latin 9992 of the Bibliothèque nationale; on it, see Douais, *Documents*, I, 253–66, and Molinier, *L'Inquisition*, 55–77.
2. The names of other members of the Roaix family are often encountered in this register and other contemporary documents referring to heresy and the Inquisition; on one such individual, see Appendix 5, pp. 244, 247. Alaman's own financial position is shown by the fact that Count Raymond VII had borrowed 4,150 *solidi*, money of Toulouse, from him on security of lands in the county. The count found some way to avoid payment, for on 3 February 1235 Alaman promised never to demand the money and to return the document recording the indebtedness, if he could find it: *HGL*, VIII, 1966. Cf. Mundy, *Liberty and Political Power*, 10, 62.
3. For examples of his activities, see p. 235, n. 105, and Wakefield, 'The Family of Niort', *Names*, XVIII (1970), 298–9. There are very many refer-

ences to him and his immediate family in Doat, Vols XXII–XXIV, and in MS 609 of the Bibliothèque municipale of Toulouse. I give only representative examples here because I propose to make a detailed study of the connection of the Roaix family with heresy. Lombarda, who died about 1227 was posthumously condemned (Doat, XXI, fol. 184); Joanne, the daughters, Blanche and Austorge, and the sons, Hugh (or Bec) and Alaman, were also on familiar terms with heretics: MS 609, fols. 201r–210v, *passim*; Doat, XXII, fols. 134v–5; XXIII, fols. 17–21v.

4. Alaman's house in Toulouse and his farmstead near Lanta were equally open to heretics: see, for example, MS 609, fol. 201r; Doat, XXII, fols. 5v, 36; XXIII, fols. 293v–4v. There seems to have been a tendency to consider acts committed before 1229 as less culpable. Cf. the protest of Raymond VII to the pope in 1234: Auvray, *Les Registres de Grégoire IX*, Vol. I, No. 2218.

5. Douais, *Documents*, II, 69, n. 2.

6. Dossat, *Les Crises de l'Inquisition toulousaine*, 344–6.

7. Doat, XXII, fols. 134v–5, 207–207v; XXIV, fol. 47v.

8. Doat XXIV, fols. 154v–5; MS 609, fols. 205v–206r.

9. Pons had been imprisoned in the Château Narbonnais (Douais, *Documents*, II, 8, n. 2); thus, he may have been arrested by officers of the count.

10. The kiss exchanged among participants and observers at the conclusion of the Cathars' religious ceremonies.

11. The term used by inquisitors to refer to the confessional assembly which Cathars called the Service.

12. 16 January.

13. The peace of 1229.

14. The prison maintained by the bishop.

15. Raymond Scriptor was one of the party murdered at Avignonet in 1242: see pp. 169–70, above.

16. Alaman's property, beyond the amount needed to meet these obligations, was confiscated by Raymond VII. The count later returned a farmstead to Hugh and Alaman of Roaix. As late as 1270, Alphonse of Poitiers, count of Toulouse, was petitioned for restitution of some of the confiscated property by a man who claimed that Alaman of Roaix had illegally deprived his father of it: Dossat, *Les Crises de l'Inquisition toulousaine*, 291, 312. On the full restoration of property rights to members of the Roaix family in 1279, see Appendix 3, n. 107.

# Appendix 5

## Testimony against Peter Garcias of Toulouse

During Lent in 1247 Peter Garcias, a citizen of Toulouse living in the quarter called Bourguet–Nau, met and talked with his relative, Friar William Garcias[1] of the Order of Friars Minor, in the convent of that order in Toulouse. Their subject was the religious beliefs of Peter Garcias, who, it appeared, was a convinced believer of the Cathars and had no hesitation in discussing his faith in what he believed was a private conversation; on one occasion he brought another person to debate with the friar. But twice at least, while Peter and William talked in the common room of the convent, their words were overheard by three or four other friars concealed in a place above the heads of the Garcias, perhaps on a balcony or perched on the boards of the ceiling.[2] Friar William was aware of their presence as he led Peter Garcias to talk about his religious ideas.

On 22 August and 10 December 1247 William Garcias and the eavesdroppers told Bernard of Caux and John of St Pierre, inquisitors, what they had heard from Peter Garcias. Other persons also testified about his reputation, one of them asserting that his father had been a believer of the Cathars, his mother an adherent of the Waldenses.[3]

The inquisitors' sentence in the case was issued on 2 February 1248: although Peter had been informed of the charge that he was suspect of heresy and had been summoned, he did not appear; he was, therefore, excommunicated as a contumacious heretic.[4] His fate thereafter is unknown. His property was confiscated. In 1268 some of it was sold by Count Alphonse; a sum assessed against another portion was donated to a religious order; and in 1268–1269 possession of yet another portion was claimed by persons who stated that Peter had transferred it to their father.[5]

The testimony of the five eavesdroppers differs in a few details, as is to be expected, but more striking is the concurrence among all, speaking at least five months after the event and in one case nine months later. It may be that the statements of the first to testify served the inquisitors as guides for prompting the others, or perhaps the friars had so often discussed among themselves what they had heard that their stories seem rehearsed. Yet we cannot doubt that the basis was Peter Garcias' words, for there are one or two striking turns of phrase and colloquialisms that break through the stiff sentences of the notary who wrote down the depositions. The result is the most circumstantial report of heretical ideas that survives among records of inquisitorial processes before 1250.

The sole record is a copy in the Collection Doat, XXII, 89–106, from which it was printed by Célestin Douais in *Documents pour servir à l'histoire de l'Inquisition dans le Languedoc*, II, 90–114. The following translation gives the deposition of Friar William Cogot on 22 August 1247 and, because Friar William had been present on only one of the two occasions of eavesdropping, that part of the testimony of Friar Déodat of Rodez which comes from the second episode is added.[6]

## The Deposition of Friar William Cogot

In the name of our crucified Lord Jesus Christ, amen. In the year 1247, 22 August, Friar William Cogot of the Order of Friars Minor, asked to tell the full and complete truth about heresy, being sworn as a witness, said that he heard Peter Garcias of Bourguet-Nau of Toulouse, when he was questioned by Friar William Garcias of the Order of Friars Minor as to whether there were two gods, say that he could in no way reach certainty about this with him with whom he had disputed for half a year.[7] Peter Garcias and Friar William Garcias were then in the common room [*schola*] of the Friars Minor of Toulouse and this witness was above, between them and the roof, in a place where he could see and hear them. As to those present with him, he said that with him were Friar Déodat of Rodez and Friar Arnold Daitz.[8] Asked about the date he said that it was this year during Lent.

Again, he said that when Friar William Garcias spoke of the text of the Apostle, 'God that sanctifieth circumcision',[9] and so on, this witness heard Peter Garcias saying that the law of Moses was nothing but shadow and vanity, and that God who gave that law was a scoundrel [*galiator*] and malign. He said this at the same time and in the same place, and the friars named above were with this witness.

Also, when Friar William Garcias spoke of that text, 'Without him was made nothing,'[10] to the Peter Garcias already mentioned, the latter said that the word 'nothing' was used to designate visible things, which are nothing. Also, Peter said that man was sin and nothing. As to date and place and those present, he [William Cogot] said the same as above.

Also, when Peter Garcias was asked by Friar William Garcias if He who was hung on the cross made these visible things, Peter answered, 'No'; for He was the best, and nothing of these visible things is good. Therefore, He made none of them. As to date and place and those present, he said the same as above.

Also, when Friar William Garcias spoke with Peter Garcias about the text, 'In Him were all things created in heaven and on earth, visible and invisible,'[11] Peter said that it should be expounded: 'Visible to the heart and invisible to the eyes of the flesh.' As to date and place and those present, he said the same as above.

Also, when Friar William Garcias spoke with Peter Garcias about the text, 'Preaching to you to be converted from these vain things [to the living God who made the heaven, the earth, and the sea and all that are in them],'[12] Peter said that Bertrand of Roaix was in the sea, that is, in prison;[13] and he had better inward eyes that Friar William Garcias and he praised Bertrand highly. As to date and place and those present, he said the same as above.

Also, he heard Peter Garcias saying that all the angels who fell from heaven, and they alone,[14] will be saved. As to date and place and those present, the same as above.

Also, he heard Peter Garcias saying that Christ and the Blessed Virgin and the Blessed John the Evangelist came down from heaven and were not of this flesh.[15] As to date and place and those present, the same as above.

Also, he heard Peter Garcias saying that John the Baptist was one of the greatest devils that ever was. As to date and place and those present, the same as above.

Also, he heard Peter Garcias, when Friar William Garcias showed him his hand and asked if flesh will rise again, saying that flesh will not rise again except as a wooden post, striking a post with his hand. As to date and place and those present he said the same as above.

Also, he heard Peter Garcias saying that Lord Jesus led no one out of hell. As to date and place and those present, he said the same as above.

Also, he heard Peter saying that matrimony was prostitution and that no one could be saved with his wife, not even he with his own wife. As to date and place and those present, he said the same as above.

Also, he heard Peter Garcias saying that that fruit forbidden to the first parents was nothing other than the pleasure of carnal coition and that Adam preferred that fruit to the woman. As to date and place and those present, the same as above.

Also, he heard Peter Garcias saying that justice ought by

no means to be carried out by condemning anyone to death. As to date and place and those present, the same as above.

Also, he heard Peter Garcias saying that if an official should judge any heretic and the latter were put to death as a heretic, the official was a murderer.[16] As to date and others [present], the same as above.

Also, he heard Peter Garcias saying that Mass was not celebrated in the church up to the time of the Blessed Sylvester nor did the church own property up to that time;[17] that the church would pass away within twenty years; that our Mass was worthless; that all the preachers of the cross are murderers; and the cross which these preachers give is nothing other than a bit of cloth on the shoulder; the same is true of the cord with which the hair is bound up. Of date and place and those present, the same as above.

Also, when Peter Garcias was repeatedly adjured and asked by Friar William Garcias whether he really believed what he had said on the foregoing topics, he replied by swearing on his faith that he believed just what he had said. As to date and others present, the same as above.

Also, when Peter was asked by William Garcias whether Peter's mother had been hereticated, he said no; but she would indeed have been, if Nicholas, a former chaplain of [the church of] the Blessed Mary of La Daurade had not prevented it.[18] And this conversation was this year, before Easter.

When this witness was asked his opinion of Peter Garcias, he answered that because of what he had heard he held him to be a believer of heretics. The above-named Friar William Cogot made this deposition at Toulouse before Friars Bernard and John, inquisitors. Witnesses were Friar Gerald, guardian of the Friars Minor of Toulouse, Friar Stephen of Lunel of the same order, and Peter Aribert, public notary, who recorded it.[19]

## The Deposition of Friar Deodat of Rodez

Also, at another time in the same place,[20] this witness heard Peter Garcias saying that the one who held the cross on Good Friday, unveiling it as he chanted, at the point where he said, 'Behold the wood of the cross,' should say, 'Behold the wood,' for there was nothing of the cross there.

Again, Peter said that all who chanted in church, singing in unintelligible fashion, deceived simple people; and that in his house he had a Passion, written in Romance, as it actually occurred.[21] Peter also said that the marriage performed by the Roman church, that is, of man and woman, for example, of him and his wife, Ayma, is prostitution; there is no matrimony except that of the soul with God. And he called the Roman church a harlot who gives poison and the power to poison to all who believe in it. And, in reference to a church which was pointed out to him, he said that it was not a church, but a building in which falsity and nonsense are uttered.

Peter also said that he had not in the carnal sense slept with his wife since Pentecost, two years ago. And when Friar William Garcias remarked to Peter that this was because she was of the same faith as his, he said no, but she was a nincompoop,[22] just as Friar William was.

Peter also said of miracles that no miracle which can be seen by the eyes is anything and that neither the Blessed Francis nor any other person performed a miracle and that God desired no justice which would condemn anyone to death. On this point, he vituperated a certain friar, a preacher of the crusade, who at Auvillars gave the cross to about seven hundred persons, saying that it was not a good deed for crusaders to march against Frederick[23] or against the Saracens or against any castle like Montségur when it opposed the church or against any place where death could occur.

Peter Garcias commended Raymond Peter of Plans[24] for probity, wisdom, and prudence, and said that he was a secretive and discreet man.[25]

Peter said to Friar William Garcias that he should not speak of this to Raymond Peter, except in the Waldensian manner.[26]

Also, Peter Garcias damned every order, except the Order of Friars Minor. He said, however, that that order was worthless, because it preached the crusade.

Peter said also that if he could lay hold of that God who would save only one out of a thousand men made by Him and would damn the others, he would break Him in pieces and rend him with nails and teeth as perfidious; and he believed Him to be false and perfidious, and he would spit in His face; and Peter added, 'May he die of gout!'[27]

Also, Peter said that only the angels who fell are to be saved, but not all such as the leaders and their assistants, only the ordinary ones, in such wise that not one out of a thousand will be damned.

Also, Peter said that there was no purgatory and that alms

given by the living are of no avail to the dead and that no one is saved unless he does perfect penance before death and that a spirit which cannot do penance in one body, if it is to be saved, passes into another body to complete penance.

Peter also said that his father and mother and Peter Cauzit[28] and the father of Willelma[29] of *Montaigo* taught him these things.

Everything on this page the witness heard this year, on the vigil of Easter, in the place mentioned above the roof and the common room, where were present the Friars Minor Arnold Daitz of Toulouse, Imbert of Rodez, and Peter Raymond of Toulouse, and Friar William Garcias[30] was below in the room, talking with Peter Garcias.

On the heretication of Peter's mother, this witness said the same as Friar William Cogot.

Also, Peter Garcias highly commended Bertrand of Roaix and vituperated Friar Raymond Gros and [said] that Raymond told Peter and Raymond Peter of Plans that he did what he did deceitfully; and if they had come to him first, he would not have remained three days in the order.[31] This witness heard this this year before Easter in the place named, where were present Friars Minor William Cogot and Arnold Daitz of Toulouse.

When this witness was asked his opinion of Peter Garcias, he replied that he thought him to be a believer of heretics because of what he heard from him. He made this deposition at Toulouse, before Friars Bernard and John, inquisitors. Witnesses already named.

# References

1. Douais (*Documents*, I, 267) states that the two men were brothers; that is not explicit in the sources, even where it would be most expected, in references to Peter Garcias' mother. A Peter Garcias of Bourguet Nau was a witness to a sale of real estate rights on 30 July 1241, together with three members of the Roaix family, of whom one, named Alaman, was probably son of the heretic discussed in Appendix 4: (*Layettes*, II, No. 2925). In the restoration of property rights by Philip III in 1279, a Peter Garcias is named: see Appendix 3, n. 107.
2. The witnesses who describe the place most clearly say that the listeners were situated between the room below and the roof, on a floor (*tabulatus*) or wall (*paries*). (Douais, *Documents*, II, 108, 113). Unless otherwise noted, all page numbers in subsequent notes are to this volume.
3. See 109–110. That is an unlikely accusation. Peter was heard to say (95) that his mother would have been hereticated but for clerical interference and that she was one of those who had taught him his faith (100–1, 105, 107, 114). William *de Montoti*, who made the accusation, had been named by Peter

as one of his preceptors in religion (107). Had William been brought out of prison to testify?

4. The sentence is on 74.

5. Dossat, *Les Crises de l'Inquisition toulousaine*, 289, 307, 313; Douais, *Documents*, I, 218, n. 4.

6. See 90–5, 97–101 respectively.

7. Déodat of Rodez, the next witness to testify, and Arnold Daitz, who was the last, both recalled that Peter had responded that there were two gods: one was good and benign and the creator of invisible and incorruptible things; the other was malign and evil and creator of the visible and transitory (95–6, 111). Déodat, when specifically questioned, said he did recall some remark about disputing for half a year (97), but William Garcias in his own testimony did not mention the point.

8. *De Acio* here, but in the record of his own deposition (111) *Daitz*.

9. Rom. 3:30. 'Sanctifieth' is a misquotation of the 'justifieth' of the biblical text, but when the verse is mentioned by other witnesses, it is quoted correctly.

10. John 1:3.

11. Col. 1:16.

12. Acts 14:14. The words in brackets are represented in the text by 'etc'.

13. Bertrand of Roaix had been sentenced to life imprisonment on 19 February 1237 (Doat, XXI, fols. 149–53). See also Appendix 3, n. 86 above.

14. *Quod omnes angeli et soli qui ceciderant de celi* . . .

15. William Garcias (103) recalled that at this point Peter added, 'Christ brought the Blessed Virgin and John the Evangelist in testimony'.

16. William Garcias reported (103–4) that Peter told him he had expressed this belief to William of Roaix when the latter was consul.

17. Because Pope Sylvester I (314–55) was the supposed recipient of the Donation of Constantine, both Cathars and Waldenses ascribed the falling away of the Roman church from true belief to his pontificate.

18. Friar Arnold Daitz recalled (114) hearing Peter speak of how he had tricked 'that rustic villain, Master Nicholas', in the matter of confession. Nicholas had co-operated in inquisitorial trials of 1237 as an official witness to proceedings: Doat, XXI, fols. 143–5v, 179–80v; 183v–5; XXIII, fols. 180v, 183, 184v.

19. Bernard of Caux and John of St Pierre together heard all the depositions in this case except two, at which only John was present (107, 108). Peter Aribert was the notary for the whole record, as he was for the sentencing of Peter Garcias.

20. Omitted here is the first part of Friar Deodat's statement which covers the same matters as the one just presented.

21. A reference to one of the vernacular translations of the New Testament used by both Cathars and Waldenses. Cf. Wakefield and Evans, *Heresies*, 64–5.

22. *Sed erat bestia*. Another witness heard this remark as 'she was stupid' (*stulta*), (106).

23. Innocent IV proclaimed a crusade against Frederick II in 1245.

24. Raymond Peter of Plans had once been brought by Peter Garcias to argue with William Garcias about justice and creation (106–7). With his two brothers and six other persons he was sentenced to life imprisonment on 25 August 1247 (48–52), being accused of having been present many times with heretics in the house where he lived (a heretical hospice?), hearing their preaching, adoring them, believing their errors, writing letters for them

for a fee, denying the truth in a previous interrogation, and refusing to confess during a time of grace previously offered. Friar Imbert, in his testimony, recalled that Peter Garcias had 'commended R. P. of Plans and P. Roger, men condemned for heresy, because they were very wise and discreet and no one knew the facts about them' (107).

25. *Homo celatus et coopertus.*

26. This paragraph is puzzling and the translation is only a guess as to the meaning of *per modum sabbatati. Sabbatatus* was a term for a Waldensian preacher.

27. *De gutta cadet ipse.* Friar Imbert remembered (107) the expression in this context. William Garcias, however, testified that Peter Garcias had denounced God, but hoped that any person who believed that spirits of men were newly created by God would die of gout (105).

28. Douais (102, n. 1) believes this to be a reference to one Raymond Cauzit, whose confession is found elsewhere, and that he was Peter Garcia's father-in-law.

29. William Garcias remembered this as a reference to 'the father of William'.

30. Imbert of Rodez and William Garcias testified on 22 August; Friar Peter Raymond of Saint Ybars on 26 August; and Friar Arnold Daitz on 10 December.

31. Raymond Gros was already dead, for Friar William Garcias testified (105) that Peter had told him 'that Friar Raymond Gros died in the faith of the heretics and that he sent Andrew the Barber as a messenger to Raymond Peter of Plans and when he would not come, he [Peter] went to Raymond.' If this was, as seems possible, the Raymond Gros whose conversion had led to a large number of prosecutions in Toulouse in 1236 (see p. 148, above, and Appendix 3, pp. 223–4), this is the only reference I have seen to the convert having become a friar.

# Appendix 6

# A Manual for Inquisitors

A little compilation illustrating the various steps in inquisitorial procedure was prepared in 1248 or 1249 by Bernard of Caux and John of St Pierre while they were temporarily assigned to Carcassonne.[1] Pope Innocent IV and the archbishop of Narbonne had ordered it to be prepared for the benefit of other friars who would pursue heretics in those parts of the ecclesiastical province of Narbonne which were politically subject to Aragon, where a separate tribunal was being established. The resulting *Processus inquisitionis* was the first of many manuals of procedure and treatises on the powers and policies of the Inquisition which would be written in the next two or three centuries.[2] In it we find model writs or suggested forms for the official commission of the inquisitors, the initial calling together of inhabitants of a locality, the abjuration of heresy required of all, an interrogatory for general use, a citation for individual suspects, a formula for absolving those who confessed and were sent to prison, a letter to be carried by one sent on pilgrimage, the sentence by which the impenitent were handed over to the secular authority for burning, and another for the deceased whose bones were to be exhumed. There is also advice on the necessity of exact procedure, confiscation of property, and provision of sustenance for prisoners.

The only known manuscript of the *Processus*, discovered by François Balme, was edited by Ad. Tardif in 'Document pour l'histoire du *processus per inquisitionem* et de l'*inquisitio heretice pravitatis*', *Nouvelle revue historique du droit français et étranger*, VII (1883), 669–78.

THE PROCEDURE OF THE INQUISITION

### Letter of Commission
To the pious and discreet men, beloved in Christ, Friars William Raymond and Peter Durand of the Order of Preachers,[3] Pons, a friar of the same order in the province of Provence,[4] a servant of little use and unworthy, sends greetings and the spirit of charity.

With full confidence in your discretion and devotion, in

virtue of the authority of the Lord Pope which is entrusted to us in this region, we have decided to send you, for remission of your sins, to make inquisition of heretics and their believers, fautors, receivers, and defenders, and also of persons who are defamed, in the province of Narbonne, with the exception of the archdeaconries of Villelongue and Villemur[5] of the diocese of Toulouse, and in the dioceses of Albi, Rodez, Mende, and Le Puy; but that same authority directing you to proceed vigorously and prudently in this business, pursuant to the mandate and decree of the Apostolic See. If both of you are unable to be present to carry out this commission, one of you nevertheless may accomplish it.

Given at Narbonne, 21 October 1244.

THE PROCEDURE OF THE INQUISITION

This is the procedure. Within the limits of inquisition entrusted to and defined for us by the prior of the province under the authority stated above, we choose a place which seems to be well suited to the purpose, from which or in which we make inquisition of other localities. Calling the clergy and people together there, we deliver a general sermon, in which we read aloud the letters of both the lord pope and the prior of the province concerning the form and the authorization of the Inquisition, and we make what explanation is necessary; thereafter, we issue a general summons, either orally to those present or by letter to those who are absent, in the following form:

*Method of Citation*

The inquisitors of heretical depravity [send] greetings in the Lord to so and so, parish priest. We enjoin and strictly instruct you, in virtue of the authority we wield, to summon in our name and by our authority all the parishioners of such and such church or inhabitants of such and such place, men from the age of fourteen, women from the age of twelve, or younger if perchance they shall have been guilty of an offence, to appear before us on such a day at such a place to answer for acts which they may have committed against the faith and to abjure heresy. And if no previous inquisition has been made in that place, we will grant indulgence from imprisonment to all from that place who have not been cited by name or who have not yet earned the indulgence, if, within a specified time, they come voluntarily as penitents to tell the exact and full truth about themselves and about others.

This we call the period of grace or of indulgence.

## Method of Abjuration and the Form of the Oath

We require each and every person who presents himself for confession to abjure all heresy and to take oath that he will tell the full and exact truth about himself and about others, living and dead, in the matter of the fact or crime of heresy or Waldensianism;[6] that he will preserve and defend the Catholic faith; that he will neither harbour nor defend heretics of any sect whatever nor befriend them nor believe in them, but rather that he will in good faith pursue and seize them and their agents[7] or, at least, will disclose them to the church or to princes and their *baillis* who are eager and able to seize them; and that he will not obstruct the Inquisition, but rather will set himself against those who impede it.

## Formula for the Interrogatory[8]

Thereafter, the person is diligently questioned about whether he saw a heretic or Waldensian, where and when, how often and with whom, and about others who were present; whether he listened to their preaching or exhortation and whether he gave them lodging or arranged shelter for them; whether he conducted them from place to place or otherwise consorted with them or arranged for them to be guided or escorted; whether he ate or drank with them or ate bread blessed by them; whether he gave or sent anything to them; whether he acted as their financial agent[9] or messenger or assistant; whether he held any deposit or anything else of theirs; whether he received the Peace from their book, mouth, shoulder, or elbow;[10] whether he adored a heretic or bowed his head or genuflected and said 'Bless us' before heretics or whether he was present at their baptisms[11] or confessions;[12] whether he was present at a Waldensian Lord's Supper, confessed his sins to them, accepted penance or learned anything from them; whether he was otherwise on familiar terms with or associated with heretics or Waldenses in any way; whether he made an agreement, heeded requests, or received gifts in return for not telling the truth about himself or others; whether he advised or persuaded anyone or caused anyone to be persuaded to do any of the foregoing; whether he knows any other man or woman to have done any of the foregoing; whether he believed in the heretics or Waldenses or their errors.

Finally, after that which he has confessed about himself or testified about other persons on all of these matters – and sometimes on others about which he was questioned, but not without good reason – has been written down, in the presence of one or both of us, with at least two other persons qualified for careful discharge of this task associated with us, he verifies everything which he caused to be recorded. In this way we authenticate the records of the Inquisition as to confessions and depositions, whether they are prepared by the notary or by another scribe.

And when a region is widely infected we make general inquisition of all persons in the manner just described, entering the names of all of them in the record, even of those who insist that they know nothing about others and have themselves committed no crime, so that if they have lied or if subsequently they commit an offence, as is often found true of a number of persons, it is on record that they have abjured and have been interrogated in detail.

## The Method of Summoning Individuals

Moreover, when we summon anyone individually we write in this form:

> In our name and by our authority, you [the priest] are to issue a summary citation to so and so, once and for all, to appear on such a day at such a place to answer for his faith (or for such and such an offence or to receive sentence of imprisonment or, more simply, penance for acts committed or to defend a deceased parent or to hear sentence in his own case or in the case of a deceased person whose heir he is).

In individual as well as multiple summons, after describing the authority by which we issue them, which is on record for the region, we list in order of rank and locality the names of persons; we state the reasons for the summons; we assign safe places and the limit of delay without contempt.[13] To no one do we deny a legitimate defence nor do we deviate from established legal procedure, except that we do not make public the names of witnesses, because of the decree of the Apostolic See, wisely made by Lord Gregory [IX] and afterward renewed by our most blessed pope, Innocent [IV], as a prerogative and absolute necessity of the faith, on which point we have letters of confirmation from several cardinals. In this matter, we proceed according to the holy counsel of prelates, with all necessary prudence and care, as well in the case of those against whom inquisition is made as in the case of those who are witnesses.

We use this form in imposing penances and issuing condemnations: We require those who wish to return to ecclesiastical unity for that reason to abjure heresy again, and we solemnly bind them by official affidavits to observance and defence of the faith, to the pursuit of heretics, and to active assistance in inquisitions, as stated above, and to acceptance and fulfilment of penance imposed at our discretion. Thereafter, having granted the boon of absolution according to the usage of the church, we impose on the penitent the penance of imprisonment with this formula:

## Method and Form of Reconciling and Punishing Those Who Return to Ecclesiastical Unity

In the name of our Lord Jesus Christ. We, inquisitors of heretical depravity, etc. Through the inquisition which by apostolic mandate we make of heretics and persons who are defamed, we find that you (so and so) as you have confessed in legal proceedings before us, have adored numerous heretics, harboured them, visited them, and believed in their errors. Having on that account been taken into custody, you nevertheless declare that you desire to return to ecclesiastical unity and to recant sincerely and unfeignedly, as recorded above; you subjugate yourself of your own will to the penalty for heretics if you act to the contrary; you recognize that you are absolved from the excommunication by which you were bound for previous acts, under the condition and reservation that if you are found to have suppressed the truth, either about yourself or about others, or if you do not carry out and fulfil the penance and commands which we lay upon you, the aforesaid absolution has no effect thereafter and you will be adjudged to be entirely non-compliant. With the co-operation and assistance of such and such prelates and men learned in law, by their counsel and that of others, in accordance with apostolic command, and by virtue of the oath you have taken, we direct you to do penance for the acts stated above, by which you have shamefully offended God and the church, and to betake yourself without delay to the decent and humane prison prepared for you in (such and such) a city, there to make your salutary and permanent abode. If, indeed, you refuse to carry out our command, either by delaying to enter or, perchance, by leaving after you have done so or by doing anything else in contradiction to what you abjured or swore or promised, whatever the time you came before us, thus revealing your fictitious confession [and your deceit] in manifesting repentance[14] we hold you guilty thenceforward as impenitent and bound by worse sins; and, pursuant to the authority we wield, we bind by the chains of excommunication as fautors, receivers, and defenders of heretics all who knowingly either harbour or defend you or in any way lend counsel and aid to your refusal to comply; and we decree that the reconciliation and mercy granted to you can have no further effect, at the same time, in full justice, relinquishing you as a heretic to the secular arm from that moment on.

*Letters concerning the Performance of Penances*

In respect of the penances which we give to those who are not to be imprisoned, we issue letters in the following form:

To all faithful Christians who shall inspect the present letter, (so and so), inquisitors, etc. Since (so and so), the bearer, sinned by the crime of heretical morbidity,[15] as revealed by his confession made in proceedings before us, and of his own will returns humbly to the bosom of Holy Church, at the same time abjuring heretical morbidity, and now has been absolved from the chains of excommunication according to the usages of the church, we decree for him that in detestation of his error he shall wear two crosses, one on the breast and one on the shoulders, yellow in colour, two palms in height, two in breadth, each arm three fingers in width. The clothing on which he wears the crosses shall never be yellow in colour. As long as he lives he shall attend mass and vespers on Sundays and feast days, as well as a general sermon if one is delivered in the village where he is, unless some impediment without fraud prevents it. He shall follow processions for (so many) years, bearing large branches in his hand, walking between the clergy and the people, in each procession in which he appears displaying himself in such aspect that he reveals to the people that he is doing penance there because of acts he committed against the faith. He shall visit over (so many) years such and such sanctuaries, and in each of these pilgrimages just stated he is required to present our letter, which we wish him to have and carry to the prelate of the church he is visiting, and to bring back to us a letter from him attesting that the pilgrimage was accomplished in proper form. Therefore, dearly beloved,[16] we request that you in no way molest or allow others to molest (so and so), who is carrying our letter and wearing crosses and fulfilling the things we have enjoined for him by reason of the acts stated above which he committed against the faith, when you find him deporting himself in all respects as a Catholic. If, however, you see him behaving otherwise or attempting to do so, you should hold him to be a perjurer and excommunicate and bound by even worse sins. And from that time on we decree that the reconciliation and mercy granted to him can have no further effect, and not only do we, pursuant to the authority we wield, bind him by the chain of excommunication as a heretic, but we do the same, as fautors, receivers, or defenders of heretics, for all who knowingly harbour or defend him or in any other way lend him aid, counsel, or favour.

### Form of Sentence for Release to the Secular Arm

We condemn by sentences such as the following heretics and their believers, having first stated and exposed their crimes and errors and other matters, as is customary in procedures of this kind:

We, the inquisitors aforesaid, having heard and carefully weighed the crimes and defaults of (so and so), named above, and especially those circumstances which ought most significantly to influence us in the work of extirpating heretical morbidity and planting the faith, either by punishment or forgiveness, with the reverend fathers (so and so) associated and acting with us, by definitive sentence adjudge (so and so), named above, to be a heretic, because he believed in the errors of heretics and is proved still to believe them and because, when examined or when convicted and confessing, he flatly refused to be recalled and to give full obedience to the mandates of the church. We relinquish him now to secular judgement and, by the authority which we wield, we not only condemn him as a heretic but also we bind with the chain of excommunication as fautors, receivers, and defenders of heretics all persons who knowingly henceforth either harbour or defend him or lend him counsel, aid, or favour.

### Form of Sentence for Those Who Died as Heretics

Likewise, we condemn deceased heretics and believers, having set forth their errors, crimes, and other matters in this way:

We, inquisitors, etc., having seen and carefully reviewed and considered the sins and defaults of (so and so), named above, and the defence offered in his behalf, and the circumstances which must be taken into account and evaluated in respect of the persons and the words of the witnesses, and other matters, with (so and so) associated and acting with us, adjudge (so and so) by definitive verdict to have died as a heretic and, condemning him and his memory with equal severity, we decree that his bones be exhumed from the cemetery, if they can be distinguished from others, and burned in detestation of so heinous an offence.

We issue and impose the condemnations and sentences here described solemnly and deliberately before a convocation of clergy and people, there requiring those on whom we impose the penances described here to abjure and to take an oath, as noted above; and an official record of the condemnations and of the penances of imprisonment is made, attested by our seals and the witness of others who are present.

The substance of letters in respect of the other penances which are imposed is entered in the records.

We do not proceed to the condemnation of anyone without clear and evident proof or without his own confession, nor, God permitting, will we do so. And all the major condemnations and penances which we have issued and do issue, we pronounce with not only the general but also the specific signed counsel of prelates.[17]

We do various other things, indeed, in procedure and in other matters which cannot easily be reduced to writing, holding in all things to the letter of the law or to specific apostolic ordinances. We cause the goods of heretics, the condemned and the imprisoned as well, to be confiscated, and we insist that this be done, as we are duty bound to do. It is in this way that heretics and believers are particularly confounded. And if justice is well done in respect of the condemned and those who relapse, if their property is surely confiscated, and if prisoners are adequately provided with necessities, the Lord will gloriously and wonderfully be made manifest in the fruit of the Inquisition.

# References

1. This is the conclusion of Yves Dossat in 'Le Plus Ancien Manuel de l'Inquisition méridionale: le *processus inquisitionis* (1248–1249)', *BPH*, 1948–1949, 33–7; also expressed in his *Les Crises de l'Inquisition toulousaine*, 167. See also, Douais *Documents*, I, 233–6, who suggested a different authorship and date.
2. See A. Dondaine, 'Le Manuel de l'inquisiteur', *AFP*, XXIX (1959), 85–194.

Printed treatises, chiefly those written in the fourteenth and later centuries, are listed in E. van der Vekené, *Bibliographie der Inquisition: ein Versuch.*

3. In the article cited in n. 1 above (36–7), Dossat suggests that Bernard of Caux and John of St Pierre copied this commission, which would be found in the archives of Carcassonne, because they themselves had only recently and provisionally been delegated there. On William Raymond and Peter Durand, see Douais, *Documents*, I, 138–43; Dossat, *Les Crises de l'Inquisition toulousaine*, 154–5, 168–9.

4. Identified by Douais, (*Documents*, I, 233, n. 1) as Pons of St Gilles, provincial prior. However, we have no assurance that Pons of St Gilles (on whom, see Appendix 3, pp. 210–22, *passim* held that office in 1244.

5. This division of authority in the diocese of Toulouse is shown also in a sentence of Bernard of Caux and John of St Pierre in 1244: Douais, *Documents*, II, 40.

6. The inquisitors were always careful to distinguish between these two sects.

7. *Nuntios*: the *nuntii* were trusted believers who served the Good Men by carrying messages, arranging meetings with believers, and obtaining escorts for the heretics on their travels.

8. The following questions may be compared with the more sophisticated interrogatories suggested by the inquisitor Bernard Gui about seventy-five years later, translated in Wakefield and Evans, *Heresies*, 384–6, 402–4.

9. *Questor*: one who received and passed on gifts intended for the heretics or held sums on deposit for them.

10. See p. 38 above.

11. *Consolamentis*: see pp. 36–9 above.

12. *Appareillamentis*: see p. 39 above.

13. *Loca tuta et contemptos dilationis sive terminos assignamus.*

14. The text reads: *Aut per hoc fictam conversionem tuam* ... [sic] *et in penitentiam declamando.*

15. *In crimine labis heretice.*

16. These words are addressed to the custodian of the place of pilgrimage.

17. This paragraph, as pointed out in Maisonneuve, *Études sur les origines de l'Inquisition*, 332, paraphrases canon 23 of the council of Narbonne (1243/1244).

# Bibliography

In addition to works cited in the notes this bibliography lists others (preceded by *) which I am conscious of having utilized but did not name and also certain ones in English which may be of interest to one who wishes to read further in that language. Those which are mentioned in more than one chapter or appendix are grouped together in Part C; the others are arranged by the chapter to which they pertain. Preceding all these are other titles which deserve mention for bibliographical purposes or because they contain a number of translations of sources.

## PART A: BIBLIOGRAPHIES

Berne-Lagarde, Pierre de, *Bibliographie du catharisme languedocien* (Institut des études cathares: Collection de textes et documents, I), Toulouse, 1957.

Duvernoy, Jean, 'La Contribution des ouvrages critiques récents à l'histoire de l'hérésie méridionale', *Bulletin de la Société ariégoise des sciences, lettres et arts*, 1968, 231–47.

Grundmann, Herbert, *Bibliographie zur Ketzergeschichte des Mittelalters (1900–1966)*, (Sussidi eruditi, 20), Rome, 1967.

Hugon, Augusto A. and Giovanni Gonnet, *Bibliografia valdese*, Torre Pellice, 1953.

Kulcsár Zsuzsánna, *Eretnekmozgalmak a XI-XIV szádban* (A Budapesti Egyetemi Könyvtár Kiadványai, XXII), Budapest, 1964.

Vekené, E[mil] van der, *Bibliographie der Inquisition: Ein Versuch*, Hildesheim, 1963.

These may be supplemented by the notes for specific matters and the general bibliographies in Borst, *Die Katharer*; Thouzellier, *Catharisme et valdéisme*; and Wakefield and Evans, *Heresies of the High Middle Ages* (cited in Part B and Part D, Ch. 2).

## PART B. SOURCES IN TRANSLATION

Maitland, Samuel R., *Facts and Documents Illustrative of the History, Doctrine and Rites of the Ancient Albigenses and Waldenses*, London, 1832.

Petry, Ray C., *A History of Christianity: Readings in the History of the Early and Medieval Church*, Englewood Cliffs, N.J., 1962.

Russell, Jeffrey B. (ed.), *Religious Dissent in the Middle Ages*, New York, 1971.

*Translations and Reprints from the Original Sources of European History*, Vol. III, No. 6: J. H. Robinson (ed.), *The Pre-Reformation Period*, Philadelphia, 1897.

Wakefield, Walter L. and Austin P. Evans (eds. and trans.), *Heresies of the High Middle Ages* (Records of Civilization: Sources and Studies, LXXXI), New York, 1969.


PART C: WORKS CITED IN MORE THAN ONE OF THE CHAPTERS OR APPENDICES

*Manuscripts*

Paris, Bibliothèque nationale, Collection Doat, Vols. XXI–XXVI, XXXI–XXXII. Copies made in the seventeenth century of documents, chiefly from inquisitorial archives, of which many of the originals have disappeared: sentences, testimony of witnesses, papal bulls, consultations on procedure, etc.

Toulouse, Bibliothèque municipale, Manuscript 609. A copy, made about 1260, of the record of inquests by Bernard of Caux and John of St Pierre in 1245–1246, with a few depositions of later date.


*Books and articles*

Albe, Ed., 'L'Hérésie albigeoise et l'Inquisition en Quercy', *Revue d'histoire de l'église de France*, V (1910), 271–93, 412–28, 460–72.

Auvray, see Gregory IX.

Biget, Jean L., 'Un Procès d'Inquisition à Albi en 1300', *Cahiers de Fanjeaux*, VI, 273–341.

*Cahiers de Fanjeaux*, Toulouse, 1966–1971. (Vol. I: *Saint Dominique en Languedoc* [1966]; Vol. II: *Vaudois languedociens et Pauvres catholiques* [1967]; Vol. III: *Cathares en Languedoc* [1968]; Vol. IV: *Paix de Dieu et guerre sainte en Languedoc au XIIe siècle* [1969]; Vol. VI: *Le Credo, la morale et l'Inquisition* [1971].)

Devic, Claude and Joseph Vaissete, *Histoire générale de Languedoc*, Auguste Molinier *et al.* (eds), 16 vols, Toulouse, 1872–1904.

Dognon, Paul, *Les Institutions politiques et administratives du pays de Languedoc du XIIIe siècle aux guerres de religion* (Bibliothèque méridionale, 2nd ser., IV), Toulouse and Paris, *ca.* 1895.

Dondaine, Antoine, 'Le Manuel de l'inquisiteur (1230–1330)', *Archivum fratrum praedicatorum*, XVII (1947), 85–194.

Dossat, Yves, *Les Crises de l'Inquisition toulousaine au XIIIe siècle (1233–1273)*, Bordeaux, 1959.

——, 'La Répression de l'hérésie par les évêques', *Cahiers de Fanjeaux*, VI, 217–72.

——, 'Les Vaudois méridionaux d'après les documents de l'Inquisition', *Cahiers de Fanjeaux*, II, 207–26.

Douais, Célestin *Documents pour servir à l'histoire de l'Inquisition dans le Languedoc* (Société de l'histoire de France, Publications, 299, 300), 2 vols, Paris, 1900.

Duvernoy, Jean, 'La Liturgie et l'église cathares', *Cahiers d'étudies cathares*, XVIII, 2nd ser., No. 33 (1967), 3–16; No. 35, 16–30.

Emery, Richard W., *Heresy and Inquisition in Narbonne* (Studies in History, Economics and Public Law, 480), New York, 1941.

Galbraith, G. R. *The Constitution of the Dominican Order, 1216 to 1360*. (Publications of the University of Manchester, XLIV), Manchester, 1925.

Gregory IX, Pope, *Les Registres de Grégoire IX (1227–1241), Recueil des bulles de ce pape*. Lucien Auvray (ed.), 4 vols, (Bibliothèque des écoles françaises d'Athènes et de Rome, 2nd ser., IX, 1–4.) Paris, 1896–1955.

Griffe, Élie, *Les Débuts de l'aventure cathare en Languedoc (1140–1190)*, Paris, 1969.

——, *Le Languedoc cathare de 1190 à 1210*, Paris, 1971.

Guiraud, Jean, *Cartulaire de Notre Dame de Prouille, précedé d'une étude sur l'albigéisme languedocien au XIIe et XIIIe siècles*, 2 vols, Paris, 1907.

——, *Histoire de l'Inquisition au moyen âge*, 2 vols, Paris, 1935–1938.

Lacger, Louis de, 'L'Albigeois pendant la crise de l'albigéisme: L'episcopat de Guilhem Peire (1185–1227)', *Revue d'histoire ecclésiastique*, XXIX (1933), 272–315, 586–633, 848–904.

*Layettes du Trésor des chartes*, A. Teulet *et al.* (eds.), 5 vols, Paris, 1866–1902.

Lea, Henry Charles, *A History of the Inquisition of the Middle Ages*, 3 vols, New York and London, 1888; reprinted 1955. (Abridged ed. by Margaret Nicolson in one volume; New York, 1961.)

Limouzin-Lamothe, Roger, *La Commune de Toulouse et les sources de son histoire (1120–1249): Etude historique et critique suivie de l'édition du Cartulaire du consulat* (Bibliothèque méridionale, 2nd ser., XXVI). Toulouse and Paris, 1932.

Luchaire, Achille, *Innocent III*, 6 vols, Paris, 1905–1908 (II, *La Croisade des albigeois* [3rd ed. 1911]; VI, *La Concile de Latran et la réforme de l'église* [1908].)

Maisonneuve, Henri, *Études sur les origines de l'Inquisition*, 2nd ed. (L'église et l'état au moyen âge, VII), Paris, 1960.

Mansi, Giovanni (ed.), *Sacrorum conciliorum nova et amplissima collectio . . .*, 53 vols, Florence, Venice, and Paris, 1759–1927.

Molinier, Auguste, 'Etude sur l'administration de Louis IX et d'Alfonse de Poitiers', in *Histoire générale de Languedoc*, VII, Part 1 (note LIX), 462–570.

Molinier, Charles, *L'Inquisition dans le Midi de la France au XIIIe et au XIVe siècle: Étude sur les sources de son histoire*, Paris, 1880.

Mundy, John H., 'Charity and Social Work in Toulouse, 1150–1250', *Traditio*, XXII (1966), 203–87.

——, *Liberty and Political Power in Toulouse, 1050–1230*, New York, 1954.

Nelli, René, 'Le Catharisme vu à travers les troubadours', *Cahiers de Fanjeaux*, III, 177–97.

Nelli, René, *La Vie quotidienne des Cathares du Languedoc au XIIIe siècle*, Paris, 1969.

Peter of Les Vaux de Cernay, *Petri Vallium Sarnaii monachi Hystoria albigensis*, Pascal Guébin and Ernest Lyon (eds), 3 vols, Paris, 1926–1939. (French translation by Henri Maisonneuve as *Histoire albigeoise* (L'Église et l'état au moyen âge, X); Paris, 1951.)

Poux, Joseph, *La Cité de Carcassonne; histoire et description*, 4 vols, Toulouse, 1931–1938.

Roquebert, Michel, *L'Epopée cathare, 1198–1212: l'invasion*, Toulouse, 1970.

Russell, Jeffrey B., *Dissent and Reform in the Early Middle Ages* (Publications of the Center for Medieval and Renaissance Studies, 1), Berkeley and Los Angeles, 1965.

Strayer, Joseph R., *The Albigensian Crusades*, New York, 1971.

Teulet, see *Layettes*.

Thouzellier, Christine, *Catharisme et valdéisme en Languedoc à la fin du XIIe et au début du XIIIe siècle, Politique pontificale-controverses* (Publications de la Faculté des lettres et sciences humaines de Paris. Série recherches, XXVII), Rev. ed., Paris, 1969.

——, *Hérésie et hérétiques: Vaudois, cathares, patarins, albigeois* (Storia e letteratura: raccolta di studi e testi, 116), Rome, 1969.

——, *Un Traité cathare inédit du début du XIIIe siècle d'après le Liber contra manicheos de Durand de Huesca* (Bibliothèque de la Revue d'histoire ecclésiastique, 37), Louvain, 1961.

Vaissete. See Devic and Vaissete.

Vicaire, M. H., *Saint Dominic and His Times*, Trans. by Kathleen Pond, New York, 1965.

Vidal, Henri, *Episcopatus et pouvoir épiscopal à Béziers à la veille de la croisade albigeoise, 1152–1209*, Montpellier, 1951.

Wakefield, Walter L., 'Friar Ferrier, Inquisition at Caunes, and Escapes from Prison at Carcassonne', *Catholic Historical Review*, LVIII (1972), 220–37.

——, 'The Family of Niort in the Albigensian Crusade and before the Inquisition', *Names*, XVIII (1970), 97–117, 286–303.

William Pelhisson, *Chronicon*, edited by Charles Molinier in *De fratre Guillelmo Pelisso veterimo inquisitionis historica*, Le Puy, 1880. Edited by Célestin Douais in *Les Sources de l'histoire de l'Inquisition dans le Midi de la France au XIIIe et XIVe siècles*, 81–118, Paris, 1881. (French translation by Jean Duvernoy as *Chronique de Guillaume Pelhisson*, Toulouse, 1958.)

William of Puylaurens, *Cronica*, edited by Bessyier in 'Guillaume de

Puylaurens et sa chronique' in *Troisièmes mélanges d'histoire du moyen âge*, A. Luchaire (ed.), 119–75 (Bibliothèque de la Faculté des lettres de Paris, XVIII), Paris, 1904.

William of Tudela, *La Chanson de la croisade albigeoise*. Edited with French translation by Eugène Martin-Chabot, 3 vols (Les classiques de l'histoire de France, XIII), Paris, 1931–1961.

Wolff, Philippe, *Commerces et marchands de Toulouse (vers 1350–vers 1450)*, Paris, 1954.

——, (ed.), *Documents de l'histoire de Languedoc*, Toulouse, 1969.

——, *et al.*, *Histoire du Languedoc*, Toulouse, 1967.

——, *Histoire de Toulouse*, Toulouse, 1958.

PART D: WORKS CITED BY CHAPTER

*Chapter I*

*Brooke, C. N. L., 'Heresy and Religious Sentiment', *Bulletin of the Institute of Historical Research*, XLI (1968), 115–31.

Couvreur, Gilles, 'Pauvreté et droits des pauvres à la fin du XIIe siècle' in *La Pauvreté: Des sociétés de pénure à la société d'abondance*, 13–37.

Delaruelle, Etienne, 'L'Idéal de pauvreté à Toulouse au XIIe siècle' in *Cahiers de Fanjeaux*, II, 64–84.

*Evans, Austin P., 'Social Aspects of Medieval Heresy' in *Persecution and Liberty: Essays in Honor of George Lincoln Burr*, 93–116, New York, 1931.

Fearns, James, 'Peter von Bruis und die religiöse Bewegungen des 12. Jahrhunderts', *Archiv für Kulturgeschichte*, XLVIII (1966), 311–35.

Grundmann, Herbert, 'Eresie e nuovi ordini religiosi nel secolo XII' in *Religiöse Bewegungen*, n. ed. Berlin, 1961.

——, *Religiöse Bewegungen im Mittelalter: Untersuchungen über die geschichtlichen Zusammenhänge zwischen der Ketzerei, den Bettelorden und der religiösen Frauenbewegungen im 12. und 13. Jahrhundert, und über die geschichtlichen Grundlagen der Deutschen Mystik* (Historische Studien, 267), Berlin, 1935; reprint with additions, 1961.

*Hérésies et sociétés dans l'Europe pré-industrielle, 11e–18e siècles*, Jacques Le Goff (ed.), (Civilisations et Sociétés, X), Paris, 1968.

Ilarino da Milano, 'Le eresie popolari del secolo XI nell'Europa occidentale', *Studi Gregoriani per la storia di Gregorio VII e della riforma Gregoriana*, G. B. Borino (ed.), II, 43–89, Rome, 1947.

McDonnell, Ernest W., 'The *vita apostolica*: Diversity or Dissent?', *Church History*, XXIV (1955), 15–31.

Magnou, Elizabeth, 'Note critique sur les sources de l'histoire de Henri l'hérétique jusqu'à son départ du Mans', *Bulletin philologique et historique (jusqu'à 1610) du Comité des travaux historique et scientifique* (1962), 539–47.

Manselli, Raoul, 'Il monaco Enrico e la sua eresia', *Bullettino dell'Isti-*

*tuto storico italiano per il medio evo e Archivio Muratoriano,* LXV (1953), 1–63.

*——,* 'Per la storia dell'eresia nel secolo XII. Studi minori', *Bullettino dell'Istituto storico italiano per il medio evo e Archivio Muratoriano,* LXVII (1955), 189–264.

*——, Studi sulle eresie del secolo XII* (Istituto storico italiano per il medio evo: Studi storici, 5), Rome, 1953.

*Manteuffel, Tadeusz, 'Les Mouvements des pauvres au moyen âge: Saints et hérétiques', *Acta poloniae historica,* XIII (1966), 5–13.

*——, Naissance d'une héresie: Les adeptes de la pauvreté volontaire au moyen âge,* translated by Anna Posner, Paris, 1970.

Mollat, Michel, 'La Notion de la pauvreté au moyen âge. Position de problèmes', *Revue d'histoire de l'église de France,* LII (1966), 6–23.

*——,* 'Le Problème de la pauvreté au XIIe siècle', in *Cahiers de Fanjeaux,* II, 23–47.

Paul, Jacques, 'Mouvements de pauvreté et réflexion theologique au XIIIe siècle' in *La Pauvreté: Des societés de pénure à la société d'abondance,* 38–46.

*La Pauvreté: Des sociétés de pénure à la société d'abondance* (Recherches et débats du Centre catholique des intellectuels françaises, 49), Paris, 1964.

*Peter the Venerable, *Contra Petrobrusianos hereticos,* James Fearns (ed.), (Corpus christianorum. Continuatio mediaevalis, X), Turnhout, 1968.

*Reagan, Joseph C., 'Did the Petrobrusians Teach Salvation by Faith Alone?', *Journal of Religion,* VII (1927), 81–91.

Russel, Jeffrey B., 'Interpretations of the Origins of Medieval Heresy', *Mediaeval Studies,* XXV (1963), 25–53.

Thouzellier, Christine, 'Tradition et résurgence dans l'hérésie médiévale. Considerations' in *Hérésie et hérétiques,* 1–15. (First published in *Hérésies et sociétes,* 105–16.)

Vacandard, Elphège, 'Les Origines de l'hérésie albigeoise', *Revue des questions historiques,* LV (1894), 50–83.

Walter, Johannes Wilhelm von, *Die ersten Wanderprediger Frankreichs: Studien zur Geschichte des Mönchtums*: Part I, *Robert von Arbrissel*; Part II, *Neue Folge,* Leipzig, 1903, 1906.


*Chapter II*

*Atlas zur Kirchengeschichte: die christlischen Welt in Geschichte und Gegenwart,* Hubert Jeden, Kenneth Scott Latourette, and Jochem Marten (eds), Freiberg-in-Br., 1970.

Borst, Arno, *Die Katharer* (Schriften der Monumenta Germaniae historica, 12), Stuttgart, 1953.

*Davison, Ellen S., *Forerunners of St Francis, and Other Studies,* Gertrude R. B. Richards (ed.), New York, 1927.

*Dondaine, Antoine, 'Les Actes du concile albigeoise de Saint Félix de Caraman', *Miscellanea Giovanni Mercati*, V, 324–55 (Studi e testi, 125), Rome, 1946.

——, 'Durand de Huesca et la polémique anti-cathare', *Archivum fratrum praedicatorum*, XXIX (1959), 228–76.

——, 'L'Origine de l'hérésie médiévale: A propos d'un livre récent', *Rivista di storia della chiesa in Italia* VI (1952), 47–78.

——, 'Aux Origines du Valdéisme: Une profession de foi de Valdès', *Archivum fratrum praedicatorum*, XVI (1946), 191–235.

Dossat, Yves, 'L'Evolution des rituels cathares', *Revue de synthèse*, XXIII (1948), 27–30.

*——, 'Remarques sur un prétendu évêque cathare du Val d'Aran en 1167', *Bulletin philologique et historique du Comité des travaux historiques et scientifiques*, 1955–1956, 339–47.

*Gonnet Giovanni, 'Un decennio di studi sull'eterodossia medioevale', *Protestantesimo*, XVII (1962), 209–39.

——, *Enchiridion fontium Valdensium* (*Recueil critique des sources concernant les Vaudois au moyen âge: Du IIIe Concile de Latran au Synode de Chanforan* [*1179–1532*], Vol. I, Torre Pellice, 1958.

——, *Il Valdismo medioevale. Prolegomeni*, Torre Pellice, 1942.

*——, 'Waldensia', *Rivista di storia e letteratura religiosa*, II (1966), 461–84.

Guiraud, Jean, 'Le Consolamentum cathare', *Revue des questions historiques*, LXXV (1904), 74–112; also in *Questions d'histoire et d'archéologie chrétienne*, 95–149, Paris, 1906.

Herder, *Atlas*. See *Atlas zur Kirchengeschichte*.

Koch, Gottfried, 'Neue Quellen und Forschungen über die Anfänge der Waldenser', *Forschungen und Fortschritten*, XXXII (1958), 141–9.

*——, 'Waldensertum und Frauenfrage im Mittelalters', *Forschungen und Fortschritten*, XXXVI (1962), 22–6.

Manselli, Raoul, *L'eresia del male* (Collano di storia diretta da Arsenio Frugoni, I), Naples, 1963.

——, 'Il valdismo originario' in *Studi sulle eresie del secolo XII*, Ch. 4.

Molinier, Charles, 'L'Eglise et la société cathare', *Revue historique*, XCIV (1906), 225–48; XCV (1907), 1–22, 263–91.

——, 'L'Endura, coûtume religieuse des derniers sectaires albigeois', *Annales de la Faculté des lettres de Bordeaux*, III (1881), 282–99.

Morghen, Raffaelo, *Medioevo cristiano* (Biblioteca di cultura moderna, 491), 2nd ed., Bari, 1958.

——, 'Problèmes sur l'origine de l'hérésie au moyen âge', *Revue historique*, CCXXXVI (1966), 1–16.

*Parcaut, Marcel, 'Pauvrété, vie evangelique et prédication chez les Vaudois', *Revue historique*, CCXLI (1969), 57–68.

Pouzet, Ph., 'Les Origines lyonnaises de la secte des Vaudois', *Revue d'histoire de l'église de France*, XXII (1936), 5–37.

Puech, Henri C., 'Catharisme médiéval et Bogomilisme' in *Convegno 'Volta' di scienze morale, storiche e filologiche, 27 maggio – 1 giugno*

*1956*. Accadamia nazionale dei Lincei, *Atti*, 8th ser., XII (1957), 56–84.

Riol, Jean-Laurent, *Dernières Connaissances sur des questions cathares (essai de critique historique)*, Albi, 1964.

*Šanjek, Franjo, 'Les "Chrêtiens bosniaques" et le mouvement cathare au moyen âge', *Revue de l'histoire des religions*, CLXXXII (1972), 131–81.

——, 'Le Rassemblement hérétique de St-Félix-de-Caraman (1167) et les églises cathares au XIIe siècle', *Revue d'histoire ecclésiastique* (1972), 767–99.

*Selge, Kurt-Victor, 'Caractéristiques du premier mouvement vaudois et crises au cours de son expansion', *Cahiers de Fanjeaux*, II, 110–42.

——, *Die ersten Waldenser. Mit Edition des* Liber antiheresis *des Durandus von Osca* (Arbeiten zur Kirchengeschichte, XXXVII), 2 vols, Berlin, 1967.

Thouzellier, Christine, 'Albigenses', in *Hérésie et hérétiques*, Ch. 8.

——, 'Hérésie et croisade au XIIe siècle' in *Hérésie et hérétiques*, Ch. 2. First published in *Revue d'histoire ecclésiastique*, XLIX (1954), 855–72.

——, 'Le "Liber antiheresis" de Durand de Huesca et le "Contra hereticos" d'Ermengaud de Béziers' in *Hérésie et hérétiques*, Ch. 3. First printed in *Revue d'histoire ecclésiastique*, LV (1960), 130–41.

——, 'Patarins' in *Hérésie et hérétiques*, Ch. 7.

Turdeneau, Emile, 'Apocryphes bogomiles et apocryphes pseudo-bogomiles', *Revue de l'histoire des religions*, CXXXVIII (1950), 22–52, 176–218.

Venckeleer, Theo, 'Un Recueil cathare: Le manuscrit A.6.10 de la Collection vaudoise de Dublin', *Revue belge de philologie et d'histoire*, XXXVIII (1960), 815–34; XXXIX (1961), 758–93.

*Warner, H. J., *The Albigensian Heresy*, 2 vols, London, 1922–1928.

Werner, Ernst, 'Παταρηνοι-patarini. Ein Beitrag zur Kirchen und Sektengeschichte des XI Jahrhunderts' in *Von Mittelalter zur Neuzeit*, Berlin, 1956.

Wolff, Philippe (ed.), *Documents de l'histoire du Languedoc*, Toulouse, 1969.

*Chapter III*

Coppolani, Jean, *Toulouse: Étude de géographie urbaine*, Toulouse, 1954.

Delaruelle, Etienne, 'L'État actuel des études sur le Catharisme', *Cahiers de Fanjeaux*, III, 19–41.

——, 'La Ville de Toulouse vers 1200 d'après quelques travaux recents', *Cahiers de Fanjeaux*, I, 107–21.

Dossat, Yves, 'Le Comté de Toulouse et la feodalité languedocienne à la veille de la croisade albigeoise', *Revue historique, scientifique et littéraire du département du Tarn*, IX (1943), 75–90.

——, 'La Société méridionale à la veille de la croisade albigeoise',

*Revue historique, scientifique et littéraire du Languedoc*, I (1944), 66–87.

Gere, Robert H., *The Troubadours, Heresy, and the Albigensian Crusade*, Ann Arbor, Mich., University Microfilms (Publ. No. 15,628, Microfilm AC-1), 1956.

Higounet, Charles, 'Un Grand Chapitre de l'histoire du XIIe siècle: La rivalté des maisons de Toulouse et de Barcelone pour la préponderance méridionale', pp. 313–22, in *Mélanges d'histoire du moyen âge dediés à la memoire de Louis Halphen*. Paris, 1951.

——, 'La Milieu social et économique languedocien vers 1200' in *Cahiers de Fanjeaux*, II, 15–22.

*——, 'Mouvements de population dans le Midi de la France du XIe au XVe siècle', *Annales: economies, sociétés, civilisations*, VIII (1953), 1–24.

——, 'Le Peuplement de Toulouse au XIIe siècle', *Annales du Midi*, LIV–LV (1942–1943), 489–98.

Le Roy Ladurie, E., *Histoire de Languedoc*, Paris, 1962.

Lopez, Robert and Irving W. Raymond, *Medieval Trade in the Mediterranean World* (Records of Civilization, LII), New York, 1955.

Mulholland, Mary Ambrose (ed.), *Early Gild Records of Toulouse*, New York, 1941.

Ourliac, Paul, 'Les Villages de la région toulousaine au XIIe siècle', *Annales: economies, sociétés, civilisations*, IV (1949), 268–77.

Rougemont, Denis de, *Love in the Western World*, translated by Montgomery Belgion, New York, 1953; reprint 1957.

Russell, Jeffrey B., 'Courtly Love as Religious Dissent', *Catholic Historical Review*, LI (1965), 31–44.

Saige, Gustave, *Les Juifs en Languedoc antérieurement au XIVe siècle*, Paris, 1881.

Sicard, Germain, 'Monocratie et féodalité: l'exemple des comtes de Toulouse (IXe–XIIIe siecles)', *Recueils de la Société Jean Bodin*, XXI: *La Monocratie*, part 2, 405–28, Brussels, 1969.

Ventura, Jordi, *Pere el catòlic i Simó de Montfort* (Biblioteca biogràfica catalana, 24), Barcelona, 1960.

Wolff, Philippe and Jean Dieuzaide, *Voix et images de Toulouse*, Toulouse, 1962.

Wood, Mary Morton, *The Spirit of Protest in Old French Literature*, New York, 1917.

*Chapter IV*

Bécamel, Marcel, 'Le Catharisme dans le diocèse d'Albi', *Cahiers de Fanjeaux*, III, 237–51.

*Castaing-Sicard, Mireille, 'Donations toulousaines du Xe au XIIIe siècle', *Annales du Midi*, LXX (1958), 27–64.

Coincy de Saint Palais, Simone, *Esclarmonde de Foix, princesse cathare*, Toulouse, 1956.

Dmitrevski, Michel, 'Notes sur le catharisme et l'Inquisition dans le

Midi de la France', *Annales du Midi*, XXXV–XXXVI (1923–1924), 294–31; XXXVII (1925–1926), 190–213.

Döllinger, J. J. I. von, *Beiträge zur Sektengeschichte des Mittelalters*, 2 vols, Munich, 1890. Reprinted New York, 1960.

Domairon, Louis, 'La Role des hérétiques de la ville de Béziers à l'epoque du déastre de 1209', *Le Cabinet historique*, IX (1863), 95–103.

Dondaine, Antoine, *Un Traité néo-manichéen du XIII siècle: le* Liber de duobus principiis, *suivi d'un fragment de rituel cathare*, Rome, 1939.

Dossat, Yves, 'Cathares et Vaudois à la veille de la croisade albigeoise', *Revue historique et littéraire de Languedoc*, II (1945), 390–7; III (1946), 70–83.

——, 'Catharisme et Gascogne', *Bulletin de la Société archéologique, littéraire et scientifique du Gers*, LXXIII (1972), 149–68.

——, 'Le Clergé méridional à la veille de la croisade albigeoise', *Revue historique et littéraire de Languedoc*, I (1944), 263–78.

Duvernoy, Jean, 'Bertrand Marty', *Cahiers d'études cathares*, XIX, 2nd ser., No. 39 (1968), 19–35.

——, 'Guilhabert de Castres', *Cahiers d'études cathares*, XVIII, 2nd ser., No. 34 (1967), 32–42.

Eudes of Rouen, *The Register of Eudes of Rouen*. Translated by Sydney M. Brown, Jeremiah F. O'Sullivan (ed.), (Records of Civilization, LXXII), New York, 1964.

Koch, Gottfried, *Frauenfrage und Ketzertum im Mittelalter. Die Frauenbewegung im Rahmen des Katharismus und des Waldensertums und ihre sozialen Wurzeln (XII–XIV Jahrhundert)* (Forschungen zur mittelalterlichen Geschichte, IX). Berlin, 1962.

Mahul, M., *Cartulaire et archives des communes de l'ancien diocèse et de l'arrondissement administratif de Carcassonne*, 6 vols in 7, Paris, 1859–1885.

Nelli, Suzette, 'Esclarmonde de Foix', *Cahiers d'études cathares*, VI, No. 24 (1955), 195–204.

Rainier Sacconi, *Summa de Catharis et Pauperibus de Lugduno*. Edited by A. Dondaine in *Un Traité néo-manichéen*, 64–78.

Rouquette, J. and Villemagne, A., *Cartulaire du Maguelonne*, Vol. II. Montpellier, 1913.

Vidal, Jean M., 'Esclarmonde de Foix dans l'histoire et le roman', *Revue de Gascogne*, n. ser., XI (1911), 53–79.

——, 'Die Stellung der Katharer zur Frau', *Studi Medievali*, 3rd ser., II (1961), 295–301.

*Chapter V*

Bévenot, Maurice, 'The Inquisition and Its Antecedents', *Heythrop Journal*, VII (1966), 257–68; 381–93; VIII (1967), 52–69, 152–68.

*Clayton, Joseph, *Pope Innocent III and His Times*, Milwaukee, 1940.

Congar, Yves, 'Henri de Marcy, abbé de Clairvaux, cardinal-éveque d'Albano et légat pontifical', *Studia Anselmiana*, XLIII; *Analecta monastica*, V (1958), 1–90.

Delehaye, Hippolyte, 'Pierre de Pavie, légat du pape Alexandre III en France', *Revue des questions historiques*, XLIX (1891), 5–61.

Fliche, Augustin and Victor Martin, *Histoire de l'église depuis les origines jusqu'à nos jours*, Vol. IX–X, Paris, 1944, 1950.

Foreville, Raymonde, 'Les Grands Courants hérétiques et les premières mesures générales de repression', Ch. 3 in Fliche and Martin, *Histoire de l'église*, Vol. IX.

——, 'Innocent III et la croisade des Albigeois', *Cahiers de Fanjeaux*, IV, 184–217.

Havet, Julien, 'L'Hérésie et le bras séculier au moyen âge jusqu'au triezième siècle', *Bibliothèque de l'Ecole des chartes*, XLI (1880) 488–517, 570–607.

*Künne, Georg, *Heinrich von Clairvaux*, Berlin, 1909.

Maillet, Henri, *L'Eglise et la répression sanglante de l'hérésie*, Karl Hanquet (ed.), (Bibliothèque de la Faculté de philosophie et lettres de l'Université de Liège, XVI), Liège, 1909.

Mandonnet, Pierre, *Saint Dominic and His Work*. Translated by M. B. Larkin, St Louis and London, 1944.

Manselli, Raoul, 'De la "persuasio" à la "coercitio" ' *Cahiers de Fanjeaux*, VI, 175–97.

*Molinier, Charles, 'L'Hérésie et la persécution au XIe siècle', *Revue des Pyrénées*, VI (1894), 26–38.

Nelson, Ernest W., 'The Theory of Persecution', 3–20, in *Persecution and Liberty: Essays in Honor of George Lincoln Burr*, New York, 1931.

Olíver, Antonio, *Tácita de propaganda y motivos literarios en las cartas antiheréticas de Innocencio III* (Collectanea theatina, XII), Rome, 1956.

Pierron, Johann B., *Die katholischen Armen. Ein Beiträge zur Entstehungsgeschichte der Bettelorden mit Berücksichtigung der Humiliaten und der Wiedervereinigten Lombarden*, Freibur im Breisgau, 1911.

Sibilia, S., *Innocenzo III, 1198–1216*, Rome, 1950.

Theloe, Hermann, *Die Ketzerverfolgungen im 11. und 12. Jahrhundert: Ein Beitrag zur Geschichte der Entstehung des päpstlichen Ketzerinquisitionsgericht* (Abhandlungen zur mittleren und neueren Geschichte, XLVIII), Berlin and Leipzig, 1913.

Thouzellier, Christine, 'La Pauvreté, arme contre l'albigéisme, en 1206' in *Hérésie et hérétiques*, Ch. 6. (First published in *Revue de l'histoire des religions*, CLI [1957], 79–92.)

Tillman, H., *Papst Innocenz III* (Bonner historische Forschungen, III), Bonn, 1954.

Zimmerman, Heinrich, *Die päpstliche Legation in der ersten Hälfte des 13. Jahrhunderts, vom Regierungsantritt Innocenz III bis zum Tode Gregors IX (1198–1241)*, Paderborn, 1913.

*Chapters VI and VII*

Belperron, Pierre, *La Croisade contre les Albigeois et l'union du Languedoc à la France, 1209–1247*, Paris, 1942; reprint 1967.

Boutaric, Edgard, 'La Guerre des Albigeois et Alphonse de Poitiers', *Revue des questions historiques*, II (1867), 155–80.

*Cartellieri, Alexander, *Philipp II, August, König von Frankreich*, 4 vols, Leipzig, 1899–1922.

Dossat, Yves, 'Simon de Montfort', *Cahiers de Fanjeaux*, IV, 281–302.

Evans, Austin P., 'The Albigensian Crusade' in K. M. Setton *et al.* (eds). *A History of the Crusades*, II, 277–324, Philadelphia, 1962.

*Holmes, Edmond G., *Holy Heretics: the Story of the Albigensian Crusade*, London, 1948.

Innocent III, Pope, *Registorum sive epistolarum libri XV*. In J. P. Migne (ed.), *Patrologiae cursus completus*, Vols CCXIV–CCXVI.

Kovarik, Robert J., *Simon de Montfort, 1165–1218, His Life and Work; a Critical Study Based on the Sources* (Microfilm), St Louis University, St Louis, Missouri.

Madaule, Jacques, *The Albigensian Crusade*, translated by Barbara Wall, New York, 1967.

Malafosse, Joseph de, 'Le Siège de Toulouse par Simon de Montfort', *Revue des Pyrénées*, IV (1892), 497–522, 725–56.

Martin-Chabot, Eugène, 'Mesaventures d'un toulousain "donat" de Saint-Sernin; Glose pour la Chanson de la croisade albigeoise' in *Mélanges d'histoire du moyen âge dediés à la memoire de Louis Halphen*, 501–5, Paris, 1951.

Oldenbourg, Zoé, *Massacre at Montségur; A History of the Albigensian Crusade*, translated by Peter Green, New York, 1961.

Petit-Dutaillis, Charles, *Étude sur la vie et le règne de Louis VIII* (1187–1226), Paris, 1894.

Renouard, Yves, 'La Famille féodale la plus marquante de l'occident au XIIIe siècle: Les Montfort' in *Études d'histoire médiévale*, Vol. II, 959–76, Paris, 1968.

Roquebert, Michel and Soula, Christian, *Citadelles du vertige*, Toulouse, 1967; reprint 1972.

Toulouse-Lautrec, R., 'Siège de Lavaur: Le combat de Montgey, avril, 1211', *Revue historique, scientifique et littéraire du département du Tarn*, IV (1885), 344–8.

Varagnac, A., 'Croisade et marchandise: Pourquoi Simon de Montfort s'en alla defaire les Albigeois', *Annales: économies, sociétés, civilisations*, I (1946), 209–18.

*Chapter VIII*

*Cardew, Alexander G., *A Short History of the Inquisition*, London, 1933.

Cauzons, Thomas de, *Histoire de l'Inquisition en France*, 2 vols, Paris, 1909–1912.

Chénon, Emile, 'L'Hérésie à La Charité-sur-Loire et les débuts de l'Inquisition monastique dans le France du nord au XIIIe siècle', *Nouvelle revue historique de droit français et étranger*, XLI (1917), 299–345.

\*Coulton, George G., *The Inquisition*, New York, 1929.

\*Darwin, Francis S., 'The Organization of the Holy Office', *Church Quarterly Review*, CXXII (1936), 196–329; 'The Holy Inquisition: Suppression of Witnesses' Names', *ibid.*, CXXV (1938), 226–46; CXXVI (1938), 19–43; 'The Holy Inquisition: Recusation, Counsel, Appeals', *ibid.*, CXLI (1945), 38–71, 176–95.

Delisle, Leopold (ed.), *Exceptiones Carcassonensium querimoniis objectae* in Martin Bouquet *et al.*, *Recueil des historiens des Gaules et de la France*, XXV, 541–614.

Dossat, Yves, 'Les Débuts de l'Inquisition à Montpellier et en Provence', *Bulletin philologique et historique du comité des travaux historiques et scientifiques*, 1961, 561–79.

——, 'La Répression de l'hérésie par les éveques', *Cahiers de Fanjeaux*, VI, 217–72.

Esser, Kajetan, 'Franziskus von Assisi und die Katharer seiner Zeit', *Archivum franciscanum historicum*, LI (1958), 225–64.

Förg, Ludwig, *Die Ketzerverfolgung in Deutschland unter Gregor IX: ihre Herkunft, ihre Bedeutung und ihre rechtlichen Grundlagen* (Historische Studien herausgegeben von Dr Emil Ebering, 218), Berlin, 1932.

\*Gandrille, Roger, *L'Organisation de l'Inquisition en France de 1233 à la fin du XVe siècle*, Orleans, 1908.

\*Gorham, Charles T., *The Medieval Inquisition: A Study in Religious Persecution*, London, 1918.

\*Guiraud, Jean, *The Mediaeval Inquisition*, translated by E. C. Messenger, London, 1929.

Haskins, Charles H., 'Robert le Bougre and the Beginnings of the Inquisition in Northern France' in *Studies in Mediaeval Culture*, New York, 1929. (First printed in *American Historical Review*, VII (1902), 437–57, 631–52.)

\*Hayward, Fernand, *The Inquisition*, translated by Malachy Carroll, New York, 1966.

Higounet, Charles, 'Les Villes et l'urbanisme' in Régine Pernoud (ed.), *Le Siècle de Saint Louis*, Paris, 1970.

\*Hinnebusch, William A., *A History of the Dominican Order: Origins and Growth to 1550*, Vol. I., New York, 1965.

Huber, Raphael M., *A Documented History of the Franciscan Order*: Vol. I: *From the Birth of St Francis to the Division of the Order under Leo X (1182–1517)*, Milwaukee, 1944.

Kaltner, Balthasar, *Konrad von Marburg und die Inquisition in Deutschland*, Prague, 1882.

Le Roy Ladurie, Emmanuel, *Les Paysans de Languedoc* (Bibliothèque générale de l'Ecole des hautes études), 2 vols, Paris, 1966.

Mann, Horace K., *The Lives of the Popes in the Middle Ages*, Vol.

XIII: *Honorius III to Celestine IV, 1216–1241*, London, 1925; reprint 1964.

*Maycock, Alan L., *The Inquisition from its Establishment to the Great Schism*, London, 1926.

Michel, R., *L'Administration royale dans la sénéchausée de Beaucaire au temps de Saint Louis* (Memoires et documents publiés par la Société de l'Ecole des chartes, IX), Paris, 1910.

Molinier, Auguste, 'Catalogue des actes de Raimond VI et de Raimond VII' in *Histoire générale de Languedoc*, VIII, 1940–2008.

*Nickerson, Hoffman, *The Inquisition: A Political and Military Study of its Establishment*, Rev. ed., Boston, 1932.

Portal, Charles, *Histoire de la ville de Cordes, Tarn (1222–1279)*, Albi and Cordes, 1902.

Santi, Louis de, 'Relations du comte de Toulouse Raimond VII avec la ville de Marseille', *Annales du Midi*, XI (1899), 200–7.

Stronski, Stanislaw, *Le Troubadour Foulquet de Marseille*, Cracow, 1910.

Tanon, L., *Histoire des tribunaux de l'Inquisition en France*, Paris, 1893.

*Thouzellier, Christine, 'L'inquisitio et Saint Dominique'; 'Réponse au R. P. Vicaire', *Annales du Midi*, LXXX (1968), 121–30, 137–8.

——, 'La Répression de l'hérésie et les débuts de l'Inquisition' in Fliche and Martin, *Histoire de l'église*, X, 300–10.

*Turberville, A. S., *Mediaeval Heresy and The Inquisition*, London, 1920; reprint 1964.

*Vacandard, Elphège, *The Inquisition: a Critical and Historical Study of the Coercive Power of the Church*, translated by B. L. Conway, New York, 1921.

*Vicaire, M. H., 'Note sur la mentalité de Saint Dominique', *Annales du Midi*, LXXX (1968), 131–6.

*——, 'Saint Dominique et les inquisiteurs', *Annales du Midi*, LXXIX (1967), 173–94.

Walsh, William T., *Characters of the Inquisition*, New York, 1940.

*Chapter IX*

Alauzier, L. de, 'L'Héritage des Trencavels', *Annales du Midi*, LXII (1950), 181–6.

Belmont, Charles, 'La Campagne de Poitou, 1242–1243: Taillebourg et Saintes', *Annales du Midi*, V (1893), 289–314.

Berger, Elie, *Histoire de Blanche de Castille, reine de France* (Bibliothèque des écoles françaises d'Athènes et de Rome, 70), Paris, 1895.

*Bisson, Thomas N., *Assemblies and Representation in Languedoc in the Thirteenth Century*, Princeton, 1964.

Boutaric, Edgard, *Saint Louis et Alfonse de Poitiers. Etude sur la réunion des provinces du Midi et de l'Oeust à la couronne et sur les origines de la centralisation administrative d'après les documents inédits*, Paris, 1870.

Dossat, Yves, 'Le Prétendu Concile de Bourges et l'excommunication du comte de Toulouse à Viviers (juillet 1240)', *Bulletin philologique et historique (jusqu'à 1610) du Comité des travaux historiques et scientifiques*, 1959, 461–71.

——, *Saisimentum comitatus tholosani* (Collection de documents inédits sur l'histoire de France, ser.-in-8vo, I), Paris, 1966.

Kantorowicz, Ernst, *Frederick the Second, 1194–1250*, translated by E. O. Lorimer, 2nd ed., London, 1951.

LaBarge, Margaret W., *Saint Louis: The Life of Louis IX of France*, London, 1968.

Merklin, Pierre, 'Les Brûlés de Béoulaygues: Un episode agenais du drame cathare (1249)', *Cahiers d'etudes cathares*, XXI (1970), 20–33.

Molinier, Auguste, 'Sur l'Expedition de Trencavel et le siège de Carcassonne, en 1240' in *Histoire générale de Languedoc*, VII, 448–61.

Molinier, Charles, *La Question de l'ensevelissement du comte de Toulouse Raimond VI en terre sainte (1222–1247): Etude accompagné de pièces inédites du XIIe et du XIIIe siècle*, Angers, 1885.

Rogozinski, Jan, 'The Counsellors of the Seneschal of Beaucaire and Nîmes, 1250–1350', *Speculum*, XLIV (1969), 421–39.

Sabarthès, A., 'L'Albigéisme à Limoux et le prétendu déplacement de cette ville', *Bulletin philologique et historique (jusqu'à 1715) du Comité des travaux historiques et scientifiques*, 1924, 193–222.

*Chapter X*

Bernard Gui, *Liber sententiarum inquisitionis Tholosanae ab anno Christi MCCCVII ad annum MCCCXXIII*. In Philip Limborch, *Historia inquisitionis*, Amsterdam, 1692.

——, *Practica inquisitionis haereticae pravitatis*, edited by Célestin Douais, Paris, 1886. Part V only, edited by Guillaume Mollat as *Manuel de l'inquisiteur*. (Les classiques de l'histoire de France au moyen âge, 8, 9). 2 vols, Paris, 1926–1927.

Cabié, Edmond, 'Comptes des inquisiteurs des diocèses de Toulouse, d'Albi et de Cahors, 1255–1256', *Revue historique, scientifique et littéraire du département du Tarn*, XXII (1905), 110–33, 215–29.

Cayla, P., 'Fragment d'un registre inédit de l'Inquisition', *Mémoires de la Société des arts et sciences de Carcassonne*, 3rd ser., VI (1941–1943), 382–9.

Clasen, Claus-Peter, 'Medieval Heresies in the Reformation', *Church History*, XXXII (1963), 392–414.

Daux, Camille, *L'Inquisition albigeois dans le Montalbanais*, Montauban, 1912.

Dossat, Yves, 'Le "Bûcher de Montségur" et les bûchers de l'Inquisition', *Cahiers de Fanjeaux*, VI, 361–78.

——, 'Un Figure d'inquisiteur: Bernard de Caux', *Cahiers de Fanjeaux*, VI, 253–72.

——, 'Innocent IV, les habitants de Limoux et l'Inquisition', *Annales du Midi*, LXI (1948–1949), 80–4.

S

——, 'Le Massacre d'Avignonet', *Cahiers de Fanjeaux*, VI, 343–59.

Douais, Célestin (ed.), *Acta capitulorum provincialium ordinis praedicatorum: Première province de Provence, province romaine, province d'Espagne (1239–1302)*, Toulouse, 1894.

Dupré-Theseider, Eugène, 'Le Catharisme languedocien et l'Italie', *Cahiers de Fanjeaux*, III, 299–313.

Duvernoy, Jean (ed.), *Le Registre de l'Inquisition de Jacques Fournier, évêque de Pamiers (1318–1325)*, (Bibliothèque méridionale, 2nd ser., XLI), 3 vols, Toulouse, 1965.

Ferlus, Jacques, *Autour de Montségur: de l'histoire ou des histoires?* Perpignan, 1960.

Fournier, Jacques, see Duvernoy.

Fournier, Pierre and Pascal Guébin. *Enquêtes administratives d'Alfonse de Poitiers: Arrêts de son parlement tenu à Toulouse et textes annexes, 1249–1271*. (Collection des documents inédits sur l'histoire de France, 109). Paris, 1959.

\* Lebois, Michèle, 'Le Complot des Carcassonnais contre l'Inquisition (1283–1285)' in *Carcassonne et sa région. Actes des XLIe et XXIVe congrès d'études régionales . . . Carcassonne, 17–19 mai, 1968.* n.p. 1970.

Leff, Gordon, *Heresy in the Later Middle Ages: The Relation of Heterodoxy to Dissent c. 1250–c. 1450*, 2 vols, Manchester and New York, 1967.

Lerner, Robert E., *The Heresy of the Free Spirit in the Later Middle Ages*, Berkeley, 1972.

Molinier, Auguste, *Correspondance administrative d'Alphonse de Poitiers*, 2 vols, Paris, 1894–1900.

Moulis, Adeline, *Montségur et le drame cathare avant, pendant, après la tragédie*, Verniolle, 1968.

Nelli, René (ed.), *Spiritualité de l'hérésie: le Catharisme*, Toulouse, 1953.

Niel, Fernand, *Montségur, temple et fortresse des Cathares d'Occitanie*, Grenoble, 1967.

Ourliac, Paul, 'La Société languedocienne du XIIIe siècle et le droit romain', *Cahiers de Fanjeaux*, VI, 199–216.

Smith, Cyril E., *The University of Toulouse in the Middle Ages: Its Origin and Growth to 1500*, Milwaukee, 1958.

Taberner, F. Valls (ed.), 'El diplomatari de Sant Ramon de Penyafort', *Analecta sacra Tarraconensia: Annuari de la Biblioteca Balmes*, V (1929), 254–61.

Timbal, Pierre, 'La Confiscation dans le droit français des XIIIe et XIVe siècles', *Nouvelle revue historique de droit français et étranger'*, 4th ser., XXII (1943), 44–79; XXIII (1944), 35–60.

Ullmann, Walter, 'The Defence of the Accused in the Medieval Inquisition', *The Irish Ecclesiastical Record*, 5th ser., LXXIII (1950), 481–9.

Vidal, Jean, 'Les Derniers Ministres de l'albigéisme en Languedoc:

leurs doctrines', *Revue des questions historiques*, LXXIX (1906), 57–107.

——, 'Doctrine et morale des derniers ministres albigeois', *Revue des questions historiques*, LXXXV (1909), 357–409; LXXXVI (1909), 5–48.

——, *Un Inquisiteur jugé par ses victimes: Jean Galand et les Carcassonnais (1285–1286)*, Paris, 1903.

——, *Le Tribunal de l'Inquisition de Pamiers: notice sur le registre de l'évêque Jacques Fournier*, Toulouse, 1906.

Walther, Daniel, 'Were the Albigenses and Waldenses Forerunners of the Reformation?', *Andrews University Seminary Studies*, VI (1968), 178–202.


APPENDIXES

*Manuscripts*
Toulouse, Archives municipales, AA 4; AA 34.

*Books and articles*
Alberic of Trois-Fontaines, *Chronica Albrici monachi Trium Fontium*, in *Monumenta Germaniae historica. Scriptores*, XXIII, 631–950.

*Annales sancti Albini Andegavensi.* See Halphen.

Bernard Gui, *De fundatione et prioribus conventuum provinciarum Tolosanae et Provinciae ordinis praedicatorum*, P. A. Amargier (ed.), (Monumenta ordinis fratrum praedicatorum historica, XXIV), Rome, 1961.

Caesarius of Heisterbach, *Dialogus miraculorum*, Joseph Strange (ed.), 2 vols, Cologne, 1851. (Translated as *The Dialogue on Miracles* by Henry von Essen Scott and Charles C. S. Bland, London, 1929.)

Davis, Georgene W., *The Inquisition at Albi, 1299–1300. Text of Register and Analysis*. (Studies in History, Economics and Public Law, 538). New York, 1948.

Dossat, Yves, 'Le Plus Ancien Manuel de l'Inquisition méridionale: le Processus inquisitionis (1248–1249)', *Bulletin philologique et historique du Comité des travaux historiques et scientifiques*, 1948–1949, 33–7.

Douais, Célestin, *Les Frères prêcheurs en Gascogne au XIIIe et XIVe siècle: chapitres, couvents, et notices; documents inédits* (Archives historiques de la Gascogne, 7–8), Paris, 1885.

——, *Les Sources de l'histoire de l'Inquisition dans le Midi de la France aux XIIIe et XIVe siècle*, Paris, 1881.

Halphen, Louis, *Recueil d'annales angevines et vendômoises*, Paris, 1903.

John of Garland, *De triumphis ecclesiae*, edited by Thomas Wright in *Johannis de Garlandia, De triumphis ecclesiae libri octo: a Latin Poem of the Thirteenth Century*, London, 1856.

Lecoy de la Marche, Albert, *Anecdotes historiques, légendes et apologues, tirées du recueil inédit d'Etienne de Bourbon, dominicain du*

*XIIIe siècle* (Société de l'histoire de France, Publications, Vol. 185), Paris, 1877.

Martène, Edmond and Ursin Durand, *Thesaurus novus anecdotorum*, 5 vols, Paris, 1717.

Molinier, Auguste, 'La Commune de Toulouse et Philippe III', *Bibliothèque de l'Ecole des chartes*, XLIII (1882), 5-40. Also in *Histoire générale de Languedoc*, X, 147-68.

Quétif, Jacques and Jacques Echard, *Scriptores ordinis praedicatorum*, 2 vols, Paris, 1719-1721.

Robert of Auxerre, *Chronicon*, in *Monumenta Germaniae historica. Scriptores*, XXVI, 219-87.

Roschach, E., *Inventaire des archives communales de Toulouse anterieures à 1790*, Toulouse, 1871.

Stephen of Bourbon. See Lecoy de la Marche.

Stephen of Salagnac and Bernard Gui. *De quatuor in quibus Deus praedicatorum ordinem insignivit*, Thomas Käppeli (ed.) (Monumenta ordinis fratrum praedicatorum, XXII), Rome, 1949.

Tardif, Ad. and F. Balme, 'Document pour l'histoire du *Processus per inquisitionem* et de l'*inquisitio heretice pravitatis*', *Nouvelle revue historique de droit français et étranger*, VII (1883), 669-78.

Thorndike, Lynn, *University Records and Life in the Middle Ages* (Records of Civilization, XXXVIII), New York, 1944.

# Index

75826

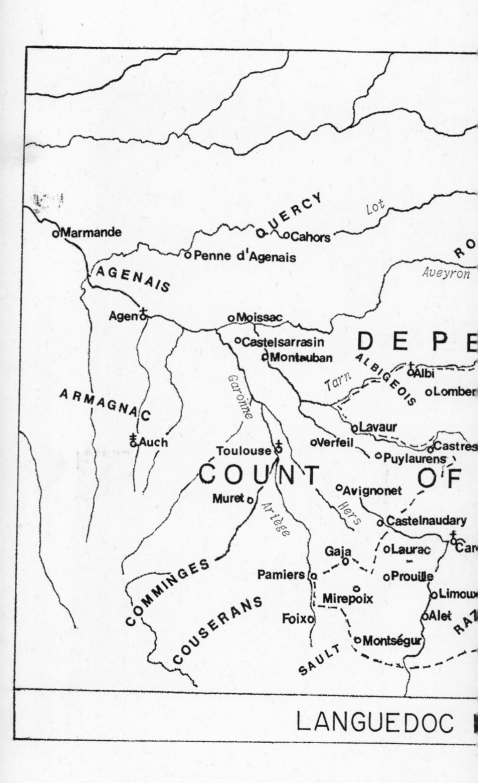

Marmande

QUERCY
Cahors
Lot

Penne d'Agenais
AGENAIS
Aveyron
RO

Agen
Moissac
Castelsarrasin
Montauban
DEPE
ALBIGEOIS
Albi
Lomber
Tarn

ARMAGNAC
Garonne
Lavaur
Verfeil
Castres
Auch
Toulouse
Puylaurens
COUNT
OF
Muret
Avignonet
Ariège
Hers
Castelnaudary
Laurac
Car
Gaja
COMMINGES
Pamiers
Prouille
Mirepoix
Limoux
COUSERANS
Foix
Alet
RAZ
SAULT
Montségur

LANGUEDOC